Numbers! Colors! Alphabet!

A Concept Guide to Children's Picture Books

Melanie Axel-Lute

Library of Congress Cataloging-in-Publication Data

Axel-Lute, Melanie.
　　Numbers! colors! alphabet! : a concept guide to children's picture book / Melanie Axel-Lute.
　　　p.cm.
　　ISBN 1-586-83-058-9 (perfect bound)
　　1. Mathematics--Study and teaching (Elementary)--Bibliography. 2. Colors--Study and teaching (Elementary)--Bibliography. 3. Alphabet--Study and teaching (Elementary)--Bibliography. 4. Picture books for children--Educational aspects--Bibliography. 5. Children's literature in mathematics education--Bibliography. I. Title.

Z5818.M3A94 2003
[QA135.6]
011.62--dc21　　　　　　　　　　　　　　　　　　　　　　　2002043332

Published by Linworth Publishing, Inc.
480 East Wilson Bridge Road, Suite L
Worthington, Ohio 43085

Copyright © 2003 by Linworth Publishing, Inc.

All rights reserved. Purchasing this book entitles a librarian to reproduce activity sheets for use in the library within a school or entitles a teacher to reproduce activity sheets for single classroom use within a school. Other portions of the book (up to 15 pages) may be copied for staff development purposes within a single school. Standard citation information should appear on each page. The reproduction of any part of this book for an entire school or school system or for commercial use is strictly prohibited. No part of this book may be electronically reproduced, transmitted, or recorded without written permission from the publisher.

ISBN: 1-58683-058-9

5 4 3 2 1

Table of Contents

Introduction vii

Chapter 1   **Abstract Concepts** 1
    Multiple Concepts (Books that introduce several different concepts) 1
    Same/Different 1
    Sets 4
    Change 5
    Real/Pretend 6

Chapter 2   **Color** 7
    Color (Books about color in general) 7
    Color Identification (Books introducing the names of colors) 9
    Books Emphasizing Particular Colors: 15
        Red 15
        Blue 16
        Yellow 16
        Green 17
        Orange 18
        Purple 18
        Black and White 18
        Brown 19
    Color Mixing (Books explaining how secondary colors are
        formed from primary ones) 19

Chapter 3   **Shapes and Position** 21
    Shape (Books introducing several different shapes) 21
    Books Introducing Specific Shapes: 24
        Circle 24
        Square 25
        Triangle 25
        Diamond-Shape 25
        Solid Shapes 26
    Position (Books showing relative location, usually using prepositions) 26
        In & Out 28
    Opposites 28
    Cause & Effect 31
    Patterns 33
    Symmetry 34
    Left & Right 34
    Point of View (Books that show events through the eyes of different characters) 34

Chapter 4   **Numbers, Counting, Math, and Money** 37
    Numbers; Things to Count (Books that show numbers or numerals in no specific
        order, or that have random numbers of things to count) 37

Number Concept (Books that help with understanding numeration) 40
Books Emphasizing a Particular Number 41
    One 41
    Two 42
    Three 42
    Four 43
    Five 43
    Six 44
    Seven 45
    Eight 45
    Nine 45
    Ten 46
    Eleven 47
    Twelve 47
    One Hundred 47
Large Numbers (1,000, 1,000,000, or more) 48
Counting Books (Books that introduce numerals in order and have a
    representative number of things to count for each numeral) 49
Counting Up (Books that give numerals in order, without things to count) 60
Counting Down (Books that give numerals in order larger to smaller,
    with or without things to count) 63
Counting by Two 67
Counting by Five 68
Counting by 10 69
Even, Odd 70
Ordinals (First, second, third, and so on) 71
Addition (Concept of addition, not math facts) 72
Subtraction (Concept of subtraction, not math facts) 75
Multiplication (Concept of multiplication, not math facts) .77
Division (Concept of division, not math facts) 79
Fractions 80
Money 81
Powers of Two 83
Powers of 10 84

Chapter 5   **Time Concepts** 85
Time (Books with general facts about time) 85
Time Sense (Understanding the passage of time) 85
Time of Day 88
    Morning 90
    Night 91
Seasons 92
    Spring 95
    Summer 96
    Fall 98
    Winter 99
Days of the Week 103
Months of the Year 103

	March	106
	November	106
	Telling Time (Using a clock)	106

Chapter 6 **Measurement and Perspective** 109
    Measurement (How, why, when to measure; see also
        specific types of measurement) 109
    Size (Bigger and smaller; comparisons) 110
    More & Less 113
    Weight (Concept of weight, comparison, weight measurement) 114
    Length & Height 114
    Distance 115
    Volume (Including cooking measurements) 116
    Perspective (How things look different from different vantage points; how
        things appear smaller when they are farther away) 116

Chapter 7 **Letters, Language, and Words** 119
    Letters & Language (Letters of the alphabet in no particular order;
        how letters form words) 119
    Alphabet Books (Books that show letters in alphabetical order, usually
        with a representative item for each letter) 120
    Alliteration (Words with the same initial sound) 131
    Rhyme (Books that emphasize rhyme, not simply stories that rhyme) 133
    Phonics (Sounds of the language) 134
    Books That Emphasize Individual Letters 134
        B 134
        C 134
        D 135
        F 135
        P 135
        R 135
        S 135
        T 136
        U 136
        W 136
    Parts of Speech 136
        Nouns 136
        Verbs 137
        Adjectives 138
        Comparative Adjectives (Small, smaller, smallest; good, better, best) 139
    Homonyms & Homophones (Words that sound alike but have different
        meanings or spellings) 139

Chapter 8 **Senses, Growth, and Emotions** 141
    Senses 141
        Sight 142
        Sound 142
        Touch 144

Hot & Cold	145
Taste	145
Smell	145
Growth (Growth of living things)	145
Maturity (How older people or animals have learned to do different things)	147
Emotions	148
Anger	151
Sadness	152
Fear	152
Happiness	154

Index by Concept 155

Index by Title 157

About the Author 166

Introduction

It's not always easy to find the right book to use in presenting a concept to young children. *Numbers! Colors! Alphabet!* is a tool that should help to make that task easier. Unlike conventional library catalogs or booklists, it zeroes in on the concepts that are used in each title, instead of the subjects of the books. Unlike lesson plan books, it lists dozens of titles that use a given concept, not just one or two.

The idea of a concept guide to children's picture books came from questions I was asked while I was working as a children's librarian in a public library. Teachers and parents would often ask for books to help introduce concepts to young children. By "concept," I mean something that needs to be understood in a broad way, instead of learned as a series of facts. Some concepts are extremely abstract—real versus pretend, for example—while others are more visual and concrete, such as colors or numbers. What is the difference between a book's subject and a concept? Eric Carle's picture book *The Very Hungry Caterpillar* is about a caterpillar who eats a lot and turns into a butterfly. That's its subject. However, in the course of telling this story, Carle uses the names of the days of the week. The story is not about the days of the week—that's not the subject of the book—but this is a concept that is presented in the book. A teacher, parent, or librarian who wanted to present or reinforce the names of the days of the week could certainly use this book. I realized that library catalog subject headings and existing indexes to children's books were frequently inadequate for finding these concepts. The listings were usually too general, like the Sears subject heading "Size and Shape." They weren't helpful for finding out which alphabet books included lowercase letters or which counting books went up to 20. I began to envision a different way of "indexing" picture books.

The purpose of *Numbers! Colors! Alphabet!* is to help librarians, media specialists, parents, and teachers to find books appropriate for young children that will introduce and illustrate these basic concepts. The books can be used to enhance lessons and to encourage discussion, to show use of a concept in everyday life, or to introduce a concept in a way that children with different learning styles can comprehend.

No index to picture books covers all that this concept guide does, or goes about it in the same way. It is annotated to show exactly what is covered in each book, and how it is covered, so that a user can find a book, for example, on telling time that shows both analog and digital clocks, and explains half hours and quarter hours. It is more specific than indexes, including, for example, entries for "circles," not just "shapes," and for individual colors, numbers and letters.

This book will be valuable for teachers using literature-based skills instruction, because it provides an extensive list of books to use in introducing each concept. Curriculum guides for teachers usually suggest only a few book titles, which are often out of print, outdated, unavailable, or in some other way inappropriate for a particular classroom. Teachers also often want new titles, because they want more titles to reinforce a concept, or simply because they're tired of the familiar ones.

Teachers emphasizing the Multiple Intelligences approach to learning will also appreciate this index. They will be able to introduce concepts using pictures as well as words. Presenting a concept in a story format taps into interpersonal and other less traditional ways of learning, since children will see "real world" examples of a concept.

All teachers, but particularly those of learning disabled or developmentally delayed children, can use books that zero in on exactly the concept to be introduced, without the confusing distraction of other concepts. A picture book will often hold the interest of a child who might otherwise not be able to listen to an explanation of a concept.

In these days of accountability, it will also be useful to have a printed source that lists books that are relevant to a particular educational concept. I have used general, layperson's terms for these concepts, rather than terms from varying state and national curriculum standards.

Parents will find a story they can use to reinforce a concept so that their time with their children can be fun as well as educational. Librarians and media specialists, who are usually the ones to whom both parents and teachers turn for help in finding books, will discover that this is an invaluable source for their own programs as well.

This index will be cost effective for teachers and librarians because although it covers a wide variety of concepts, it is selective in its choice of books, based on printed reviews as well as my own experience as a librarian, book reviewer, and member of the Garden State Children's Book Award committee. It does not attempt to be comprehensive in its listing of picture books and does not list them by subject. It will thus be less expensive, as well as more focused, than a picture book index like *A to Zoo: Subject Access to Children's Picture Books* (Carolyn and John Lima, Bowker, 1998).

Numbers! Colors! Alphabet! is organized simply. Each concept is listed, and, if necessary, defined, followed by an annotated list of picture books that illustrate that concept. There is also a suggested age level for which the book is an appropriate introduction to the concept. If there is more than one book by the same author for a given concept, the books are listed in one entry. An entry will look like this:

Numeroff, Laura Joffe, *If You Give a Mouse a Cookie.* **Ill. by Felicia Bond. HarperCollins, 1985. ISBN 0060245867.**
Shows the chain of events that start when you give a mouse a cookie. See also *If You Give a Moose a Muffin* [1991: ISBN 0060244054], and *If You Give a Pig a Pancake* [1998: ISBN 0060266864]. **PS, K, Pr**

Author and title are followed by illustrator (if different from the author), publisher, publication date, and ISBN. If more than one edition of the book is in print, the hardback or library bound edition is listed. If only a paperback edition is in print, the entry is marked "(pbk)." Although the bibliographic information was accurate at the time the book was completed, children's books go out of print very rapidly, so it would be best to check this information before ordering.

A short annotation follows, giving both a description of the book and, if necessary, some information on the scope of the book's coverage of the concept. For example, the annotations to the counting books will tell you what range of numbers is included. Does the book include zero? Does it go up to 10, 12, 20, or even higher? It will tell you if the numerals, or written forms of the numbers, are used. A surprising number of counting books for young children have the words "one" and "two" instead of the numerals 1 and 2, a difference which may determine a book's usefulness for you. The annotations to the alphabet books will tell you if lowercase or uppercase letters, or both, are used.

The concepts are grouped with other related concepts, and there is an alphabetical index to them. To find a book on a specific concept, just locate that concept's listings by using the table of contents or the index. The table of contents gives an explanation of the concepts that are not self-explanatory. At the end of the annotation are age level suggestions:

T for toddler (ages 2–3)
PS for Preschool (ages 3–5)
K for Kindergarten (ages 5–6)
Pr for Primary (grades 1–3)

Many books fit into more than one concept area and so have been repeated in each of these concept lists. This may seem repetitive to the browser, but it is necessary to make these books easy to locate for the user who is looking in a single category.

Instead of comprehensiveness, *Numbers! Colors! Alphabet!* aims for quality, usefulness, and availability. To be listed, books must be well written, they must be useful introductions to the concept, and they must be currently in print or published after 1995. Except for the simplest books aimed at the youngest child, they must have some story line, rhyme, or other interesting "hook." Holiday books, nonfiction, and TV and movie tie-ins are not included, nor are cookie-cutter series of books covering each letter or number. Alphabet books that are actually introductions to their subject, rather than to the alphabet (such as *A to Z of Dogs*), have been excluded. Board books have been included only if they provide some of the best representations of the concept for young children. Thousands of picture books were analyzed for inclusion based on these principles, and the rigorously chosen lists in *Numbers! Colors! Alphabet!* are the result. Inevitably, some excellent books have been missed. I would be happy to know of other good introductions to concepts for possible inclusion in an addendum or a second edition of *Numbers! Colors! Alphabet!*

Chapter One

Abstract Concepts

Multiple Concepts [Books that introduce several different concepts]

Le Jars, David, *One, Two, Red, and Blue.* **Two-Can, 2000. ISBN 1587280159.**
Briefly introduces many concepts, such as numerals to 10, colors, differences, shapes, position, and weather. **PS**

Lobel, Anita, *One Lighthouse, One Moon.* **Greenwillow, 2000. ISBN 0688155391.**
Colorful footwear for each day of the week; a cat's activities for each month of the year; and seashore-related pictures for numbers one to ten, plus one hundred stars. Numerals are not used. **PS, K**

Same/Different

Anno, Mitsumasa, *All in a Day.* **Paper Star, 1999. ISBN 0698117727 (pbk).**
Pictures by different illustrators show what is happening around the world at the same moment on one day. **K, Pr**

Appelbaum, Diana, *Cocoa Ice.* **Ill. by Holly Mead. Orchard, 1997. ISBN 0531300404.**
Cocoa is harvested in the tropics, while ice is harvested in Maine. **K**

Axworthy, Anni, ill, *Guess What I Am.* **Words by Louise Jackson and Paul Harrison. Candlewick, 1998. ISBN 0763606251.**
Pages with cutouts compare cats and tigers, goldfish and sharks, and the like. **PS, K**

Baker, Keith, *Who Is the Beast?* **Harcourt Brace, 1990. ISBN 0152960570.**
Tiger points out the similarities between himself and the animals who are afraid of him. Some colors are identified. **T, PS, K**

Ballard, Robin, *My Day, Your Day.* **Greenwillow, 2001. ISBN 0688177964.**
Compares children's activities at day care with their parents' activities at work. **PS**

Boynton, Sandra, *Pajama Time!* **Workman, 2000. ISBN 0761119752.**
Animals wear different kinds of pajamas. Board book. **T, PS**

Brown, Margaret Wise, *Two Little Trains.* **Ill. by Leo and Diane Dillon. HarperCollins, 2001. ISBN 0060283769.**
Two trains—a real one and a toy one—travel on contrasting journeys. Many prepositions are used to describe their trips. **PS**

Cannon, Janell, *Stellaluna.* **Harcourt, 1993. ISBN 0152802177.**
A bat raised by birds learns to appreciate their similarities and differences. **K, Pr**

Crimi, Carolyn, *Outside, Inside.* **Ill. by Linnea Asplind Riley. Simon & Schuster, 1995. ISBN 0671886886.**
Contrasts what goes on inside a house with what is going on outside. **PS**

Dooley, Norah, *Everybody Bakes Bread.* **Ill. by Peter J. Thornton. Lerner, 1995. ISBN 087614864X.**
Carrie visits many neighbors who are baking bread of different kinds. **K, Pr**

Eaton, Deborah, and Susan Halter, *No One Told the Aardvark.* **Ill. by Jim Spence. Charlesbridge, 1997. ISBN 0881068713 (pbk).**
A boy complains that animals are fortunate in not having to conform to human rules about eating, bathing, and so on. **PS, K**

Fox, Mem, *Whoever You Are.* **Ill. by Leslei Staub. Harcourt Brace, 1997. ISBN 0152007873.**
Shows the similarities and differences between children all over the world. **PS, K**

Giganti, Paul, Jr., *How Many Snails? A Counting Book.* **Ill. by Donald Crews. Greenwillow, 1988. ISBN 0688063705.**
The reader is asked to count things and to determine differences: for example, count all the flowers, then just the yellow ones. **PS, K**

Katz, Karen, *The Colors of Us.* **Henry Holt, 1999. ISBN 0805058648.**
Lena observes that everyone's skin is a different shade of brown, from peachy tan to darkest chocolate. **PS, K, Pr**

King, Stephen Michael, *Henry and Amy (Right-Way-Round and Upside Down).* **Walker, 1998. ISBN 0802786863.**
Henry, who does everything topsy-turvy, meets Amy, who does everything right, and they both learn from each other. **PS, K**

Lionni, Leo, *A Color of His Own.* **Dragonfly, 1997. ISBN 0679887857 (pbk).**
A chameleon, tired of not having a color of his own, joins forces with another chameleon so that they will at least always be the same color as each other. **PS, K**

Lionni, Leo, *Fish Is Fish.* **Knopf, 1987. ISBN 0394827996 (pbk).**
When a tadpole becomes a frog and leaves his friend the fish behind, the fish becomes jealous and wishes to be able to see the world beyond the pond. **PS, K**

Lobel, Arnold, *Frog and Toad Are Friends.* **HarperCollins, 1970. ISBN 0060239573.**
Five stories. In "A Lost Button," Frog and Toad look for a button that has all the characteristics of Toad's missing one. **PS, K**

Manna, Giovanni, *You and Me.* **Barefoot Books, 2000. ISBN 1841482633.**
A girl and boy pretend to be opposite or contrasting things, like a valley and a hill, a tiger and a bear, or dark and bright. **PS, K**

Masurel, Claire, *Ten Dogs in the Window: A Countdown Book.* **Ill. by Pamela Paparone. North-South, 1997. ISBN 1558587543.**
Ten dogs in the window are purchased one by one by people who resemble them. **PS, K**

McKee, David, *Elmer.* **Lothrop, Lee & Shepard, 1989. ISBN 0688091717.**
A multicolored patchwork elephant wishes he were gray like the others, but they appreciate his differences. See also other books about Elmer, including a board book *Elmer's Colors* [1994: ISBN 0688137628]. **PS**

Miller, David, *Just Like You and Me.* **Dial, 1999. ISBN 0803725868.**
Collage pictures show how people do many of the same things as animals. **PS, K**

Mitchell, Lori, *Different Just Like Me.* **Charlesbridge, 1999. ISBN 0881069752.**
A girl observes the differences and similarities between the people she meets. **PS, K, Pr**

Murphy, Stuart J., *A Pair of Socks.* **Ill. by Lois Ehlert. HarperCollins, 1996. ISBN 0060258799.**
A sock looks for its mate. **PS, K**

Pandell, Karen, *Animal Action ABC.* **Ill. by Art Wolfe and Nancy Sheehan. Dutton, 1996. ISBN 0525454861.**
Photographs of animals and children illustrate action words from "arch" through "leap" and "zap." Letters are shown in upper case. **PS, K, Pr**

Pinkwater, Daniel Manus, *The Big Orange Splot.* **Scholastic, 1993. ISBN 0590445103 (pbk).**
> An orange splot that appears on Mr. Plumbean's house inspires him to decorate his house quite differently from all the identical houses on his street. **Pr**

Singer, Marilyn, *On the Same Day in March.* **Ill. by Frané Lessac. HarperCollins, 2000. ISBN 0060281871.**
> Shows the weather at different places in the world on the same day in March. **K, Pr**

Sets

Baker, Alan, *Gray Rabbit's Odd One Out.* **Kingfisher, 1995. ISBN 1856975851.**
> As Gray Rabbit searches for his lost book, he sorts his toys into various categories. **PS, K**

Giganti, Paul, Jr., *How Many Snails? A Counting Book.* **Ill. by Donald Crews. Greenwillow, 1988. ISBN 0688063705.**
> The reader is asked to count things and to determine differences: for example, count all the flowers, then just the yellow ones. **PS, K**

Jenkins, Emily, *Five Creatures.* **Ill. by Tomek Bogacki. Frances Foster, 2001. ISBN 0374323410.**
> A girl, her parents, and two cats share a house and have some similarities and some differences: four adults and one child, three with orange hair and two with gray, and so on. **PS, K, Pr**

Jocelyn, Marthe, *Hannah's Collections.* **Dutton, 2000. ISBN 0525464425.**
> Hannah has too many collections to share just one with her class, so she creates a piece of sculpture with pieces from many collections. Story includes different things to count. **PS, K**

Keenan, Sheila, *More or Less a Mess.* **Ill. by Patrick Girouard. Scholastic, 1997. ISBN 0590602489 (pbk).**
> To clean up her room, a girl sorts things into different categories. **PS, K**

Lobel, Arnold, *Frog and Toad Are Friends.* **HarperCollins, 1970. ISBN 0060239573.**
> Five stories. In "A Lost Button," Frog and Toad look for a button that has all the characteristics of Toad's missing one. **PS, K**

Murphy, Stuart J., *Dave's Down-to-Earth Rock Shop.* **Ill. by Cat Bowman Smith. HarperCollins, 2000. ISBN 0060280182.**
> With their new hobby of rock collecting, Amy and Josh learn that there are many different ways of classifying the same things. **K, Pr**

Murphy, Stuart J., *Seaweed Soup*. Ill. by Frank Remkiewicz. HarperCollins, 2001. **ISBN 0064467368.**
Turtle sets the table for his friends using sets of dishes. **PS, K**

Reid, Margarette S., *The Button Box*. Ill. by Sarah Chamberlain. Dutton, 1990. **ISBN 0525445900.**
A boy sorts out different buttons in his grandmother's button box. **PS, K, Pr**

Change

Axworthy, Anni, ill, *Guess What I'll Be*. **Words by Louise Jackson and Paul Harrison. Candlewick, 1998. ISBN 076360626X.**
Pages with cut-outs lead the reader to discover what various animals such as a tadpole and a grub will grow up to be. **PS, K**

Baker, Jeannie, *Window*. **Greenwillow, 1991. ISBN 0688089186.**
Collage construction illustrations chronicle the changes in a boy's neighborhood as he grows up. Wordless. **PS, K, Pr**

Ballard, Robin, *When I Am a Sister*. **Greenwillow, 1998. ISBN 0688153976.**
A little girl finds out how things will change when her father and stepmother have a baby. **PS**

Burton, Virginia Lee, *The Little House*. **Houghton Mifflin, 1978. ISBN 0395181569.**
Over the years, a little house, built out in the country, is gradually surrounded by the city. **PS, K, Pr**

Carle, Eric, *The Very Hungry Caterpillar*. **Putnam, 1983. ISBN 0399208534.**
A caterpillar eats his way through the days of the week, including groups of one to five foods, then changes into a butterfly. **T, PS**

Ford, Miela, *What Color Was the Sky Today?* Ill. by Sally Noll. Greenwillow, 1997. **ISBN 0688145582.**
The sky changes color as the weather changes during the course of a day. Simple text. **PS**

Murphy, Mary, *Some Things Change*. **Houghton Mifflin, 2001. ISBN 0618003347.**
Little Penguin learns about things that can change. **T, PS**

Shannon, George, *Tomorrow's Alphabet*. **Ill. by Donald Crews. Greenwillow, 1996. ISBN 0688135048.**
Examples like "D is for puppy—tomorrow's dog." Uppercase letters. **K, Pr**

Thornhill, Jan, *Before & After: A Book of Nature Timescapes*. **National Geographic, 1997. ISBN 0792270932.**
Detailed pictures of various natural areas are shown at one time and then a few seconds or up to a year later. **PS, K, Pr**

Zolotow, Charlotte, *When the Wind Stops.* **Ill. by Stefano Vitale. HarperCollins, rev. ed., 1995. ISBN 0060269715.**
A boy learns that the end of one thing is the beginning of another: day to night, fall to winter, and others. **PS, K, Pr**

Real/Pretend

Bittner, Wolfgang, *Wake Up, Grizzly!* **Ill. by Gustavo Rosemffet. North-South, 1996. ISBN 1558585184.**
A boy and his father pretend to be bears. **PS, K**

Brown, Margaret Wise, *Two Little Trains.* **Ill. by Leo and Diane Dillon. HarperCollins, 2001. ISBN 0060283769.**
Two trains—a real one and a toy one—travel on contrasting journeys. Many prepositions are used to describe their trips. **PS**

Carrick, Carol, *Patrick's Dinosaurs.* **Ill. by Donald Carrick. Houghton Mifflin, 1983. ISBN 0899191894.**
As his older brother Hank tells him about dinosaurs, Patrick imagines he sees them. **K, Pr**

Crews, Nina, *You Are Here.* **Greenwillow, 1998. ISBN 068815753X.**
Two girls go on an imaginary journey. Illustrated with photo collages. **PS, K**

Lionni, Leo, *Alexander and the Wind-up Mouse.* **Knopf, 1987. ISBN 0394829115 (pbk).**
A real mouse befriends a toy wind-up mouse and thinks the toy has a better life, but when the toy is discarded, the mouse finds a way to turn him into a real mouse. **PS, K, Pr**

Chapter Two

Color

Color *[Books about color in general]*

Bannerman, Helen, *The Story of Little Babaji*. **Ill. by Fred Marcellino. HarperCollins, 1996. ISBN 0062050648.**
Little Babaji fools the tigers who take his colorful new clothes. **PS, K, Pr**

Carle, Eric, *The Mixed-up Chameleon*. **HarperCollins, 1987. ISBN 069004397X.**
A chameleon who wishes to be like other animals finds himself with parts of many animals, each in a different color. **PS**

Deeter, Catherine, *Seymour Bleu*. **Simon & Schuster, 1998. ISBN 0689801378.**
Artist Seymour Bleu searches for inspiration in places of many colors. Includes exotic color names like indigo, azure, viridian. **Pr**

DeRolf, Shane, *The Crayon Box That Talked*. **Ill. by Michael Letzig. Random, 1999. ISBN 0679886117.**
The different colored crayons don't get along until a little girl draws a picture with them and shows them how they can work together. **PS, K**

Ehlert, Lois, *Color Zoo*. **Lippincott Williams & Wilkins, 1989. ISBN 0397322593.**
Pages with cutouts in different shapes make abstract portraits of various animals. Shapes used are star, circle, square, triangle, rectangle, heart, oval, diamond, octagon, hexagon. See also the similar *Color Farm* [1990: ISBN 0397324413]. **PS, K**

Ford, Miela, *What Color Was the Sky Today?* **Ill. by Sally Noll. Greenwillow, 1997. ISBN 0688145582.**
> The sky changes color as the weather changes during the course of a day. Simple text. **PS**

Heller, Nicholas, *Goblins in Green.* **Ill. by Jos. A. Smith. Greenwillow, 1995. ISBN 0688128025.**
> Goblins with names from A to Z try on clothes. Each description includes words starting with that letter, plus one with the next letter. **PS, K**

Hissey, Jane, *Old Bear's Surprise Painting.* **Philomel, 2001. ISBN 0399237097.**
> The toys make colorful patterns that don't quite work out as they planned, but Old Bear puts them together to make one picture. **K**

Kleven, Elisa, *The Lion and the Little Red Bird.* **Dutton, 1992. ISBN 0525448985.**
> A bird discovers that the reason the lion's tail changes color is that he uses it for painting. **K, Pr**

Lester, Julius, *Sam and the Tigers.* **Ill. by Jerry Pinkney. Dial, 1996. ISBN 0803720289.**
> Sam loses his colorful clothes to the tigers, then outwits them, in this African-American retelling of "Little Black Sambo." **PS, K, Pr**

Lionni, Leo, *A Color of His Own.* **Dragonfly, 1997. ISBN 0679887857 (pbk).**
> A chameleon, tired of not having a color of his own, joins forces with another chameleon so that they will at least always be the same color as each other. **PS, K**

McKee, David, *Elmer.* **Lothrop, Lee & Shepard, 1989. ISBN 0688091717.**
> A multicolored patchwork elephant wishes he were gray like the others, but they appreciate his differences. See also other books about Elmer, including a board book *Elmer's Colors* [1994: ISBN 0688137628]. **PS**

Priceman, Marjorie, *It's Me, Marva! A Story about Color and Optical Illusions.* **Knopf, 2001. ISBN 0679889930 (pbk).**
> Marva's invention causes her trouble with colors and optical illusions. **K, Pr**

Strete, Craig Kee, *They Thought They Saw Him.* **Ill. by Jose Aruego and Ariane Dewey. Greenwillow, 1996. ISBN 0688141943.**
> A chameleon escapes from those who want to eat him by changing colors. **PS, K**

Strom, Maria Diaz, *Rainbow Joe and Me.* **Lee & Low, 1999. ISBN 1880000938.**
> Eloise, who loves to paint with colors, learns how a blind man perceives color. **K, Pr**

Walsh, Ellen Stoll, *Mouse Magic.* **Harcourt, 2000. ISBN 0152003266.**
   The crow wizard shows Kit the mouse how to mix secondary colors, and how complementary colors seem to move when placed next to each other. **PS, K**

Watt, Mélanie, *Leon the Chameleon.* **Kids Can Press, 2001. ISBN 155074867X.**
   Instead of turning the same color as something he's on, like the other chameleons, Leon turns the complementary color. **PS, K**

Wilson, April, *April Wilson's Magpie Magic: A Tale of Colorful Mischief.* **Dial, 1999. ISBN 0803723547.**
   An artist draws a black-and-white bird, which comes to life and interacts with drawings of other colors. Wordless. **PS, K**

Color Identification [Books introducing the names of colors]

Baker, Alan, *Brown Rabbit's Day.* **Kingfisher, 1995. ISBN 1856975843.**
   Brown Rabbit spends his day making some gelatin molds for his friends in yellow, green, red, and purple. **T, PS**

Baker, Alan, *Brown Rabbit's Shape Book.* **Kingfisher, 1999. ISBN 1856979504.**
   Brown Rabbit opens a package of colored shape balloons: includes triangle, circle, rectangle, square, oval, sausage-shape, pear-shape, plus red, orange, green, purple. **T, PS**

Baker, Alan, *White Rabbit's Color Book.* **Kingfisher, 1994. ISBN 1856979539.**
   White Rabbit goes from one paint pot to another, changing his color, mixing secondary colors from primary ones. **PS**

Bartlett, Alison, *Cat Among the Cabbages.* **Dutton, 1997. ISBN 0525457550.**
   A cat wanders around a colorful garden, looking at things of different sizes. **T, PS**

Bassède, Francine, *George Paints His House.* **Orchard, 1999. ISBN 0531301508.**
   George asks his animal friends for help deciding what color to paint his house. **PS, K**

Blackstone, Stella, *Can You See the Red Balloon?* **Ill. by Debbie Harter. Orchard, 1998. ISBN 0531300773.**
   Asks the reader to find items of a particular color in a busy picture. **PS**

Bond, Michael, *Paddington's Colors.* **Ill. by John Lobban. Puffin, 1996. ISBN 0140557644 (pbk).**
   Paddington Bear does his spring cleaning, showing different colors. Also shows how to mix colors. **PS**

Bourgoing, Pascal, *Colors.* Ill. by P. M. Valet and Sylvaine Perols. Scholastic, 1991. ISBN 0590452363 (spiral binding).
Transparent overlays help introduce colors and how to mix them. **PS, K, Pr**

Boynton, Sandra, *Blue Hat, Green Hat.* Little Simon, 1995. ISBN 0671493205.
Animals display clothing in different colors. Board. **T, PS**

Brown, Margaret Wise, *My World of Color.* Ill. by Loretta Kruoinksi. Hyperion, 2002. ISBN 0786825197.
Scenes of things in nature illustrate rhymes about many colors. **T, PS**

Bulloch, Ivan, *Pick a Color!* Ill. by Lydia Monks. World Book/Two-Can, 2000. ISBN 158728006X.
Photos of children and drawings of animals introduce colors. **T, PS**

Burton, Katherine, *One Gray Mouse.* Ill. by Kim Fernandes. Kids Can Press, 1997. ISBN 1550742256.
Pictures of groups consisting of from one to ten animals, with colors identified, for example: "Five pink pigs in yellow pig wigs." Numerals included. **T, PS**

Cabrera, Jane, *Cat's Colors.* Puffin, 2000. ISBN 014056487X (pbk).
A cat describes 10 different colors. Bright and jazzy. **T, PS**

Carle, Eric, *Hello, Red Fox.* Simon & Schuster, 1998. ISBN 0689817754.
Little frog invites his friends to a party—but they are different colors from their names. Shows how staring at one color can produce an afterimage of the complementary color. **PS, K**

Carter, David A., *More Bugs in Boxes.* Simon & Schuster, 1990. ISBN 0671695770.
Pop-up book shows different colored bugs in different colored boxes, including some less common colors like fuchsia and olive drab. **PS**

Chocolate, Debbi, *Kente Colors.* Ill. by John Ward. Walker, 1996. ISBN 0802783880.
Identifies and gives meanings for the colors of African Kente cloth. **PS**

Cousins, Lucy, *Maisy's Colors.* Candlewick, 1999. ISBN 076360237X.
Maisy the mouse plays with things of various colors. Board. **T, PS**

Crews, Donald, *Freight Train.* Morrow, 1978. ISBN 0688841651.
A train has cars of eight different colors. **T, PS**

Dena, Anaël, *Colors.* Ill. by Christel Desmoinaux. Gareth Stevens, 1997. ISBN 0836819845.
There are many things of one color in each picture. Also explains mixing colors. **PS, K**

Dodd, Emma, *Dog's Colorful Day: A Messy Story about Colors and Counting.* **Dutton, 2001. ISBN 0525465286.**
> A dog with one black spot acquires nine more spots of different colors. Numerals 1 to 10 are shown in order at one point in the story. **PS, K**

Dodds, Dayle Ann, *The Color Box.* **Ill. by Giles Laroche. Little, Brown, 1992. ISBN 0316188204.**
> A monkey explores different colors. Cutouts give a peep to the next color to be visited. **PS**

Emberley, Ed, *Go Away, Big Green Monster!* **Little, Brown, 1993. ISBN 0316236535.**
> Cutouts show a big green monster with yellow eyes and other colored body parts. **PS**

Emberley, Ed, and Anne Miranda, *Glad Monster, Sad Monster: A Book about Feelings.* **Little, Brown, 1997. ISBN 0316573957.**
> Different colored monsters explain different feelings. Lift-the-flap pages make masks for children to use in acting out the feelings. **PS, K**

Emberley, Rebecca, *My Colors; Mis Colores.* **Little, Brown, 2000. ISBN 0316233471.**
> A representative item in each color, identified in English and Spanish. **T, PS**

Fleming, Denise, *Lunch!* **Henry Holt, 1992. ISBN 0805016368.**
> Large pictures show all the different colored things a messy mouse eats. **T, PS**

French, Vivian, *Oh, No, Anna!* **Ill. by Alex Ayliffe. Peachtree, 1997. ISBN 1561451258.**
> Baby Anna finds things of various colors and gets into trouble with each one. Simple text, foldout pages. **T, PS**

Garne, S. T., *By a Blazing Blue Sea.* **Ill. by Lori Lohstoeter. Harcourt Brace, 1999. ISBN 0152017801.**
> There are many colors in the life of a Caribbean fisherman. **PS, K**

Godwin, Laura, *Little White Dog.* **Ill. by Dan Yaccarino. Hyperion, 1998. ISBN 0786802979.**
> The animals are hard to find as each one is in a place that matches its color. **T, PS**

Haring, Keith, *Big.* **Hyperion, 1998. ISBN 0786803908.**
> Large-size board book shows funny pictures of oversized clothes in different colors. **T, PS**

Harshman, Marc, and Cheryl Ryan, *Red Are the Apples.* **Ill. by Wade Zahares. Gulliver/Harcourt, 2001. ISBN 0152019170.**
> A garden in the fall is described in terms of many colorful things. **PS, K**

Hill, Eric, *Spot's Big Book of Colors, Shapes and Numbers.* **Putnam, 1994. ISBN 0399226796.**
> Large pages with multiple illustrations show colors, simple shapes, and numbers, with numerals, 1 to 10. **PS**

Hoban, Tana, *Colors Everywhere.* **Greenwillow, 1995. ISBN 0688127622.**
> Colorful photographs of everyday objects. Wordless. **PS, K**

Hoban, Tana, *Of Colors and Things.* **Greenwillow/Mulberry, 1996. ISBN 0688045855 (pbk).**
> Each page has four pictures of things in one color. **PS**

Hooper, Patricia, *How the Sky's Housekeeper Wore Her Scarves.* **Ill. by Susan L. Roth. Little, Brown, 1995. ISBN 0316372552.**
> The sky's housekeeper has a different scarf for each chore, and finally wears them all one rainy-sunny day, forming a rainbow. **PS, K**

Hubbard, Patricia, *My Crayons Talk.* **Ill. by G. Brian Karas. Henry Holt, 1996. ISBN 080503529X.**
> A girl imagines that each color in her box of crayons has a something to say. **PS, K**

Inkpen, Mick, *Kipper's Book of Colors.* **Harcourt Brace, Red Wagon, 1995. ISBN 0152006478.**
> Pictures Kipper with things of various colors. Board book and hardcover editions. **T**

Jackson, Ellen, *Brown Cow, Green Grass, Yellow Mellow Sun.* **Ill. by Victoria Raymond. Hyperion, 1995. ISBN 0786800100.**
> A colorful story of where butter comes from. **PS**

Jonas, Ann, *Color Dance.* **Greenwillow, 1989. ISBN 0688059902.**
> Children dance with transparent scarves, identifying and mixing colors. **PS, K**

Kalan, Robert, *Rain.* **Ill. by Donald Crews. Mulberry, 1991. ISBN 0688104797 (pbk).**
> Rain comes down on things of many colors, and ends with a rainbow. Very simple text. **T, PS**

Leuck, Laura, *Teeny, Tiny Mouse: A Book about Colors.* **Ill. by Pat Schories. BridgeWater, 1998. ISBN 0816745471.**
> A mother and child mouse go through their house, pointing out things of different colors. **PS**

MacKinnon, Debbie, *Eye Spy Colors.* **Ill. by Anthea Sieveking. Charlesbridge, 1998. ISBN 0881063347.**
> Photographs on pages with cutouts introduce colors. **PS**

Martin, Bill, Jr., *Brown Bear, Brown Bear, What Do You See?* Ill. by Eric Carle. Henry Holt, 1983. ISBN 0805002014.
　　Animals of different colors are introduced. Simple text. **T, PS**

McMillan, Bruce, *Growing Colors*. Lothrop, Lee & Shepard, 1988. ISBN 0688078443.
　　Photographs of fruits and vegetables illustrate colors. **T, PS**

Miller, Margaret, *I Love Colors*. Little Simon, 1999. ISBN 0689823568.
　　Photos of babies holding or wearing things of different colors. Board. **T**

Onyefulu, Ifeoma, *Chidi Only Likes Blue: An African Book of Colors*. Cobblehill/Dutton, 1997. ISBN 0525652434.
　　Photographs of things in Nigeria, with descriptions of them, showing different colors. **PS, K, Pr**

Peek, Merle, *Mary Wore Her Red Dress and Henry Wore His Green Sneakers*. Houghton Mifflin, 1998. ISBN 0395900220 (pbk).
　　Animal children each wear clothing of a different color to a party. **T, PS**

Pinkney, Sandra L., *A Rainbow All Around Me*. Ill. by Myles C. Pinkney. Scholastic, 2002. ISBN 043930928X.
　　Photographs of children illustrate colors. **PS**

Rau, Dana Meachen, *Bob's Vacation*. Children's Press, 1999. ISBN 0516215434.
　　Simple text tells of Bob the snowman, who goes on a tropical vacation to find colors other than the white of snow. **T, PS**

Rogers, Alan, *Green Bear*. World Book/Two-Can, 1997. ISBN 0716644053.
　　Green Bear likes green best, but paints his house to match the seasons. **T, PS**

Rogers, Alan, *Ship Shape*. Two-Can 2000. ISBN 1587281554.
　　Blue Tortoise, Green Bear, Red Rhino, and Yellow Hippo make a boat out of simple shapes. **PS**

Rotner, Shelley, and Anne Woodhull, *Colors Around Us*. Ill. by Shelley Rotner. Little Simon, 1996. ISBN 0689809808.
　　Many photographs illustrate each color, and tabs to lift show the color's name and a surprise. **T, PS**

Ryan, Pat Muñoz, and Jerry Pallotta, *The Crayon Counting Book*. Ill. by Frank Mazzola, Jr. Charlesbridge, 1996. ISBN 088106954X.
　　Colorful crayons are counted by 2s from 0 to 24 and from 1 to 23, illustrating even and odd numbers. **PS, K**

Seuss, Dr., *My Many Colored Days*. Ill. by Steve Johnson and Lou Fancher. Knopf, 1996. ISBN 0679875972.
Days are illustrated by different colors, which represent the mood of the day. **PS, K, Pr**

Shields, Carol Diggory, *Colors: Animagicals*. Ill. by Svjetlan Junakovic. Handprint, 2000. ISBN 1929766041.
Rhymes about colors are riddles whose pictured answers are hidden under folded pages. **PS, K**

Siddals, Mary McKenna, *Tell Me a Season*. Ill. by Petra Mathers. Clarion, 1997. ISBN 0395710219.
In this book with very simple text, each season and time of day is represented by a different color. **T, PS**

Sis, Peter, *Ballerina!* Greenwillow, 2001. ISBN 0688179444.
A little girl wears different colored costumes as she dances. **PS**

Thong, Roseanne, *Red Is a Dragon: A Book of Colors*. Ill. by Grace Lin. Chronicle, 2001. ISBN 0811831779.
Colors are introduced by pictures and rhymes reflecting Chinese-American culture. **PS, K**

Van Fleet, Matthew, *One Yellow Lion*. Dial, 1992. ISBN 0803710992.
Fold-out pages illustrate animals of different colors from 1 to 10 (with numerals). **T, PS**

Wallis, Diz, *Mandarins and Marigolds: A Child's Journey Through Color*. Gareth Stevens, 1995. ISBN 083681391X.
On a gray day, a boy discovers colors one by one. Lush pictures and prose. **PS, K**

Walsh, Ellen Stoll, *Mouse Paint*. Harcourt Brace Jovanovich, 1989. ISBN 0152560254.
White mice play in jars of paint, mixing orange, green, and purple from red, yellow, and blue. **T, PS**

Whippo, Walt, *Little White Duck*. Ill. by Joan Paley. Little, Brown, 2000. ISBN 0316032271.
The white duck, green frog, black bug, and red snake interact in the familiar song. **PS, K**

Yolen, Jane, *Color Me a Rhyme: Nature Poems for Young People*. Ill. by Jason Stemple. Wordsong/Boyds Mills, 2000. ISBN 156397892X.
Short poems illustrated with photographs of natural objects illustrate colors. **K, Pr**

Young, Ed, *Seven Blind Mice.* **Philomel, 1992. ISBN 0399222618.**
> Seven blind mice of different colors each feel a different part of an elephant and get a very different idea of what it is like. **PS, K, Pr**

Books Emphasizing Particular Colors

Red

Asbury, Kelly, *Rusty's Red Vacation.* **Henry Holt, 1997. ISBN 0805040218.**
> Rusty goes camping on his vacation, and everything is red. **T, PS**

dePaola, Tomie, *Charlie Needs a Cloak!* **Simon & Schuster, 1988. ISBN 0671664670 (pbk).**
> Charlie the shepherd takes an entire year to make himself a red cloak, starting by shearing the sheep in the spring, spinning and dyeing in the summer, and weaving and sewing in the fall, so that the cloak is ready for winter. **PS, K**

Johnston, Tony, *The Bull and the Fire Truck.* **Scholastic, 1996. ISBN 0590475975.**
> A bull who hates everything red has an unfortunate run-in with a fire truck. **PS**

Kellogg, Steven, *The Missing Mitten Mystery.* **Dial, 2000. ISBN 0803725663.**
> A girl loses her red mitten in the snow and imagines what could have happened to it. **PS, K**

Lacome, Julie, *Ruthie's Big Old Coat.* **Candlewick, 2000. ISBN 0763609692.**
> Ruthie's red hand-me-down coat is too big for her, so she and her friend Fiona wear it together and play in it. Contains a scene where one girl uses the toilet. **PS, K**

Lia, Simone, *Red's Great Chase.* **Dutton, 1999. ISBN 0525462139.**
> A blue monster chases Red up, down, around, through, and all over the world—until she tags Red and it's her turn to be It. **PS**

Merriam, Eve, *Ten Rosy Roses.* **Ill. by Julia Gorton. HarperCollins, 1999. ISBN 0060278870.**
> Ten red roses are picked one by one by different children. **T, PS**

Rogers, Alan, *Red Rhino.* **World Book/Two-Can, 1997. ISBN 0716644029 (pbk).**
> Red Rhino has a red balloon, which he loses among other red things. **T, PS**

Sharratt, Nick, *The Time It Took Tom.* **Ill. by Stephen Tucker. Little Tiger, 1999. ISBN 1888444630.**
> Tom paints everything in the living room red, and then he and his mother redo it. The story uses units of time from seconds to years. **PS, K**

Sis, Peter, *Fire Truck*. Greenwillow, 1998. ISBN 0688158781.
: Matt imagines that he is a red fire truck, complete with one driver, two ladders, and so on up to ten boots. **PS, K**

Walton, Rick, *That's My Dog!* Ill. by Julia Gorton. Putnam, 2001. ISBN 0399233520.
: A boy describes his big red dog, using many adjectives, including comparative ones. **PS, K**

Yorinks, Arthur, *Tomatoes from Mars*. Ill. by Mort Drucker. HarperCollins, 1999. ISBN 0062050702.
: Earth is attacked by giant tomatoes from Mars. **K, Pr**

Blue

Asbury, Kelly, *Bonnie's Blue House*. Henry Holt, 1997. ISBN 0805040226.
: Bonnie describes what she does at her home, which is all blue. **T, PS**

Bogacki, Tomek, *The Story of a Blue Bird*. Farrar, Straus & Giroux, 1998. ISBN 0374371970.
: A little blue bird goes looking for "nothing" and learns to fly in the process. **PS, K**

Kellogg, Steven, *The Mystery of the Stolen Blue Paint*. Dutton, 1993. ISBN 0140546723 (pbk).
: Belinda accuses the younger children of taking her blue paint. **PS, K, Pr**

Lionni, Leo, *Little Blue and Little Yellow*. Mulberry, 1995. ISBN 0688132855.
: Little Blue and Little Yellow hug each other and become green. **PS, K**

Martin, Bill, Jr., and Bernard Martin, *Chicken Chuck*. Ill. by Steven Salerno. Winslow, 2000. ISBN 1890817317.
: Chicken Chuck eats a magic seed and sprouts a blue feather, which makes him think he's superior to the other animals. **PS, K**

Rogers, Alan, *Blue Tortoise*. World Book/Two-Can, 1997. ISBN 0716644002 (pbk).
: Blue Tortoise makes his way slowly to a picnic, along with other blue creatures. **T, PS**

Sis, Peter, *Ship Ahoy!* Greenwillow, 1999. ISBN 068816644X.
: In this wordless book done all in blue, a boy imagines his sofa to be many kinds of ships. **T, PS**

Yellow

Asbury, Kelly, *Yolanda's Yellow School*. Henry Holt, 1997. ISBN 0805040234.
: Yolanda describes her day at school, which is all yellow. **T, PS**

Cohen, Caron Lee, *Three Yellow Dogs.* **Ill. by Peter Sis. Mulberry Books, 1997. ISBN 0688152864 (pbk).**
Very simple text introduces the number three and the color yellow. **T, PS**

Lionni, Leo, *Little Blue and Little Yellow.* **Mulberry, 1995. ISBN 0688132855.**
Little Blue and Little Yellow hug each other and become green. **PS, K**

Rogers, Alan, *Yellow Hippo.* **World Book/Two-Can, 2001. ISBN 1587281570.**
Simple story of Yellow Hippo and her yellow belongings. **T, PS**

Spinelli, Eileen, *In My New Yellow Shirt.* **Ill. by Hideko Takahashi. Henry Holt, 2001. ISBN 0805062424.**
In his new yellow shirt, a boy imagines himself to be a duck, a banana, and other yellow things. **PS, K**

Weitzman, Jacqueline Preiss, *You Can't Take a Balloon into the Metropolitan Museum.* **Ill. by Robin Preiss Glasser. Dial, 1998. ISBN 0803723016.**
Left outside the Metropolitan Museum of Art, a yellow balloon floats around New York, causing chaos. Interspersed in the wordless illustrations are photos of actual museum holdings. **PS, K**

Green

Arnold, Tedd, *Green Wilma.* **Dial, 1993. ISBN 0803713134.**
When Wilma wakes up green one morning, she starts acting like a frog. **PS, K, Pr**

Baker, Keith, *Little Green.* **Harcourt, 2001. ISBN 0152928596.**
A boy watches a green hummingbird. **PS, K**

Lionni, Leo, *Little Blue and Little Yellow.* **Mulberry, 1995. ISBN 0688132855.**
Little Blue and Little Yellow hug each other and become green. **PS, K**

Rogers, Alan, *Green Bear.* **World Book/Two-Can, 1997. ISBN 0716644053.**
Green Bear likes green best, but paints his house to match the seasons. **T, PS**

Sis, Peter, *Dinosaur!* **Greenwillow, 2000. ISBN 0688170498.**
While a boy is taking a bath, several green dinosaurs appear. Wordless. **PS**

Weitzman, Jacqueline Preiss, *You Can't Take a Balloon into the Museum of Fine Arts.* **Ill. by Robin Preiss Glasser. Dial, 2002. ISBN 0803725701.**
Left outside the Museum of Fine Arts, a green balloon floats around Boston, causing chaos. Interspersed in the wordless illustrations are photos of actual museum holdings. **PS, K**

Orange

Bunting, Eve, *The Pumpkin Fair.* **Ill. by Eileen Christelow. Clarion, 1997. ISBN 0395700604.**
There are all kinds of pumpkin activities at the pumpkin fair. **PS, K**

Kellogg, Steven, *The Mystery of the Flying Orange Pumpkin.* **Dutton, 1992. ISBN 0140546707.**
Children plant a pumpkin for Halloween, but the new owner of the property claims the pumpkin is his. A cheerful trick provides a way for the children to have a jack-o'-lantern and the man to have a pie. **PS, K, Pr**

Weitzman, Jacqueline Preiss, *You Can't Take a Balloon into the National Gallery.* **Ill. by Robin Preiss Glasser. Dial, 2000. ISBN 0803723032.**
Left outside the National Gallery, an orange balloon floats around Washington, D.C., causing chaos. Interspersed in the wordless illustrations are photos of actual museum holdings. **PS, K**

Purple

Cornette, *Purple Coyote.* **Ill. by Rochette. Doubleday, 1999. ISBN 0385326645.**
A boy is curious to discover why a coyote is the unusual color of purple. **PS, K**

Johnson, Crockett, *Harold and the Purple Crayon.* **HarperCollins, 1977. ISBN 0060229357.**
Harold draws himself an adventure with his purple crayon. **PS, K**

Pearson, Tracy Campbell, *The Purple Hat.* **Farrar, Straus & Giroux, 1997. ISBN 0374361533.**
Annie loses her favorite purple hat, and everyone brings her other purple hats until she finds her own. **PS, K**

Rau, Dana Meachen, *Purple Is Best.* **Ill. by Mike Cressy. Children's, 1999. ISBN 0516216384.**
Sue paints with blue and Fred paints with red until their colors mix and make purple. Simple text. **PS**

Black and White

Lewis, Paul Owen, *You Are Cordially Invited to P. Bear's New Year's Party!* **Tricycle, 1999. ISBN 1883672996 (pbk).**
A polar bear invites only black and white animals to his party. One arrives at one o'clock, two at two o'clock, and so on through twelve midnight. **PS, K**

Myers, Christopher, *Black Cat.* **Scholastic, 1999. ISBN 0590033751.**
Painted photographs illustrate the story of a black cat wandering the city streets. **PS, K**

Rau, Dana Meachen, *Bob's Vacation.* **Children's Press, 1999. ISBN 0516215434.**
Simple text tells of Bob the snowman, who goes on a tropical vacation to find colors other than the white of snow. **T, PS**

Tildes, Phyllis Limbacher, *Animals Black and White.* **Charlesbridge, 1996. ISBN 0881069612.**
Clues help identify many different black and white animals. See also board book *Baby Animals Black and White* (no text) [1998: ISBN 0881063134]. **PS, K**

Brown

Katz, Karen, *The Colors of Us.* **Henry Holt, 1999. ISBN 0805058648.**
Lena observes that everyone's skin is a different shade of brown, from peachy tan to darkest chocolate. **PS, K, Pr**

Russo, Marisabina, *The Big Brown Box.* **Greenwillow, 2000. ISBN 068817096X.**
Sam has fun playing with a large box, but doesn't want to share it with his little brother. **PS, K**

Color Mixing [Books explaining how secondary colors are formed from primary ones]

Baker, Alan, *White Rabbit's Color Book.* **Kingfisher, 1994. ISBN 1856979539.**
White Rabbit goes from one paint pot to another, changing his color, mixing secondary colors from primary ones. **PS**

Bond, Michael, *Paddington's Colors.* **Ill. by John Lobban. Puffin, 1996. ISBN 0140557644 (pbk).**
Paddington Bear does his spring cleaning, showing different colors. Also shows how to mix colors. **PS**

Bourgoing, Pascal, *Colors.* **Ill. by P. M. Valet and Sylvaine Perols. Scholastic, 1991. ISBN 0590452363 (spiral binding).**
Transparent overlays help introduce colors and how to mix them. **PS, K, Pr**

Brown, Margaret Wise, *The Color Kittens.* **Ill. by Alice and Martin Provensen. Golden, 2000. ISBN 0307102343.**
Two kittens mix paint and make different colors. **PS, K**

Dena, Anaël, *Colors.* **Ill. by Christel Desmoinaux. Gareth Stevens, 1997. ISBN 0836819845.**
There are many things of one color in each picture. Also explains mixing colors. **PS, K**

Edwards, Pamela Duncan, *Warthogs Paint: A Messy Color Book.* **Ill. by Henry Cole. Hyperion, 2001. ISBN 078680470X.**
The messy warthogs decide to paint their walls and get their red, blue, and yellow paints mixed. **PS, K**

Jonas, Ann, *Color Dance.* **Greenwillow, 1989. ISBN 0688059902.**
Children dance with transparent scarves, identifying and mixing colors. **PS, K**

Lionni, Leo, *Little Blue and Little Yellow.* **Knopf, 1990. ISBN 0394810406.**
Little Blue and his friend Little Yellow hug each other until they both become green. **PS, K**

Walsh, Ellen Stoll, *Mouse Magic.* **Harcourt, 2000. ISBN 0152003266.**
The crow wizard shows Kit the mouse how to mix secondary colors, and how complementary colors seem to move when placed next to each other. **PS, K**

Walsh, Ellen Stoll, *Mouse Paint.* **Harcourt Brace Jovanovich, 1989. ISBN 0152560254.**
White mice play in jars of paint, mixing orange, green, and purple from red, yellow, and blue. **T, PS**

Chapter Three

Shapes and Positions

Shape [Books introducing several different shapes]

Axelrod, Amy, *Pigs on the Ball: Fun with Math and Sports.* **Ill. by Sharon McGinley-Nally. Simon & Schuster, 1998. ISBN 0689815654.**
The pigs go to a miniature golf course. Circle, triangle, hexagon, square, oval, semicircle, diamond, rectangle, octagon. Curved lines, parallel lines, angles, right angle. **K, Pr**

Baker, Alan, *Brown Rabbit's Shape Book.* **Kingfisher, 1999. ISBN 1856979504.**
Brown Rabbit opens a package of colored shape balloons: includes triangle, circle, rectangle, square, oval, sausage-shape, pear-shape, plus red, orange, green, purple. **T, PS**

Blackstone, Stella, *Bear in a Square.* **Ill. by Debbie Harter. Barefoot Books, 1998. ISBN 1901223582.**
Asks the reader to find simple shapes—square, heart, circle, rectangle, "moon"(crescent shape), triangle, diamond, zigzag, oval. **PS, K**

Burns, Marilyn, *The Greedy Triangle.* **Ill. by Gordon Silveria. Scholastic, 1995. ISBN 0590489917.**
A triangle wants more sides, and turns into a quadrilateral, pentagon, hexagon and so on, before becoming a triangle again. Information for adults and suggested activities. **K, Pr**

Carle, Eric, *The Secret Birthday Message.* **Crowell, 1981. ISBN 0690723474.**
In order to find his birthday present, Tim has to follow a message that directs him below, behind, and so on, various shapes. **PS, K**

Dodds, Dayle Ann, *The Shape of Things.* **Ill. by Julie Lacome. Candlewick, 1996. ISBN 1564026981 (pbk).**
Square, circle, triangle, rectangle, oval, and diamond are introduced, then turned into complete pictures. **PS, K**

Ehlert, Lois, *Color Zoo.* **Lippincott Williams & Wilkins, 1989. ISBN 0397322593.**
Pages with cutouts in different shapes make abstract portraits of various animals. Shapes used are star, circle, square, triangle, rectangle, heart, oval, diamond, octagon, hexagon. See also the similar *Color Farm* [1990, 0397324413]. **PS, K**

Emberley, Ed, *The Wing on a Flea: A Book about Shapes.* **Little, Brown, 2001. ISBN 0316234877.**
Bright illustrations and rhymes introduce shapes. Also 1961 edition with different illustrations. **PS, K**

Emberley, Rebecca, *My Shapes: Mis Formas.* **Little, Brown, 2000. ISBN 0316233552.**
A shape and an item in that shape are identified in English and Spanish. Includes square, circle, triangle, diamond, rectangle, oval, star, crescent, teardrop. Board. **T, PS**

Falwell, Cathryn, *Shape Space.* **Houghton Mifflin, 1992. ISBN 0395613051.**
A little girl plays with rectangles, triangles, semicircles, circles, and squares. **PS**

Friedman, Aileen, *A Cloak for the Dreamer.* **Ill. by Kim Howard. Scholastic, 1995. ISBN 0590489879.**
The tailor's sons make cloaks of different colored shapes—rectangle, square, and circle—but the circles don't fit into a solid cloak until they're recut into hexagons. **Pr**

Greene, Rhonda Gowler, *When a Line Bends, A Shape Begins.* **Ill. by James Kaczman. Houghton Mifflin, 1997. ISBN 0395786061.**
Shows how many shapes begin with the bending of a line. **PS, K, Pr**

Henkes, Kevin, *Circle Dogs.* **Ill. by Dan Yaccarino. Greenwillow, 1998. ISBN 0688154468.**
Two dogs who sleep in circle shapes live in a square house. **PS, K, Pr**

Hill, Eric, *Spot's Big Book of Colors, Shapes and Numbers.* **Putnam, 1994. ISBN 0399226796.**
Large pages with multiple illustrations show colors, simple shapes, and numbers, with numerals, 1 to 10. **PS**

Hoban, Tana, *Shapes, Shapes, Shapes*. Morrow, 1986. ISBN 0688058329.
   Each color photo of everyday things contains different shapes to identify. **PS, K**

Lorenz, Joanna, *Let's Look at Shapes*. Ill. by Lucy Tizard. Lorenz, 1999. ISBN 0754803023.
   Oversized board book has photographs of many things for each shape, including solid shapes. **T, PS**

Maccarone, Grace, *The Silly Story of Goldie Locks and the Three Squares*. Ill. by Anne Kennedy. Scholastic, 1996. ISBN 059054344X (pbk).
   Goldie Locks visits a house where things are in the shapes of triangles, circles, squares, and rectangles. **PS, K**

Maccarone, Grace, *Three Pigs, One Wolf, and Seven Magic Shapes*. Ill. by David Neuhaus. Scholastic, 1997. ISBN 0590308572 (pbk).
   Three pigs are each given a collection of shapes and each one makes something different, but the house is the most useful creation. **Pr**

MacDonald, Suse, *Sea Shapes*. Harcourt Brace/Voyager, 1998. ISBN 0152017003 (pbk).
   Sea creatures are used to introduce shapes. **PS, K**

MacKinnon, Debbie, *Eye Spy Shapes*. Ill. by Anthea Sieveking. Charlesbridge, 2000. ISBN 0881061352.
   Photographs glimpsed through cutout shapes illustrate circles, squares, triangles, rectangles, and stars. **PS**

Murphy, Stuart J., *Circus Shapes*. Ill. by Edward Miller. HarperCollins, 1998. ISBN 0060274360.
   Acts in a circus introduce square, circle, rectangle, and triangle. **PS**

Neuschwander, Cindy, *Sir Cumference and the First Round Table: A Math Adventure*. Ill. by Wayne Geehan. Charlesbridge, 1999. ISBN 1570911606.
   King Arthur tries many different shapes for the table for his knights. **Pr**

Onyefulu, Ifeoma, *A Triangle for Adaora: An African Book of Shapes*. Dutton, 2000. ISBN 0525463828.
   Photos of traditional African things introduce many shapes. **PS, K, Pr**

Rocklin, Joanne, *Not Enough Room!* Ill. by Cristina Ong. Scholastic, 1998. ISBN 0590399624 (pbk).
   Two girls who have to share a square room try dividing it into rectangles and triangles. **PS, K**

Rogers, Alan, *Ship Shape*. Two-Can, 2000. ISBN 1587281554.
   Blue Tortoise, Green Bear, Red Rhino, and Yellow Hippo make a boat out of simple shapes. **PS**

Thong, Roseanne, *Round Is a Mooncake: A Book of Shapes.* **Ill. by Grace Lin. Chronicle, 2000. ISBN 0811826767.**
A variety of round, square, and rectangular things are shown in a Chinese-American neighborhood. **PS**

Ziefert, Harriet, *Squarehead.* **Ill. by Todd McKie. Houghton Mifflin, 2001. ISBN 0618083782.**
Squareheaded George only likes square things until a dream of outer space shows him the beauty of other shapes. **PS, K**

Books Introducing Specific Shapes

Circle

Baranski, Joan Sullivan, *Round Is a Pancake.* **Ill. by Yu-Mei Han. Dutton, 2001. ISBN 0525461736.**
Round things are shown all over a fairy-tale kingdom. **PS**

Dotlich, Rebecca Kai, *What Is Round?* **Photos by Maria Ferrari. Harper Festival, 1999. ISBN 0694012084.**
Photos of many things that are round. **PS, K**

Emberley, Ed, *Ed Emberley's Picture Pie: A Circle Drawing Book.* **Little, Brown, 1984. ISBN 0316234265 (pbk).**
Shows how many different things can be drawn starting with a circle or part of a circle. **K, Pr**

Engel, Diana, *Circle Song.* **Marshall Cavendish, 1999. ISBN 0761450408.**
A loving good-night story, with round moons, faces, and other round things. **PS**

Grover, Max, *Circles and Squares Everywhere!* **Browndeer/Harcourt Brace, 1996. ISBN 0152000917.**
Simple text and more elaborate pictures show many things in the shape of circles and squares. **PS, K**

Hoban, Tana, *So Many Circles, So Many Squares.* **Greenwillow, 1998. ISBN 0688151655.**
Colored photographs of everyday things that are in the shape of circles or squares. Wordless. **PS, K**

Neuschwander, Cindy, *Sir Cumference and the Dragon of Pi.* **Ill. by Wayne Geehan. Charlesbridge, 1999. ISBN 1570911649 (pbk).**
Radius must discover the value of pi in order to change his father back from a dragon. **Pr**

Rau, Dana Meachen, *Circle City.* **Ill. by Susan Miller. Children's, 1999. ISBN 0516216325.**
A girl sees many circles as she walks through the city. Simple text, small format. **PS**

Square

Dotlich, Rebecca Kai, *What Is Square?* **Photos by Maria Ferrari. Harper Festival, 1999. ISBN 0694012076.**
Photos of many things that are square. **PS, K**

Grover, Max, *Circles and Squares Everywhere!* **Browndeer/Harcourt Brace, 1996. ISBN 0152000917.**
Simple text and more elaborate pictures show many things in the shape of circles and squares. **PS, K**

Hoban, Tana, S*o Many Circles, So Many Squares.* **Greenwillow, 1998. ISBN 0688151655.**
Colored photographs of everyday things that are in the shape of circles or squares. Wordless. **PS, K**

Ziefert, Harriet, *Squarehead.* **Ill. by Todd McKie. Houghton Mifflin, 2001. ISBN 0618083782.**
Squareheaded George only likes square things until a dream of outer space shows him the beauty of other shapes. **PS, K**

Triangle

Burns, Marilyn, *The Greedy Triangle.* **Ill. by Gordon Silveria. Scholastic, 1995. ISBN 0590489917.**
A triangle wants more sides, and turns into a quadrilateral, pentagon, hexagon, and so on, before becoming a triangle again. Information for adults and suggested activities. **K, Pr**

Dotlich, Rebecca Kai, *What Is a Triangle?* **Ill. by Maria Ferrari. Harper Festival, 2000. ISBN 0694013927.**
Photographs of many things that are triangular in shape. **PS, K**

Diamond-Shape

Bateson-Hill, Margaret, *Shota and the Star Quilt.* **Ill. by Christine Fowler. Zero to Ten, 1998. ISBN 1840890215.**
A Lakota family makes a quilt to celebrate the homes they might lose, but the quilt changes the developer's mind. Text in Lakota and English. Directions for using diamond shapes to make a star quilt. **K, Pr**

Solid Shapes

Baker, Alan, *Brown Rabbit's Shape Book*. **Kingfisher, 1999. ISBN 1856979504.**
Brown Rabbit opens a package of colored shape balloons: includes triangle, circle, rectangle, square, oval, sausage-shape, pear-shape, plus red, orange, green, purple. **T, PS**

Hoban, Tana, *Cubes, Cones, Cylinders, & Spheres*. **Greenwillow, 2000. ISBN 0688153259.**
Photographs of everyday things that have various solid shapes. **PS, K, Pr**

Lorenz, Joanna, *Let's Look at Shapes*. Ill. by Lucy Tizard. **Lorenz, 1999. ISBN 0754803023.**
Oversized board book has photographs of many things for each shape, including solid shapes. **T, PS**

Murphy, Stuart J., *Captain Invincible and the Space Shapes*. Ill. by Rémy Simard. **HarperCollins, 2001. ISBN 0060280220.**
In outer space, Captain Invincible encounters solid shapes like pyramids and cubes. **PS, K**

Van Fleet, Matthew, *Spotted Yellow Frogs*. **Dial, 1998. ISBN 0803723504.**
Lift-the-flap book showcases three-dimensional shapes and patterns that resolve into pictures of animals. **PS, K**

Position [Books showing relative location, usually using prepositions]

Appelt, Kathi, *Elephants Aloft*. Ill. by Keith Baker. **Harcourt Brace, 1993. ISBN 015225384X.**
Pictures tell the story of two elephants' travel from India to Africa. The only words are prepositions. **T, PS**

Axtell, David, *We're Going on a Lion Hunt*. **Henry Holt, 2000. ISBN 0805061592.**
Two girls look for a lion through the grass, a lake, a swamp, a cave. Over, under, around, and through. **PS, K**

Berenstain, Stan, and Jan Berenstain, *Bears in the Night*. **Random, 1971. ISBN 0394822862.**
Bears sneak out of bed, to the window, down the tree, and so on. Simple text. **T, PS**

Berenstain, Stan, and Jan Berenstain, *The Berenstain Bears and the Spooky Old Tree*. **Random, 1978. ISBN 0394939107.**
Three bears dare to go into a spooky tree: up, through, down, out, without. **PS, K**

Berenstain, Stan, and Jan Berenstain, *Inside Outside Upside Down*. **Random, 1968. ISBN 0394811429.**
>Brief text. A young bear hides in a box and rides to town. **T, PS**

Brown, Margaret Wise, *Two Little Trains*. **Ill. by Leo and Diane Dillon. HarperCollins, 2001. ISBN 0060283769.**
>Two trains—a real one and a toy one—travel on contrasting journeys. Many prepositions are used to describe their trips. **PS**

Bryant-Mole, Karen, *Where Is Mortimer?* **Gareth Stevens, 2000. ISBN 0836826221.**
>A teddy bear demonstrates contrasting prepositions. Illustrated with photos. **PS**

Carle, Eric, *The Secret Birthday Message*. **Crowell, 1981. ISBN 0690723474.**
>In order to find his birthday present, Tim has to follow a message that directs him below, behind, and so on, various shapes. **PS, K**

Cohen, Caron Lee, *Where's the Fly?* **Ill. by Nancy Barnet. Greenwillow, 1996. ISBN 0688140440.**
>Starting with the fly on the dog's nose, this book shows increasingly distant perspectives, all the way to the ocean on the earth. **PS, K**

Crebbin, June, *Into the Castle*. **Ill. by John Bendall-Brunello. Candlewick, 1996. ISBN 1564028224.**
>Three children, a horse, and a dog search a castle for a monster. **PS, K**

Heller, Ruth, *Behind the Mask: A Book about Prepositions*. **Grosset & Dunlap, 1995. ISBN 0448411237.**
>Colorful pictures illustrate and explain prepositions. **K, Pr**

Hill, Eric, *Where's Spot?* **Putnam, 1980. ISBN 0399207589.**
>A lift-the-flap book showing places to look for a missing dog. **T, PS**

Hines-Stephens, Sarah, *Bean Soup*. **Ill. by Anna Grossnickle Hines. Red Wagon, 2000. ISBN 0152021647.**
>A dog and a cat demonstrate opposite prepositions. Board book. **T**

Hoban, Tana, *Over, Under & Through and Other Spatial Concepts*. **Macmillan, 1973. ISBN 007448207.**
>Black-and-white photographs illustrate various prepositions. **PS**

Jorgensen, Gail, *Gotcha!* **Ill. by Kerry Argent. Scholastic, 1995. ISBN 0690962086.**
>Bertha Bear chases a fly that disrupted her birthday party. **PS**

Lavis, Steve, *Little Mouse Has an Adventure*. **Ragged Bears, 2000. ISBN 1929927096.**
>Little Mouse takes a walk. Prepositions describe his route. **T, PS**

Lia, Simone, *Red's Great Chase.* **Dutton, 1999. ISBN 0525462139.**
> A blue monster chases Red up, down, around, through, and all over the world—until she tags Red and it's her turn to be It. **PS**

McGuirk, Leslie, *Tucker off His Rocker.* **Dutton, 2000. ISBN 0525463984.**
> In this small format book, Tucker the dog goes on an elaborate journey, using many prepositions. **PS**

Miller, Margaret, *Where Does It Go?* **Greenwillow, 1992. ISBN 0688109284.**
> Asks children to determine the appropriate place to put something, like a sock or a toothbrush. Photographs illustrate several humorous wrong answers as well as the right one. **PS, K**

Murphy, Stuart J., *The Greatest Gymnast of All.* **Ill. by Cynthia Jabar. HarperCollins, 1998. ISBN 0060276088.**
> Zoë goes through her gymnastics routine demonstrating opposite positions. **PS, K**

Penner, Lucille Recht, *Where's that Bone?* **Ill. by Lynn Adams. Kane, 2000. ISBN 1575650975 (pbk).**
> Jill helps her dog keep track of the bones he buries, using positions marked on maps. **PS, K**

Roche, Denis, *Ollie All Over.* **Houghton Mifflin, 1997. ISBN 0395811244.**
> A little puppy hides from his mother in various places. Board. **T, PS**

In & Out

Pluckrose, Henry, *Inside and Outside.* **Ill. by Steve Shott. Children's Press, 1995. ISBN 0516082388.**
> Photos explain and demonstrate inside and outside. **PS**

Opposites

Berenstain, Stan, and Jan Berenstain, *Inside Outside Upside Down.* **Random, 1968. ISBN 0394811429.**
> Brief text. A young bear hides in a box and rides to town. **T, PS**

Bernhard, Durga, *Earth, Sky, Wet, Dry: A Book of Nature Opposites.* **Orchard, 2000. ISBN 053130213X.**
> Illustrations of opposites, using scenes from nature. **T, PS**

Bernhard, Durga, *To & Fro, Fast & Slow.* **Walker, 2001. ISBN 0802787827.**
> Going back and forth between her mother's country home and her father's city apartment, a girl experiences many different opposites. The only words are the opposites. **PS, K**

Blackstone, Stella, *How Big Is a Pig?* Ill. by Clare Beaton. Barefoot Books, 2000. ISBN 1841480770.
Animals illustrate opposites. 3-D felt pictures. **PS**

Bond, Michael, *Paddington's Opposites.* Ill. by John Lobban. Puffin, 1996. ISBN 0140557652 (pbk).
Paddington Bear illustrates opposites in large, simple pictures. **T, PS**

Boynton, Sandra, *Pajama Time!* Workman, 2000. ISBN 0761119752.
Animals wear different kinds of pajamas. Board book. **T, PS**

Cabrera, Jane, *Panda Big and Panda Small.* DK, 1999. ISBN 0789434857.
A big panda and a small panda like opposite things. **PS**

Corey, Dorothy, *You Go Away.* Ill. by Diane Paterson. Whitmen, 2nd ed., 1999. ISBN 0807594423.
Shows people going away and coming back. Very simple text. **T**

Crews, Nina, *A High, Low, Near, Far, Loud, Quiet Story.* Greenwillow, 1999. ISBN 0688167942.
Two children's activities during the day are used to illustrate opposites. Photos. **PS, K**

Crimi, Carolyn, *Outside, Inside.* Ill. by Linnea Asplind Riley. Simon & Schuster, 1995. ISBN 0671886886.
Contrasts what goes on inside a house with what is going on outside. **PS**

Dena, Anaël, *Opposites.* Ill. by Christel Desmoinaux. Gareth Stevens, 1997. ISBN 083681987X.
Many things in each picture illustrate a pair of opposites. **PS, K**

Emberley, Rebecca, *My Opposites; Mis Opuestos.* Little, Brown, 2000. ISBN 0316233455.
Simple pictures of opposites, identified in English and Spanish. **T**

Hendra, Sue, *Opposites.* Candlewick, 1999. ISBN 0763608947.
The reader is asked to pick the correct opposite for each word. Lifting a flap tells if the answer is correct. **PS**

Hines-Stephens, Sarah, *Bean Soup.* Ill. by Anna Grossnickle Hines. Red Wagon, 2000. ISBN 0152021647.
A dog and a cat demonstrate opposite prepositions. Board book. **T**

Hoban, Tana, *Exactly the Opposite.* **Greenwillow, 1990. ISBN 0688088619.**
Colored photographs with no words illustrate opposite concepts. **PS, K, Pr**

Inkpen, Mick, *Kipper's Book of Opposites.* **Harcourt Brace, Red Wagon, 1995. ISBN 0152006680.**
Kipper illustrates several simple opposites. Board. Hardcover edition 1994. **T**

King, Stephen Michael, *Henry and Amy (Right-Way-Round and Upside Down).* **Walker, 1998. ISBN 0802786863.**
Henry, who does everything topsy-turvy, meets Amy, who does everything right, and they both learn from each other. **PS, K**

MacKinnon, Debbie, *What Size?* **Ill. by Anthea Sieveking. Dial, 1995. SBN 0803717458.**
Photographs of children playing illustrate things of different sizes, including long and short, thick and thin, high and low, wide and narrow. **PS**

Manna, Giovanni, *You and Me.* **Barefoot Books, 2000. ISBN 1841482633.**
A girl and boy pretend to be opposite or contrasting things, like a valley and a hill, a tiger and a bear, or dark and bright. **PS, K**

McLenighan, Valjean, *Stop — Go, Fast — Slow.* **Ill. by Margrit Fiddle. Children's, 1982. ISBN 0516036173.**
Explains and presents opposites. Simple text. **PS**

Meister, Carl, *Catch That Cat!* **Ill. by David Brooks. Children's Press, 1999. ISBN 0516216147.**
A girl and her cat illustrate various opposites. Simple text. **T, PS**

Milgrim, David, *My Friend Lucky.* **Atheneum, 2002. ISBN 0689842538.**
Cartoon-like illustrations of a boy and his dog show opposites. **PS, K**

Minters, Frances, *Too Big, Too Small, Just Right.* **Ill. by Janie Bynum. Harcourt, 2001. ISBN 0152021574.**
Two rabbit friends find what is just right out of opposites like heavy and light, dark and bright. Simple text. **PS**

Murphy, Stuart J., *The Greatest Gymnast of All.* **Ill. by Cynthia Jabar. HarperCollins, 1998. ISBN 0060276088.**
Zoë goes through her gymnastics routine demonstrating opposite positions. **PS, K**

Schroeder, Pamela J. P., and Jean M. Donisch, *Opposites.* **Rourke, 1996. ISBN 0866255796.**
Photograph collages show opposites. **PS, K**

Serfozo, Mary, *What's What? A Guessing Game*. Ill. by Keiko Narahashi. Margaret K. McElderry, 1996. ISBN 0689806531.
Descriptions of things that illustrate opposites. **PS, K**

Stevens, Janet, *Tops & Bottoms*. Harcourt Brace, 1995. ISBN 0152928510.
When they share a garden, Hare tricks Bear into always choosing the less useful part of the crops: tops when carrots are planted, bottoms when lettuce is planted. **PS, K, Pr**

Stickland, Paul, and Henrietta Stickland, *Dinosaur Roar!* Dutton, 1994. ISBN 0525452761.
Dinosaurs illustrate opposites. **PS, K**

Swinburne, Stephen R., *What's Opposite?* Boyds Mills, 2000. ISBN 1563978814.
Photographs illustrate opposites, some of which are left up to the reader to name. **PS, K**

Tullet, Hervé, *Night Day: A Book of Eye-Catching Opposites*. Little, Brown, 1999. ISBN 0316842443.
Pages with cutouts illustrate many opposites, including unusual ones like "pills/candy" and "complete/ruined." **PS**

Cause & Effect

Aardema, Verna, *Why Mosquitoes Buzz in People's Ears: A West African Tale*. Ill. by Leo and Diane Dillon. Dial, 1984. ISBN 0803760892.
Mosquito's thoughtless joke starts a chain of events that ends in the death of an owlet. **PS, K, Pr**

Ada, Alma Flora, *The Rooster Who Went to His Uncle's Wedding: A Latin American Folktale*. Ill. by Kathleen Kuchera. Paper Star, 1998. ISBN 0698116828 (pbk).
Rooster needs to have his beak cleaned, which is accomplished by a chain of events. **PS, K, Pr**

Aylesworth, Jim, *Aunt Pitty Patty's Piggy*. Ill. by Barbara McClintock. Scholastic, 1999. ISBN 0590899872.
Nelly must make a chain of events happen to get her aunt's pig to go through the gate. **PS, K, Pr**

Coursen, Valerie, *Mordant's Wish*. Henry Holt, 1997. ISBN 0805043748.
Mordant the mole's wish for a turtle friend sparks a chain of events that leads to the wish coming true. **K, Pr**

dePaola, Tomie, *Charlie Needs a Cloak!* **Simon & Schuster, 1988. ISBN 0671664670 (pbk).**
Charlie the shepherd takes an entire year to make himself a red cloak, starting by shearing the sheep in the spring, spinning and dyeing in the summer, and weaving and sewing in the fall, so that the cloak is ready for winter. **PS, K**

George, Lindsay Barrett, *Around the Pond: Who's Been Here?* **Greenwillow, 1996. ISBN 0688143768.**
While picking blueberries, two children discover signs of many animals around the pond. See also *In the Snow: Who's Been Here?* [1995: ISBN 0688123201]. **PS, K, Pr**

Glaser, Omri, *Round the Garden*. **Ill. by Byron Glaser and Sandra Higashi. Harry N. Abrams, 1999. ISBN 0810941376.**
A tear makes a puddle, which eventually becomes the rain to water the onions, which cause fresh tears. Simple text. **T, PS**

Kalan, Robert, *Jump, Frog, Jump!* **Ill. by Byron Barton. Morrow, 1995. ISBN 068813954X.**
In this cumulative tale, a frog escapes from many predators, including some boys with a basket. **PS**

McGuire, Richard, *What Goes Around Comes Around*. **Viking, 1995. ISBN 0670863963.**
A doll falling out of a window sets off a complicated chain of events around the world, which finally brings the doll back home. **PS, K**

Noble, Trinka Hakes, *The Day Jimmy's Boa Ate the Wash*. **Ill. by Steven Kellogg. Dial, 1980. ISBN 0803717237.**
Jimmy's snake causes a lot of trouble on a class trip to a farm. **PS, K**

Numeroff, Laura Joffe, *If You Give a Mouse a Cookie*. **Ill. by Felicia Bond. HarperCollins, 1985. ISBN 0060245867.**
Shows the chain of events that start when you give a mouse a cookie. See also *If You Give a Moose a Muffin* [1991: ISBN 0060244054] and *If You Give a Pig a Pancake* [1998: ISBN 0060266864]. **PS, K, Pr**

Whippo, Walt, *Little White Duck*. **Ill. by Joan Paley. Little, Brown, 2000. ISBN 0316032271.**
The white duck, green frog, black bug, and red snake interact in the familiar song. **PS, K**

Wormell, Mary, *Why Not?* **Farrar, Straus & Giroux, 2000. ISBN 0374384223.**
A kitten learns why he should not annoy the other animals. **PS**

Patterns

Axelrod, Amy, *Pigs in the Corner: Fun with Math and Dance.* **Ill. by Sharon McGinley-Nally. Simon & Schuster, 2001. ISBN 068982470X.**
Mr. Pig calls a square dance, and the dancers must figure out left and right and other directions. **K, Pr**

Bateson-Hill, Margaret, *Shota and the Star Quilt.* **Ill. by Christine Fowler. Zero to Ten, 1998. ISBN 1840890215.**
A Lakota family makes a quilt to celebrate the homes they might lose, but the quilt changes the developer's mind. Text in Lakota and English. Directions for using diamond shapes to make a star quilt. **K, Pr**

Harris, Trudy, *Pattern Fish.* **Ill. by Anne Canevari Green. Millbrook, 2000. ISBN 0761317120.**
Sea creatures are used to illustrate both patterns (yellow—black, yellow—black) and sequences of actions (stretch—spurt—glide). **PS, K, Pr**

Hissey, Jane, *Old Bear's Surprise Painting.* **Philomel, 2001. ISBN 0399237097.**
The toys make colorful patterns that don't quite work out as they planned, but Old Bear puts them together to make one picture. **K**

Marshall, Janet, *Look Once Look Twice.* **Ticknor & Fields, 1995. ISBN 0395716446.**
Each lowercase letter is patterned in a design that is revealed to be part of something starting with that letter. Patterns are stylized and not easy to guess. **PS, K**

Murphy, Stuart J., *Beep Beep, Vroom Vroom!* **HarperCollins, 2000. ISBN 0060280166.**
Molly plays with her brother's red, blue, and yellow cars and tries to line them up in the same sequence he had left them. **PS, K**

Murphy, Stuart J., *A Pair of Socks.* **Ill. by Lois Ehlert. HarperCollins, 1996. ISBN 0060258799.**
A sock looks for its mate. **PS, K**

Pluckrose, Henry, *Pattern.* **Ill. by Chris Fairclough. Children's, 1995. ISBN 0516454552.**
Photographs introduce patterns. **PS, K, Pr**

Van Fleet, Matthew, *Spotted Yellow Frogs.* **Dial, 1998. ISBN 0803723504.**
Lift-the-flap book showcases three-dimensional shapes and patterns that resolve into pictures of animals. **PS, K**

Symmetry

Murphy, Stuart J., *Let's Fly a Kite.* Ill. by Brian Floca. HarperCollins, 2000. ISBN 0060280344.
Learning about symmetry helps Hannah and Bob find ways to share fairly. **PS, K**

Left & Right

Axelrod, Amy, *Pigs in the Corner: Fun with Math and Dance.* Ill. by Sharon McGinley-Nally. Simon & Schuster, 2001. ISBN 068982470X.
Mr. Pig calls a square dance, and the dancers must figure out left and right and other directions. **K, Pr**

Murphy, Stuart J., *Bug Dance.* Ill. by Christopher Santoro. HarperCollins, 2002. ISBN 0060289104.
The bugs learn a dance in their gym class, which consists of moving to the left and right, forward and back. **PS, K**

Smith, Mavis, *Which Way, Ben Bunny?* Scholastic, 1996. ISBN 0590622455.
Ben Bunny searches for his stolen carrot, following directions given to him by a crow. Lifting flaps on the right or left will tell the reader if he's chosen correctly. **PS**

Point of View *[Books that show events through the eyes of different characters]*

Alborough, Jez, *Watch Out! Big Bro's Coming!* Candlewick, 1997. ISBN 0763601306.
When mouse says Big Bro is coming, each animal imagines a creature larger than himself. **PS, K**

Browne, Anthony, *Voices in the Park.* DK, 1998. ISBN 078942522X.
A girl, her father, and their dog meet a boy, his mother, and their dog at the park. The simple incident is retold from four different points of view. **Pr**

Lobel, Arnold, *Ming Lo Moves the Mountain.* Mulberry, 1993. ISBN 0688109950 (pbk).
A wise man teaches Ming Lo to "move" the mountain that is too near their home. They are to dismantle their house and do a dance that consists of walking backwards. **K, Pr**

McMillan, Bruce, *Mouse Views: What the Class Pet Saw*. **Holiday House, 1993. ISBN 0823410080.**
  Photos show the world of a school from the point of view of a mouse. **PS, K**

Stoeke, Janet Morgan, *A Friend for Minerva Louise*. **Dutton, 1997. ISBN 0525458697.**
  A chicken looks at the new baby's things and interprets them in her own way. See also *Minerva Louise* [1988: ISBN ISBN 0525443746], *A Hat for Minerva Louise* [1994: ISBN 0525453288], *Minerva Louise at School* [1996: ISBN 0525454942], and *Minerva Louise at the Fair* [2000: ISBN 0525464395]. **PS, K**

Van Allsburg, Chris, *Two Bad Ants*. **Houghton Mifflin, 1988. ISBN 0395486688.**
  Two ants discover some sugar in a kitchen, shown from their point of view. **PS, K, Pr**

Wolff, Ferida, *A Weed Is a Seed*. **Ill. by Janet Pederson. Houghton Mifflin, 1996. ISBN 0395722918.**
  Rhymes show that many things can be good or bad, depending on your point of view. **K, Pr**

Wormell, Mary, *Hilda Hen's Scary Night*. **Harcourt Brace, 1995. ISBN 0152009906.**
  In the farmyard at night, Hilda Hen is frightened by ordinary things that seem to be something else. **PS, K**

Young, Ed, *Seven Blind Mice*. **Philomel, 1992. ISBN 0399222618.**
  Seven blind mice of different colors each feel a different part of an elephant and get a very different idea of what it is like. **PS, K, Pr**

Chapter Four

Numbers, Counting, Math, and Money

Numbers; Things to Count [Books that show numbers or numerals in no specific order, or that have random numbers of things to count]

Arenson, Roberta, ill., *One, Two, Skip a Few: First Number Rhymes.* **Barefoot, 1998. ISBN 190122399X.**
Traditional rhymes having to do with numbers, from "One potato, two potato" to "As I was going to St. Ives." **PS, K, Pr**

Axelrod, Amy, *Pigs Go to Market: Fun with Math and Shopping.* **Ill. by Sharon McGinley-Nally. Simon & Schuster, 1997. ISBN 0689810695.**
On Halloween Mrs. Pig wins a five-minute shopping spree in the supermarket. The reader is invited to count, multiply, and measure. **Pr**

Berenstain, Stan, and Jan Berenstain, *The Berenstain Bears Go Up and Down.* **Random, 1999. ISBN 0679887202.**
Different numbers of bears play on the escalators. **PS, K**

Bond, Felicia, *Tumble Bumble.* **Front Street, 1996. ISBN 1886910154.**
A bug meets several other animal friends, making ten in all. No numerals. **PS, K**

Burns, Marilyn, *How Many Feet? How Many Tails?* **Ill. by Lynn Adams. Scholastic, 1996. ISBN 0690673602 (pbk).**
Counting animals' tails and feet to solve simple riddles, such as "What has 8 feet, 2 tails, and pulls a wagon?" **PS, K**

Capucilli, Alyssa Satin, *Mrs. McTats and Her Houseful of Cats.* Ill. by Joan Rankin. Margaret K. McElderry, 2001. ISBN 0689831854.
>Mrs. McTats has one cat named Abner. She then adds 24 more, in groups of two to six, which she names in alphabetical order, plus a dog she names Zoom. **PS, K**

Carle, Eric, *The Very Hungry Caterpillar.* Putnam, 1983. ISBN 0399208534.
>A caterpillar eats his way through the days of the week, including groups of one to five foods, then changes into a butterfly. **T, PS**

Chorao, Kay, *Number One Number Fun.* Holiday House, 1995. ISBN 0823411427.
>Animals in a circus invite the reader to add and subtract as they do their tricks. **PS, K**

Cohen, Caron Lee, *How Many Fish?* Ill. by S. D. Schindler. Harper Collins, 1998. ISBN 0060277130.
>Very simple text about six little fish, one of whom gets caught under a pail. **T, PS**

Crews, Donald, *Ten Black Dots.* Greenwillow, rev. ed., 1986. ISBN 0688060676.
>Shows things you can make with from 1 to 10 black dots. Numerals. **PS, K, Pr**

Cuyler, Margery, *100th Day Worries.* Ill. by Arthur Howard. Simon & Schuster, 2000. ISBN 080503191X.
>Jessica can't find 100 things to take to school for the hundredth day, but she does come up with 10 groups of 10 things. **K, Pr**

Dena, Anaël, *Numbers.* Ill. by Christel Desmoinaux. Gareth Stevens, 1997. ISBN 0836819861.
>Pictures with the appropriate number of things illustrate numerals 1 to 10. Also included are 100 rabbits to count (with numerals) and other counting games. **PS, K**

Edwards, Roberta, *Five Silly Fishermen.* Ill. by Sylvie Wickstrom. Random, 1989. ISBN 0679800921 (pbk).
>Easy-reader text about five fishermen who think one of them is missing, because each one counts the other four but not himself. **PS, K**

Enderle, Judith Ross, and Stephanie Gordon Tessler, *Where Are You, Little Zack?* Ill. by Brian Floca. Houghton Mifflin, 1997. ISBN 0395730929.
>In their search for Zack, the three duck brothers search all over New York City and encounter various numbers of things, including 80,000 fans at Yankee Stadium. **PS**

Friedman, Aileen, *The King's Commissioners.* Ill. by Susan Guevara. Scholastic, 1995. ISBN 0590489895.
>The king and his advisors count the commissioners in different ways—by twos, by fives and by tens. **K, Pr**

Giganti, Paul, Jr., *Each Orange Had 8 Slices: A Counting Book.* Ill. by Donald Crews. Greenwillow, 1992. ISBN 0688104282.
Many things to count and add or multiply: for example, two oranges with eight slices and two seeds in each slice. **K, Pr**

Giganti, Paul, Jr., *How Many Snails? A Counting Book.* Ill. by Donald Crews. Greenwillow, 1988. ISBN 0688063705.
The reader is asked to count things and to determine differences: for example, count all the flowers, then just the yellow ones. **PS, K**

Harris, Trudy, *100 Days of School.* Ill. by Beth Griffis Johnson. Millbrook, 1999. ISBN 0761312714.
Different ways of arriving at the number 100. **K, Pr**

Inkpen, Mick, *Kipper's Book of Numbers.* Harcourt Brace, Red Wagon, 1995. ISBN 015200646X.
One Kipper plays with groups of other animals, up to ten. Includes numerals. Board. **T**

Jocelyn, Marthe, *Hannah's Collections.* Dutton, 2000. ISBN 0525464425.
Hannah has too many collections to share just one with her class, so she creates a piece of sculpture with pieces from many collections. Story includes different things to count. **PS, K**

Jonas, Ann, *Splash.* Mulberry, 1995. ISBN 0688110517.
As different animals jump into and out of a pond, the reader is asked to tell how many are in the pond. **PS, K**

Koller, Jackie French, *One Monkey Too Many.* Ill. by Lynn Munsinger. Harcourt Brace, 1999. ISBN 0152000062.
A bike for one ends up with two monkeys, a golf cart for two ends up with three, and so on up to seven, with disastrous results. **PS, K**

Mallat, Kathy, *Seven Stars, More!* Walker, 1998. ISBN 0802786758.
Trying to get to sleep, Abby counts many things, but can only count as high as seven. Numerals are shown. **PS**

Merriam, Eve, *12 Ways to Get to 11.* Ill. by Bernie Karlin. Aladdin, 1996. ISBN 0689808925 (pbk).
Shows different groups of things that add up to 11. No numerals in the text. **K, Pr**

Murphy, Stuart J., *Animals on Board.* Ill. by R. W. Alley. HarperCollins, 1998. ISBN 0060274433.
Truckloads of animals are added up. **K, Pr**

Murphy, Stuart J., *Ready, Set, Hop!* **Ill. by Jon Buller. HarperCollins, 1996. ISBN 0060258772.**
Two frogs have a contest to see who can take fewer hops to get places. **Pr**

Naylor, Phyllis Reynolds, *Ducks Disappearing.* **Ill. by Tony Maddox. Atheneum, 1997. ISBN 0689319029.**
A boy counts the ducks he sees in the motel's courtyard, then notices later that there are fewer. He is able to solve the mystery of the ducks' disappearance. **PS, K, Pr**

Plummer, David, and John Archambault, *Counting Kittens.* **Ill. by Liisa Chauncy Guida. Silver Press, 1997. ISBN 0382396499.**
Trying to keep track of ten kittens is not easy. No numerals. **PS, K**

Schlein, Miriam, *More Than One.* **Ill. by Donald Crews. Greenwillow, 1996. ISBN 0688141021.**
Explains how one pair is two, one week is seven days, and other examples. **K, Pr**

Wells, Rosemary, *Bunny Party.* **Viking, 2001. ISBN 0670035017.**
Ruby invites seven stuffed animals to Grandma's birthday party, but Max adds some guests of his own. **PS, K**

Ziefert, Harriet, *A Dozen Dogs: A Read-and-Count Story.* **Ill. by Carol Nicklaus. Random, 1985. ISBN 0394869354 (pbk).**
Twelve dogs at the beach introduce many things to count. **PS**

Number Concept [Books that help with the understanding of numeration]

Birch, David, *The King's Chessboard.* **Ill. by Devis Grebu. Scott Foresman, 1993. ISBN 0140548807 (pbk).**
A wise man, forced to accept a reward from an Indian king, asks for one grain of rice on the first square of a chessboard, to be doubled on each following square. **K, Pr**

Demi, *One Grain of Rice: A Mathematical Folktale.* **Scholastic, 1997. ISBN 059093998X.**
The raja rewards the rani with one grain of rice to be doubled each day for thirty days, which soon adds up to much more than the raja bargained for. Shows how the total reaches one billion. **Pr**

Gag, Wanda, *Millions of Cats.* **Paper Star, 1996. ISBN 0698113632 (pbk).**
A man finds hundreds of cats, thousands of cats, millions and billions and trillions of cats. **PS, K**

Holtzman, Caren, *No Fair!* **Ill. by Joan Holub. Scholastic, 1997. ISBN 0590922300.**
Kristy and David try to discover what gives each one an equal chance. For

example, having more yellow marbles than blue ones does not give a fair chance of picking one or the other. **PS, K, Pr**

Hopkins, Lee Bennett, *Marvelous Math: A Book of Poems.* **Ill. by Karen Barbour. Simon & Schuster, 1997. ISBN 068980658.**
Short poems about mathematics, from a variety of authors. **K, Pr**

Munsch, Robert, *Moira's Birthday.* **Ill. by Michael Martchenko. Annick, 1989. ISBN 0920303854.**
Moira is supposed to invite six kids to her birthday party, but ends up inviting six grades (plus kindergarten). It takes ingenuity to feed them all and to clean up the mess. **PS, K, Pr**

Murphy, Stuart J., *Dinosaur Deals.* **Ill. by Kevin O'Malley. HarperCollins, 2001. ISBN 0060289260.**
While trading dinosaur cards, two boys learn about equivalent values. **K, Pr**

Rocklin, Joanne, *The Case of the Missing Birthday Party.* **Ill. by John Speirs. Scholastic, 1996. ISBN 0590673599 (pbk).**
Knowing about place value helps some children figure out the house number of the location of a birthday party. **Pr**

San Souci, Robert D., *Six Foolish Fishermen.* **Ill. by Doug Kennedy. Hyperion, 2000. ISBN 0786803851.**
These fishermen have a lot of trouble with logic, including the familiar problem of skipping oneself when counting. Cajun dialog. **K, Pr**

Scieszka, John, and Lane Smith, *Math Curse.* **Viking, 1995. ISBN 0670861944.**
A youngster starts seeing everything in terms of zany math problems. **Pr**

Ziefert, Harriet, *Math Riddles.* **Ill. by Andrea Baruffi. Viking, 1997. ISBN 0670874981.**
Riddles that involve some use of math. **K, Pr**

Books Emphasizing a Particular Number

One

Hoberman, Mary Ann, *One of Each.* **Ill. by Marjorie Priceman. Little, Brown, 1997. ISBN 0316367311.**
Oliver Tolliver has only one of each thing, but discovers that it's more fun to have two. **PS, K**

Schlein, Miriam, *More Than One.* **Ill. by Donald Crews. Greenwillow, 1996. ISBN 0688141021.**
Explains how one pair is two, one week is seven days, and other examples. **K, Pr**

Thompson, Lauren, *One Riddle, One Answer.* Ill. by Linda S. Wingerter. Scholastic, 2001. ISBN 0590313355.
>A sultan's daughter devises a riddle for her suitors to solve: "Placed above, it makes greater things small. Placed beside, it makes small things great. In matters that count, it always comes first. Where others increase, it keeps all things the same." The answer is One. **Pr**

Two

Aker, Suzanne, *What Comes in 2's, 3's, and 4's?* Ill. by Bernie Karlin. Aladdin, 1992. ISBN 0671792474 (pbk).
>Things of which there are two, three, and four. **PS, K**

Hoberman, Mary Ann, *One of Each.* Ill. by Marjorie Priceman. Little, Brown, 1997. ISBN 0316367311.
>Oliver Tolliver has only one of each thing, but discovers that it's more fun to have two. **PS, K**

Narahashi, Keiko, *Two Girls Can!* Margaret K. McElderry/Simon & Schuster, 2000. ISBN 0689826184.
>Celebrates all the things two girls can do together, but also shows that dancing can be done by any number. **T, PS**

Three

Aker, Suzanne, *What Comes in 2's, 3's, and 4's?* Ill. by Bernie Karlin. Aladdin, 1992. ISBN 0671792474 (pbk).
>Things of which there are two, three, and four. **PS, K**

Alter, Anna, *The Three Little Kittens.* Holt, 2001. ISBN 0805064710.
>Three kittens lose their mittens and find them again. **T, PS**

Barton, Byron, *The Three Bears.* HarperCollins, 1991. ISBN 0060204230.
>Goldilocks sneaks into the bears' house, eats some porridge, breaks a rocker, and falls asleep, after making comparisons. Simple text. **T, PS**

Berenstain, Stan, and Jan Berenstain, *The Berenstain Bears and the Spooky Old Tree.* Random, 1978. ISBN 0394939107.
>Three bears dare to go into a spooky tree: up, through, down, out, without. **PS, K**

Blackstone, Stella, *Baby Rock, Baby Roll.* Ill. by Denise & Fernando. Holiday House, 1997. ISBN 082341311X.
>Three babies do many things. **T, PS**

Cohen, Caron Lee, *Three Yellow Dogs.* Ill. by Peter Sis. Mulberry Books, 1997. ISBN 0688152864 (pbk).
>Very simple text introduces the number three and the color yellow. **T, PS**

Finch, Mary, *The Three Billy Goats Gruff.* Ill. by Roberta Arenson. Barefoot, 2001. ISBN 1841483494.
A colorfully illustrated edition of the traditional story of three goats outwitting a troll. **PS, K**

Galdone, Paul, *Three Little Kittens.* Clarion, 1986. ISBN 0899194265.
The familiar rhyme about three kittens who lose their mittens. **T, PS**

Most, Bernard, *A Trio of Triceratops.* Harcourt Brace, 1998. ISBN 0152014489.
Three dinosaurs do many things—from trimming trees to telling tales—that start with T. **PS, K**

Sathre, Vivian, *Three Kind Mice.* Ill. by Rodger Wilson. Harcourt Brace, 1997. ISBN 0152012664.
Three mice bake a cake for the cat's birthday. **PS**

Siomades, Lorianne, *Three Little Kittens.* Boyds Mills, 2000. ISBN 1563978458.
Simple picture story of the three little kittens who lose their mittens. **T, PS**

Wahl, Jan, *Three Pandas.* Ill. by Naava. Boyd Mills, 2000. ISBN 1563977494.
Three pandas leave their home in the bamboo forest and go to a Chinese city. **PS, K, Pr**

Four

Aker, Suzanne, *What Comes in 2's, 3's, and 4's?* Ill. by Bernie Karlin. Aladdin, 1992. ISBN 0671792474 (pbk).
Things of which there are two, three, and four. **PS, K**

Herman, Gail, *The Littlest Duckling.* Ill. by Ann Schweninger. Viking, 1996. ISBN 0670851132.
Four ducklings, first, second, third and last, go swimming, and the last one almost gets lost. **PS**

Payne, Nina, *Four in All.* Ill. by Adam Payne. Front Street, 2001. ISBN 1886910162.
Cut-paper illustrations of a girl building a house and inviting animal friends to visit are accompanied by four nouns for each picture, such as "roof window chimney door" and "fork plate knife spoon." **PS, K, Pr**

Five

Bishop, Claire Huchet, *The Five Chinese Brothers.* Ill. by Kurt Wiese. Putnam, 1996. ISBN 0698113587 (pbk).
Five identical brothers pose as each other and use their magic powers to escape an unjust execution. **PS, K, Pr**

Christelow, Eileen, *Five Little Monkeys Jumping on the Bed*. **Clarion, 1989. ISBN 0899197698.**

An expanded version of the familiar rhyme in which five monkeys fall off the bed one by one. See also the author's *Five Little Monkeys with Nothing to Do* [1996: ISBN 0395758300] and *Five Little Monkeys Sitting in a Tree* [1991: ISBN 0395544343]. **PS, K**

Edwards, Roberta, *Five Silly Fishermen*. **Ill. by Sylvie Wickstrom. Random, 1989. ISBN 0679800921 (pbk).**

Easy-reader text about five fishermen who think one of them is missing, because each one counts the other four but not himself. **PS, K**

Floca, Brian, *Five Trucks*. **DK, 1999. ISBN 0789425610.**

Five trucks work at an airport. **PS**

Jenkins, Emily, *Five Creatures*. **Ill. by Tomek Bogacki. Frances Foster, 2001. ISBN 0374323410.**

A girl, her parents, and two cats share a house and have some similarities and some differences: four adults and one child, three with orange hair and two with gray, and so on. Sets. **PS, K, Pr**

Jewell, Nancy, *Five Little Kittens*. **Ill. by Elizabeth Sayles. Clarion, 1999. ISBN 0395775175.**

Five kittens go through their day, eating, playing, and kissing mama good-night. **PS**

Paparone, Pamela, *Five Little Ducks: An Old Rhyme*. **North-South, 1995. ISBN 1558584730.**

Five little ducks go out, but only four come back, then three, two, one, and zero, but finally all return. No numerals. **PS, K**

Six

Cohen, Caron Lee, *How Many Fish?* **Ill. by S. D. Schindler. HarperCollins, 1998. ISBN 0060277130.**

Very simple text about six little fish, one of whom gets caught under a pail. **T, PS**

Coxe, Molly, *6 Sticks*. **Random, 1999. ISBN 0679886893 (pbk).**

Minimal text shows different things that two mice can make out of six sticks. **PS, K**

Curtis, Matt, *Six Empty Pockets*. **Ill. by Mary Newell DePalma. Children's, 1997. ISBN 0516203991.**

Short text tells what Charles puts in each of his six pants pockets. **PS**

Enderle, Judith Ross, and Stephanie Gordon Tessler, *Six Sandy Sheep*. **Ill. by John O'Brien. Boyds Mills, 1997. ISBN 1563975823.**

At the beach, six sheep go into the water one by one. No numerals. **PS, K**

McDermott, Gerald, *Anansi the Spider: A Tale from the Ashanti.* **Henry Holt, 1987. ISBN 0805003118 (pbk).**
Each of Anansi's six sons has a talent that comes in handy when Anansi is in trouble. **PS, K, Pr**

Moran, Alex, *Six Silly Foxes.* **Ill. by Keith Baker. Green Light/Harcourt, 2000. ISBN 015202560X.**
Simple text tells of six fox siblings and their changing emotions. **PS**

Spinelli, Eileen, *Six Hogs on a Scooter.* **Ill. by Scott Nash. Orchard, 2000. ISBN 0531302121.**
Six hogs try many different ways—from scooter to hot-air balloon—to get where they're going. **PS, K**

Ziefert, Harriet, *A Dozen Dozens.* **Ill. by Chris Demarest. Puffin, 1998. ISBN 0670877891.**
Rhymes show different things in dozens or half dozens. **K, Pr**

Seven

Baker, Keith, *Quack and Count.* **Harcourt Brace, 1999. ISBN 0152928588.**
Seven ducks divide themselves into different groupings, such as 6 and 1 and 2 and 5. **PS, K, Pr**

Lanteigne, Helen, *The Seven Chairs.* **Ill. by Maryann Kovalski. Orchard, 1998. ISBN 0531301109.**
Tells what happens to each of the seven different chairs made by one man. **PS, K, Pr**

Mallat, Kathy, *Seven Stars, More!* **Walker, 1998. ISBN 0802786758.**
Trying to get to sleep, Abby counts many things, but can only count as high as seven. Numerals are shown. **PS**

Eight

Elya, Susan Middleton, *Eight Animals on the Town.* **Ill. by Lee Chapman. Putnam, 2000. ISBN 0399234373.**
Eight animals go to a market, each looking for the appropriate food. Numerals are shown in the corners of the pages. Text is mainly in English, but includes Spanish words. **PS, K**

Nine

Brett, Jan, *Comet's Nine Lives.* **Putnam, 1996. ISBN 0399229310.**
A cat on Nantucket Island loses eight of his nine lives. **PS, K, Pr**

Hayes, Sarah, *Nine Ducks Nine.* **Candlewick, 1996. ISBN 1564028305 (pbk).**
A fox chases nine ducks who go away one by one. **PS, K**

Ten

Crews, Donald, *Ten Black Dots.* **Greenwillow, rev. ed., 1986. ISBN 0688060676.**
Shows things you can make with from 1 to 10 black dots. Numerals. **PS, K, Pr**

Geddes, Anne, *10 in the Bed.* **Cedco, 2000. ISBN 0768322839.**
Ten babies climb out of bed one by one. Story can be read with book right side up or upside down, so the reader can see how many babies are in or out of the bed at one time. Numerals. **PS, K**

Goldstone, Bruce, *Ten Friends.* **Ill. by Heather Cahoon. Henry Holt, 2001. ISBN 0805062491.**
Describes the different combinations that could make 10 friends: 5 shepherds and 5 sheep, or 4 scuba divers, 3 chauffeurs and 3 bus drivers, for example. Numerals are used. **K, Pr**

Guettier, Benedicte, *The Father Who Had Ten Children.* **Dial, 1999. ISBN 0803724462.**
A father has a lot of work to do to take care of 10 children, but when he goes out alone on his boat, he misses them. **PS, K, Pr**

LeSeig, Theo, *Ten Apples up on Top!* **Ill. by Roy McKie. Random, 1961. ISBN 0394800192.**
Animals balance apples on their heads, starting with one and going up to ten. No numerals. **PS, K**

Maccarone, Grace, *Monster Math Picnic.* **Ill. by Marge Hartelius. Scholastic, 1998. ISBN 0590371274 (pbk).**
Ten monsters divide up in different groups to do different activities. **PS, K, Pr**

Michelson, Richard, *Ten Times Better.* **Ill. by Leonard Baskin. Marshall Cavendish, 2000. ISBN 076145070X.**
Poems about animals introduce numbers 1 to 10, and those 10 times as much, 10 to 100. **Pr**

Ochiltree, Dianne, *Ten Monkey Jamboree.* **Ill. by Anne-Sophie Lanquetin. Margaret K. McElderry/Simon & Schuster, 2001. ISBN 0689834020.**
Ten monkeys divide themselves up in many different combinations. **PS, K, Pr**

Sturges, Philemon, *Ten Flashing Fireflies.* **Ill. by Anna Vojtech. North-South, 1995. ISBN 155858420X.**
Ten fireflies are captured one by one. Rhymes without numerals show how many of the ten are free and how many are in the jar. **PS, K, Pr**

Eleven

Merriam, Eve, *12 Ways to Get to 11*. Ill. by Bernie Karlin. Aladdin, 1996. ISBN 0689808925 (pbk).
Shows different groups of things that add up to 11. **K, Pr**

Twelve

Hutchings, Amy, and Richard Hutchings, *The Gummy Candy Counting Book*. Ill. by Richard Hutchings. Scholastic, 1997. ISBN 0590341278 (pbk).
Gummy candies are counted up to 12. Then the group of 12 is divided up in different ways. **PS, K**

Slater, Teddy, *Stay in Line*. Ill. by Gioia Fiammenghi. Scholastic, 1996. ISBN 0590227130 (pbk).
Twelve children on a trip to the zoo arrange themselves in different groups. **K, Pr**

Ziefert Harriet, *A Dozen Dogs: A Read-and-Count Story*. Ill. by Carol Nicklaus. Random, 1985. ISBN 0394869354 (pbk).
Twelve dogs at the beach introduce many things to count. **PS**

Ziefert, Harriet, *A Dozen Dozens*. Ill. by Chris Demarest. Puffin, 1998. ISBN 0670877891.
Rhymes show different things in dozens or half dozens. **K, Pr**

One Hundred

Cuyler, Margery, *100th Day Worries*. Ill. by Arthur Howard. Simon & Schuster, 2000. ISBN 080503191X.
Jessica can't find 100 things to take to school for the hundredth day, but she does come up with 10 groups of 10 things. **K, Pr**

Harris, Trudy, *100 Days of School*. Ill. by Beth Griffis Johnson. Millbrook, 1999. ISBN 0761312714.
Different ways of arriving at the number 100. **K, Pr**

Lee, Chinlun, *The Very Kind Rich Lady and Her One Hundred Dogs*. Candlewick, 2001. ISBN 0763612901.
A woman's one hundred dogs are illustrated and named. **PS, K, Pr**

Medearis, Angela Shelf, *The 100th Day of School*. Ill. by Joan Holub. Scholastic, 1996. ISBN 059025944X (pbk).
Children celebrate the one hundredth day of school with activities relating to 100. **PS, K, Pr**

Pinczes, Elinor J., *One Hundred Hungry Ants*. Ill. by Bonnie MacKain. Houghton Mifflin, 1993. ISBN 0395631165.
One hundred ants line up in rows of two, four, five, and ten, but still arrive too late for the picnic. **PS, K, Pr**

Rockwell, Anne, *100 School Days*. Ill. by Lizzie Rockwell. HarperCollins, 2002. ISBN 0060291443.
On the way to the hundredth day of school, a class celebrates days 10, 20, 30, and so on. **K, Pr**

Slate, Joseph, *Miss Bindergarten Celebrates the 100th Day of Kindergarten*. Ill. by Ashley Wolff. Dutton, 1998. ISBN 0525460004.
Children from A to Z and their teacher find many items representing 100. **K**

Szekeres, Cyndy, *I Can Count 100 Bunnies and So Can You!* Scholastic, 1998. ISBN 0590383612.
Ninety-nine bunnies gather for the arrival of a new baby bunny. All numerals are shown. **PS, K, Pr**

Wells, Rosemary, *Emily's First 100 Days of School*. Hyperion, 2000. ISBN 0786805072.
Emily relates what happens on each of the 100 days, demonstrating other uses of numbers as well. Numerals. **PS, K, Pr**

Large Numbers [1,000, 1,000,000, or more]

Gag, Wanda, *Millions of Cats*. Paper Star, 1996. ISBN 0698113632 (pbk).
A man finds hundreds of cats, thousands of cats, millions and billions and trillions of cats. **PS, K**

Isadora, Rachel, *123 Pop!* Viking, 2000. ISBN 0670888591.
Pop-art style pictures illustrate numerals 1 to 20, plus 100, 500, 1,000, and 1,000,000. **PS**

Nolan, Helen, *How Much, How Many, How Far, How Heavy, How Long, How Tall Is 1000?* Ill. by Tracy Walker. Kids Can, 1997. ISBN 1550741640.
Different representations of 1,000, from counting freckles to going long distances. **K, Pr**

Packard, Edward, *Big Numbers and Pictures That Show Just How Big They Are*. Ill. by Salvatore Murdocca. Millbrook, 2000. ISBN 0761315705.
Using peas, grains of sand, and other common items, cartoons attempt to show numbers as large as a million billion trillion. **PS, K, Pr**

Schwartz, David M., *How Much Is a Million?* Ill. by Steven Kellogg. Morrow, 1985. ISBN 0688040497.
> Humorous text and illustrations present the concept of a million, a billion, and a trillion. **K, Pr**

Schwartz, David M., *On Beyond a Million: An Amazing Math Journey.* Ill. by Paul Meisel. Doubleday, 1999. ISBN 0385322178.
> While trying to count popcorn kernels, a group of children learns about counting by powers of 10 all the way to googolplex. **Pr**

Wells, Robert E., *Can You Count to a Googol?* Albert Whitman, 2000. ISBN 0807510602.
> Starting with 1, and multiplying each time by 10 up to a googol, this book gives humorous examples of that amount. **Pr**

Counting Books [Books that introduce numerals in order and have a representative number of things to count for each numeral]

Anderson, Lena, *Tea for Ten.* R&S, 2000. ISBN 9129645573.
> One by one, ten friends stop by to visit Hedgehog. **PS**

Anno, Masaichiro, and Mitsumasa Anno, *Anno's Mysterious Multiplying Jar.* Ill. by Mitsumasa Anno. Putnam, 1983. ISBN 0399209514.
> One island has two countries, each country has three mountains, and so on up to ten. Explains factorials. Includes numerals. **Pr**

Anno, Mitsumasa, *Anno's Counting Book.* Harper Trophy, 1986. ISBN 0064431231 (pbk).
> Detailed pictures depict things for numerals 1 through 12 as a village grows and moves through the months of the year (not named). **K, Pr**

Appelt, Kathi, *Bat Jamboree.* Ill. by Melissa Sweet. Morrow, 1996. ISBN 0688138829.
> Bats from 1 to 10 and down again (55 in all) perform in a show. Numerals shown. **PS, K**

Appelt, Kathi, *Rain Dance.* Ill. by Emilie Chollat. Harper Festival, 2001. ISBN 0694012912.
> Simple, large pictures of animals, minimal text, and numerals 1 through 10. **T, PS**

Baker, Keith, *Big Fat Hen.* Harcourt Brace, 1994. ISBN 0152928693.
> A version of "One, Two, Buckle My Shoe." Numerals 1 to 10. **T, PS**

Bassède, Francine, *George's Store at the Shore.* Orchard, 1998. ISBN 0531300838.
> George prepares his beach store for business with items 1 to 10. Numerals. **T, PS**

Beaton, Clare, *One Moose, Twenty Mice.* **Barefoot Books, 1999. ISBN 1902283376.**
: Groups of animals from 1 to 20. Fabric collage pictures and numerals. **PS, K**

Bennett, David, *One Cow Moo Moo!* **Ill. by Andy Cooke. Henry Holt, 1990. ISBN 0805014160.**
: A boy sees one cow, two horses and so on up to ten mice running and wonders why. Numerals included. **PS, K**

Blackstone, Stella, *Grandma Went to Market: A Round-the-World Counting Rhyme.* **Ill. by Bernard Lodge. Houghton Mifflin, 1996. ISBN 0395740452.**
: Grandma visits places around the world, buying one flying carpet, two temple cats, and so on, up to ten. No numerals. **PS, K**

Bohdal, Susi, *1, 2, 3 What Do You See? An Animal Counting Book.* **North-South, 1997. ISBN 1558586466.**
: The appropriate number of animals for each numeral 1 to 10. **T, PS**

Bowdish, Lynea, *One Glad Man.* **Ill. by Kristin Sorra. Children's, 1999. ISBN 0516215957.**
: A lonely man is sad until animals from one to ten move into his house. No numerals are shown. **PS**

Bowen, Betsy, *Gathering: A Northwoods Counting Book.* **Little, Brown, 1995. ISBN 0395981336.**
: Colored woodcuts illustrate numerals 0 through 12 as well as seasons spring through winter. **K**

Boynton, Sandra, *Doggies: A Counting and Barking Book.* **Little Simon, 1995. ISBN 0671493183.**
: Noisy dogs from 1 to 10, with numerals. Board. **T, PS**

Boynton, Sandra, *Hippos Go Berserk!* **Simon & Schuster, 1996. ISBN 0689808542.**
: Groups of hippos from one to nine arrive at a party, then leave again in the morning. Numerals shown. **PS**

Brooks, Alan, *Frogs Jump: A Counting Book.* **Ill. by Steven Kellogg. Scholastic, 1996. ISBN 0590455281.**
: Numerals from 1 to 12 are illustrated by animal activities interpreted in unusual ways: for example, monkeys swing golf clubs, not on trees. **PS, K**

Brusca, María Cristina, and Tona Wilson, *Three Friends/ Tres Amigos: A Counting Book/Un Cuento para Contar.* **Ill. by Maria Cristina Brusca. Henry Holt, 1995. ISBN 0805037071.**
: Scenes of cowboys in the Southwest (without numerals) illustrate a story using numbers one to ten and ten to one. In Spanish and English. **PS, K**

Burton, Katherine, *One Gray Mouse*. Ill. by Kim Fernandes. Kids Can Press, 1997. ISBN 1550742256.
Pictures of groups consisting of from 1 to 10 animals, with colors identified, for example: "Five pink pigs in yellow pig wigs." Numerals included. **T, PS**

Cabrera, Jane, *Over in the Meadow*. Holiday House, 2000. ISBN 0823414906.
Different animal moms and their babies illustrate numerals 1 to 12 in this familiar old song. **PS, K**

Carle, Eric, *1, 2, 3 to the Zoo: A Counting Book*. Putnam, 1998. ISBN 0698116453 (pbk).
Wordless pictures of groups of zoo animals, with numerals 1 through 10. **T, PS**

Carlstrom, Nancy White, *Let's Count It Out, Jesse Bear*. Ill. by Bruce Degen. Simon & Schuster, 1996. ISBN 0689804784.
Rhymes about each number 1 to 10, plus numerals through 20 and explanation of adding one each time. Also, counting backwards from 10. **PS, K, Pr**

Carter, David A., *How Many Bugs in a Box?* Little Simon, 1988. ISBN 0671649655.
Pop-up pictures show from 1 to 10 bugs hiding in different kinds of boxes. Numerals. **PS, K**

Chester, Jonathan and Kirsty Melville, *Splash! A Penguin Counting Book*. Tricycle, 1997. ISBN 1883672562.
Photos show from 1 to 10 penguins, with numerals. **T, PS**

Clark, Emma Chichester, *Little Miss Muffet's Count-Along Surprise*. Doubleday, 1997. ISBN 0385325177.
Little Miss Muffet is joined by one spider, two lemurs, and so on up to ten crocodiles, who have a party for her. Numerals 1 to 10. **PS, K**

Cousins, Lucy, *Count with Maisy*. Candlewick, 1997. ISBN 076360156X.
Maisy counts things from 1 to 10. Numerals shown. Oversized board pages. **T, PS**

Crews, Donald, *Ten Black Dots*. Greenwillow, rev. ed., 1986. ISBN 0688060676.
Shows things you can make with from 1 to 10 black dots. Numerals. **PS, K, Pr**

Dale, Penny, *Ten Play Hide-and-Seek*. Candlewick, 1998. ISBN 0763606545.
A little boy finds his nine stuffed animals one by one as they play hide-and-seek. No numerals in the text. **PS**

Dena, Anaël, *Numbers*. Ill. by Christel Desmoinaux. Gareth Stevens, 1997. ISBN 0836819861.
Pictures with the appropriate number of things illustrate numerals 1 to 10. Also included are 100 rabbits to count (with numerals) and other counting games. **PS, K**

Dodd, Emma, *Dog's Colorful Day: A Messy Story about Colors and Counting.* **Dutton, 2001. ISBN 0525465286.**

A dog with one black spot acquires nine more spots of different colors. Numerals 1 to 10 are shown in order at one point in the story. **PS, K**

Dorros, Arthur, *Ten Go Tango.* **Ill. by Emily Arnold McCully. HarperCollins, 2000. ISBN 0060276908.**

Animals doing various dance steps illustrate numerals 1 to 10. **PS**

Duke, Kate, *One Guinea Pig Is Not Enough.* **Dutton, 1998. ISBN 0525459189.**

One guinea pig plus one makes two. One more is added each time to make 10, then 10 more to make 20. Large numerals. **PS, K**

Edwards, Pamela Duncan, *Roar! A Noisy Counting Book.* **Ill. by Henry Cole. HarperCollins, 2000. ISBN 006028384X.**

A lion cub roars at groups of from 1 to 9 other animals, finally joining the 9 other lion cubs to make 10. Large numerals. **PS**

Edwards, Pamela Duncan, *Warthogs in the Kitchen: A Sloppy Counting Book.* **Ill. by Henry Cole. Hyperion, 1998. ISBN 0786803991.**

Eight warthogs messily mix a batch of cupcakes. Story uses numerals 1 to 10, plus 0. **PS**

Ehlert, Lois, *Fish Eyes: A Book You Can Count On.* **Harcourt Brace Jovanovich, 1992. ISBN 0152280510 (pbk).**

Counting fish from 1 to 10, with cutouts for their eyes. Numerals. **PS, K**

Emberley, Rebecca, *My Numbers; Mis Numeros.* **Little, Brown, 2000. ISBN 0316233501.**

Numerals 1 through 10, with an appropriate number of things in Spanish and English. Board book. **T, PS**

Evans, Lezlie, *Can You Count Ten Toes? Count to 10 in 10 Different Languages.* **Ill. by Denis Roche. Houghton Mifflin, 1999. ISBN 0395904994.**

Numbers one to ten in ten languages. Includes a map showing where these languages are spoken. **K, Pr**

Falwell, Cathryn, *Feast for 10.* **Clarion, 1993. ISBN 0395620376.**

Numerals 1 to 10 are used in describing a trip to the grocery store and then again in describing the preparing of a feast. **PS**

French, Vivian, *Let's Go, Anna!* **Ill. by Alex Ayliffe. David & Charles, 2000. ISBN 1862330743.**

Anna and her father go shopping. Introduces numbers 1 to 5. Items to count are all together on last foldout page. **T, PS**

Freymann, Saxton, and Joost Elffers, *One Lonely Sea Horse.* **Arthur A. Levine, 2000. ISBN 0439110149.**
   Numerals from 1 to 10 are illustrated by sea creatures fashioned from vegetables. **PS**

Geddes, Anne, *1 2 3.* **Cedco, 1995. ISBN 1559120061.**
   Photos of babies in costumes are used to count from 1 to 10. With numerals. **PS**

Girnis, Meg, *1, 2, 3 for You and Me.* **Ill. by Shirley Leamon. Whitman, 2001. ISBN 080756107X.**
   Photographs of Down's syndrome children illustrate this counting book with numerals 1 through 20. **PS**

Glass, Julie, *Counting Sheep.* **Ill. by Mike Wohnoutka. Scholastic, 2000. ISBN 0375906193.**
   As he tries to go to sleep, a boy counts animals by ones, twos, threes, fours, and fives. No numerals. **PS, K**

Golding, Kim, *Counting Kids.* **DK, 2000. ISBN 0789426781.**
   Photos of children, with numerals 1 to 10. **T, PS**

Gollub, Matthew, *Ten Oni Drummers.* **Ill. by Kazuko G. Stone. Lee & Low, 2000. ISBN 1584300116.**
   One by one, ten oni appear at night. Numbers are given in Japanese as well as English, but no numerals are used. **PS, K**

Grossman, Bill, *My Little Sister Ate One Hare.* **Ill. by Kevin Hawkes. Crown, 1996. ISBN 0517596008.**
   Starting with one hare, a girl eats various unusual things, up to ten peas (which make her sick). Numerals. **K, Pr**

Grossman, Virginia, *Ten Little Rabbits.* **Ill. by Sylvia Long. Chronicle, 1995. ISBN 0811810577 (pbk).**
   Rabbits 1 to 10 each illustrate a Native American activity. Includes numerals and information about Native Americans at the end of the book. **PS, K, Pr**

Grover, Max, *Amazing & Incredible Counting Stories: A Number of Tall Tales.* **Harcourt Brace/Browndeer, 1995. ISBN 0152000909.**
   Silly paragraph-long stories use numbers 1 through 25, plus 50, 75, 100, and millions. There are numerals and things to count. **K, Pr**

Gunson, Christopher, *Over on the Farm: A Counting Picture Book Rhyme.* **Scholastic, 1997. ISBN 0590134450.**
   Animal mothers have one through ten babies. No numerals. **PS**

Halsey, Megan, *Circus 1—2—3.* **HarperCollins, 2000. ISBN 0688171044.**
   Simple pictures of a circus act for each numeral 1 to 10. **T, PS**

Hill, Eric, *Spot Can Count.* **Putnam, 1999. ISBN 0399234543.**
  Spot counts things from 1 to 10 on the farm. Numerals are under flaps to lift. **T, PS**

Hill, Eric, *Spot's Big Book of Colors, Shapes and Numbers.* **Putnam, 1994. ISBN 0399226796.**
  Large pages with multiple illustrations show colors, simple shapes, and numbers, with numerals, 1 to 10. **PS**

Hoban, Tana, *Count and See.* **Simon & Schuster, 1972. ISBN 0027448002.**
  Large black-and-white photos illustrate numerals 1 to 15, plus 20, 30, 40, 50, and 100. **PS, K**

Hoban, Tana, *Let's Count.* **Greenwillow, 1999. ISBN 0688160085.**
  Colorful photos illustrate numerals 1 to 15, plus 20, 30, 40, 50, and 100. **PS, K**

Hughes Shirley, *Alfie's 123.* **Lothrop, Lee & Shepard, 2000. ISBN 0688177050.**
  More than one example of things from 1 to 10 in the life of preschooler Alfie. Numerals. **PS**

Hulme, Joy N., *Sea Squares.* **Ill. by Carol Schwartz. Hyperion, 1993. ISBN 1562825208 (pbk).**
  From one to ten sea animals provide examples of square numbers, such as four seals with four flippers each and eight octopuses with eight legs each. **PS, K, Pr**

Hunt, Jonathan, and Lisa Hunt, *One Is a Mouse.* **Macmillan, 1995. ISBN 0027457818.**
  Each numeral from 1 to 10 is introduced by an animal. **T, PS**

Hunt, Judith A., ill. *The Timbertoes 1 2 3 Counting Book.* **Boyds Mills, 1997. ISBN 1563976277.**
  Simple pictures and large numerals introduce numbers 1 to 12. **PS**

Hutchings, Amy, and Richard Hutchings, *The Gummy Candy Counting Book.* **Ill. by Richard Hutchings. Scholastic, 1997. ISBN 0590341278 (pbk).**
  Gummy candies are counted up to 12. Then the group of 12 is divided up in different ways. **PS, K**

Hutchins, Pat, *1 Hunter.* **Morrow, 1982. ISBN 0688006140.**
  A hunter is observed by animals in groups of 2 through 10. No words other than numerals and names of animals. **T, PS**

Isadora, Rachel, *123 Pop!* **Viking, 2000. ISBN 0670888591.**
  Pop-art style pictures illustrate numerals 1 to 20, plus 100, 500, 1,000, and 1,000,000. **PS**

Jahn-Clough, Lisa, *123 Yippie.* **Houghton Mifflin, 1998. ISBN 0395870038.**
  A party happens with one house, two children, and other groups of animals up to ten. Then each group leaves, ten to one. **T, PS**

Jennings, Linda, *Nine Naughty Kittens.* **Ill. by Caroline Jayne Church. Little Tiger, 1999. ISBN 1888444622.**
  Lift-the-flap pages add one more kitten each time, up to ten. No numerals. **PS**

Keats, Ezra Jack, *One Red Sun: A Counting Book.* **Viking, 1999. ISBN 0670884782.**
  Numerals 1 to 10 are illustrated by simple everyday pictures. Board book edition. **T, PS**

Kellogg, Steven, *Give the Dog a Bone.* **SeaStar, 2000. ISBN 1587170019.**
  A variation on the old song "This Old Man," with hilarious dog-related incidents from 1 to 10, with numerals. **PS, K**

King, Dave, *Counting Book.* **DK, 1998. ISBN 0789434482.**
  Pictures of things 1 to 20, 30, 40, and so on to 100 and 1,000. Numerals are hidden in the pictures, and other counting activities are included for each picture. **PS, K**

Kneen, Maggie, *When You're Not Looking . . . A Storytime Counting Book.* **Simon & Schuster, 1996. ISBN 0689800266.**
  Detailed pictures hide objects from 1 to 10. Numerals. **K, Pr**

Kuskin, Karla, *James and the Rain.* **Ill. by Reg Cartwright. Simon & Schuster, 1995. ISBN 0671888080.**
  As James walks in the rain, he is joined by one cow, then other groups of animals two through ten. No numerals. An earlier edition was published in 1957 with different illustrations. **PS, K**

Lavis, Steve, *Cock-a-Doodle-Doo: A Farmyard Counting Book.* **Lodestar/Dutton, 1996. ISBN 0525675426.**
  Numerals 1 to 10 and noisy farm animals. **T, PS**

Lee, Huy Voun, *1, 2, 3, Go!* **Henry Holt, 2000. ISBN 080506205X.**
  Number words in English and Chinese, plus active children to count, from one to ten. No numerals. **K, Pr**

LeSeig, Theo, *Ten Apples up on Top!* **Ill. by Roy McKie. Random, 1961. ISBN 0394800192.**
  Animals balance apples on their heads, starting with one and going up to ten. No numerals. **PS, K**

Lesser, Carolyn, *Spots: Counting Creatures from Sky to Sea.* **Ill. by Laura Regan. Harcourt Brace, 1999. ISBN 0152006664.**
  Different animals with spots are counted, 1 to 10, with numerals presented at the book's end. **PS, K**

Leuck, Laura, *My Baby Brother Has Ten Tiny Toes.* **Ill. by Clara Vulliamy. Albert Whitman, 1997. ISBN 0807553107.**
> A girl introduces her baby brother, showing his one tiny nose, his two sparkling eyes, and so on up to ten toes. No numerals. **K**

Lewis, Paul Owen, *You Are Cordially Invited to P. Bear's New Year's Party!* **Tricycle, 1999. ISBN 1883672996 (pbk).**
> A polar bear invites only black and white animals to his party. One arrives at one o'clock, two at two o'clock, and so on through twelve midnight. **PS, K**

MacDonald, Suse, *Look Whooo's Counting.* **Scholastic, 2000. ISBN 0590683209.**
> Owl learns to count from 1 to 10. Numerals shown. **PS, K**

McGrath, Barbara Barbieri, *The Baseball Counting Book.* **Ill. by Brian Shaw. Charlesbridge, 1999. ISBN 0881063320.**
> Rhymes about baseball items from 0 to 20 (with numerals). **PS, K**

McGrath, Barbara Barbieri, *The Cheerios Counting Book.* **Ill. by Rob Bolster and Frank Mazzola, Jr. Scholastic, 1998. ISBN 0590683578.**
> Counting Cheerios and fruit from 1 to 20, then by tens from 10 to 100. Also introduces zero. Numerals. **PS, K**

McMillan, Bruce, *Counting Wildflowers.* **Mulberry, 1995. ISBN 0688140270 (pbk).**
> Colored circles and photographs of flowers illustrate numerals 1 to 20. **PS**

Miranda, Anne, *Monster Math.* **Ill. by Polly Powell. Harcourt Brace, 1999. ISBN 0152018352.**
> Monsters arrive for a party, one by one to ten, then in tens up to 50. Mother shoos them away in groups. No numerals. **PS, K**

Moore, Elaine, *Roly-Poly Puppies: A Counting Book.* **Ill. by Jacqueline Rogers. Scholastic, 1996. ISBN 0590466658.**
> One puppy is joined by others one at a time, up to 10. Numerals. **T, PS**

Mora, Pat, *Uno, Dos, Tres: One, Two, Three.* **Ill. by Barbara Lavallee. Clarion, 1996. ISBN 0395672945.**
> Two girls buy birthday presents for their mother, from one to ten in Spanish and English. No numerals. **PS, K, Pr**

Murphy, Stuart J., *Every Buddy Counts.* **Ill. by Fiona Dunbar. Scholastic, 1997. ISBN 0060267720.**
> Using numerals and number words, a girl counts things from 1 to 10 to cheer herself up. **T, PS**

Nikola-Lisa, W., *One Hole in the Road.* **Ill. by Dan Yaccarino. Henry Holt, 1996. ISBN 0805042857.**
> Using numerals 1 to 10, this book tells the story of a hole in the road that becomes a flood from burst pipes. **T, PS**

Noll, Sally, *Surprise!* **Greenwillow, 1997. ISBN 0688151701.**
>Numbers counting things one to ten are part of a story of a girl opening a present. Numerals not included. **T, PS**

Numeroff, Laura, *Monster Munchies.* **Ill. by Nate Evans. Beginner/Random, 1998. ISBN 0679891633.**
>Monsters one through twenty eat a variety of silly things. No numerals. **PS, K**

Parker, Vic, *Bearobics: A Hip-Hop Counting Story.* **Ill. by Emily Bolam. Viking, 1997. ISBN 067087034X.**
>Animals from one to ten (plus a million ants) have a wild time dancing in this rhythmic story without numerals. **PS, K, Pr**

Piers, Helen, *Is There Room on the Bus? An Around-the-World Counting Story.* **Ill. by Hannah Giffard. Simon & Schuster, 1996. ISBN 0689806108.**
>Sam drives his bus around the world, picking up one lion, two cows, and so on up to ten bees, which cause an accident. Numerals. **PS, K, Pr**

Pomeroy, Diana, *One Potato: A Counting Book of Potato Prints.* **Harcourt Brace, 1996. ISBN 0152003002.**
>Simple pictures, with numerals, of fruits and vegetables from 1 to 10, 20, 30, 40, 50, and 100. Also *Wildflower ABC* [1997: ISBN 0152010416]. **PS, K**

Roche, Denis, *Only One Ollie.* **Houghton Mifflin, 1997. ISBN 0395811236.**
>Ollie decides to count things, using numerals from 1 to 10. **T, PS**

Root, Phyllis, *One Duck Stuck.* **Ill. by Jane Chapman. Candlewick, 1998. ISBN 0763603341.**
>Groups of animals from 2 fish to 10 dragonflies try to help one duck stuck in the marsh. Numerals. **PS, K**

Roth, Carol, *Ten Dirty Pigs: An Upside-Down, Turn-Around Bathtime Counting Book.* **Ill. by Pamela Paparone. North-South, 1999. ISBN 0735810893.**
>Shows one to ten dirty pigs getting clean. The reverse of the book shows them getting dirty again. No numerals. **PS**

Roth, Susan L., *Night-Time Numbers: A Scary Counting Book.* **Barefoot, 1999. ISBN 1841480010.**
>Collage pictures show mildly scary things to count, with numerals 1 through 10. **PS, K**

Ryan, Pam Muñoz, *One Hundred Is a Family.* **Ill. by Benrei Huang. Hyperion, 1996. ISBN 078681120X (pbk).**
>Shows different kinds of families, which number from one to ten, then by tens to a hundred. Numerals not shown. **PS, K**

Saul, Carol P., *Barn Cat: A Counting Book.* Ill. by Mary Azarian. Little, Brown, 1998. ISBN 0316761133.
One barn cat watches other animals 2 through 10. Numerals. **PS, K**

Schnur, Steven, *Night Lights.* Ill. by Stacey Schuett. Farrar, Straus & Giroux, 2000. ISBN 0374355223.
Before she goes to bed, Melinda counts lights, starting with one seashell night-light, through twenty airplanes, then to fifty, a hundred, a thousand, and a million stars. No numerals. **PS, K**

Schumaker, Ward, *In My Garden: A Counting Book.* Chronicle, 2000. ISBN 0811826899.
Large numerals illustrate things in a garden from 1 to 10, 20, 30, 40, 50, and 233. **PS, K**

Sendak, Maurice, *One Was Johnny: A Counting Book.* Harper & Row, 1991. ISBN 0064432513 (pbk).
Johnny's house is invaded by others, one by one up to 10, but he rids himself of them, one by one from 10 to 1. Numerals. Small format. **PS, K**

Siddals, Mary McKenna, *Millions of Snowflakes.* Ill. by Elizabeth Sayles. Scholastic, 1998. ISBN 0395715318.
A child sees one snowflake, then two, three, four, five, and millions. No numerals. **T, PS**

Sierra, Judy, *Counting Crocodiles.* Ill. by Will Hillenbrand. Harcourt Brace, 1997. ISBN 0152001921.
A monkey persuades some crocodiles to line up and be counted, so that he can use them as a bridge to get across the sea. The crocs are counted both up and down in groups of one to ten, without numerals. **PS, K, Pr**

Sis, Peter, *Fire Truck.* Greenwillow, 1998. ISBN 0688158781.
Matt imagines that he is a red fire truck, complete with one driver, two ladders, and so on up to ten boots. Numerals are shown. **PS, K**

Sloat, Teri, *From One to One Hundred.* Scott Foresman, 1995. ISBN 0140556435 (pbk).
Each illustration includes several groups of things of the featured number 1 to 10, then by tens from 20 to 100. Numerals are used. **PS, K, Pr**

Spowart, Robin, *Ten Little Bunnies.* Scholastic, 2001. ISBN 0439208637.
Simple book shows bunnies from one to ten, without numerals. **T, PS**

Stow, Jenny, *Following the Sun.* Carolrhoda, 1996. ISBN 157505048X.
Starting with just 1 animal and reaching 10, animals follow the sun as it goes across the sky. Numerals. **PS, K**

Sturges, Philemon, *Ten Flashing Fireflies.* **Ill. by Anna Vojtech. North-South, 1995. ISBN 155858420X.**
Ten fireflies are captured one by one. Rhymes without numerals show how many of the ten are free and how many are in the jar. **PS, K, Pr**

Szekeres, Cyndy, *I Can Count 100 Bunnies and So Can You!* **Scholastic, 1998. ISBN 0590383612.**
Ninety-nine bunnies gather for the arrival of a new baby bunny. All numerals are shown. **PS, K, Pr**

Tafuri, Nancy, *Who's Counting?* **Greenwillow, 1986. ISBN 0688061303.**
Large, simple pictures and numerals introduce numbers 1 to 10. **T**

Tryon, Leslie, *1 Gaping Wide-Mouthed Hopping Frog.* **Athenuem, 1993. ISBN 0689317859.**
A frog letter carrier introduces numerals 1 through 10. **PS**

Tudor, Tasha, *1 Is One.* **Simon & Schuster, 2000. ISBN 0689828438.**
Numerals 1 to 20 are illustrated with simple rhymes. **PS**

Van Fleet, Matthew, *One Yellow Lion.* **Dial, 1992. ISBN 0803710992.**
Foldout pages illustrate animals of different colors from 1 to 10 (with numerals) **T, PS**

Wallace, Nancy Elizabeth, *Count Down to Clean Up!* **Houghton Mifflin, 2001. ISBN 0618101306.**
Ten bunnies disperse one by one to gather what they need, then meet to clean up a park. **PS**

Walton, Rick, *How Many How Many How Many.* **Ill. by Cynthia Jabar. Candlewick, 1996. ISBN 1564026566 (pbk).**
From 1 Jack-Be-Nimble to 12 months, this counting book shows numerals for each number. **PS**

Walton, Rick, *One More Bunny: Adding from One to Ten.* **Ill. by Paige Miglio. Lothrop, Lee & Shepard, 2000. ISBN 0688168477.**
Demonstrates adding one bunny at a time, from 1 to 10. Numerals shown. **PS, K, Pr**

Wells, Rosemary, *Max's Toys.* **Dial, 1998. ISBN 0803722710.**
Using the numerals 1 through 10, this board book tells a short story about Max and Ruby playing with their toys. **T**

Wilson, Anna, and Alison Bartlett, *Over in the Grasslands.* **Little, Brown, 2000. ISBN 0316939102.**
Large numerals 1 to 10 and animals from African grasslands appear in this variation on "Over in the Meadow." **PS, K**

Winter, Jeanette, *Josefina.* **Harcourt Brace, 1996. ISBN 0152010912.**
    A Mexican artist makes clay figures 1 through 10. Numbers also given in Spanish. Numerals. **K, Pr**

Wojtowycz, David, *Animals Antics from 1 to 10.* **Holiday House, 2000. ISBN 082341552X.**
    Large numerals and amusing pictures of alliterative animals illustrate numbers 1 to 10. **PS, K**

Wormell, Christopher, *A Number of Animals.* **Creative Editions, 1993. ISBN 156846083X.**
    A chick searches for his mother among different numbers of farm animals, 1 to 10. Large numerals. **PS, K**

Yektai, Niki, *Bears at the Beach: Counting 10 to 20.* **Millbrook, 1996. ISBN 0761300473.**
    Pictures show items from 10 to 20 (with numerals) as bears have a day at the beach. **PS, K**

Counting Up [Books that give numerals in order, without things to count]

Alda, Arlene, *Arlene Alda's 123.* **Tricycle, 1998. ISBN 1883672716.**
    Photos of things that resemble numerals 1 to 10 and 10 to 1. **PS, K**

Appelt, Kathi, *Toddler Two-Step.* **Ill. by Ward Schumaker. Harper, 2000. ISBN 0694012440.**
    Counting up to ten and down again as children do dance steps. No numerals. **T, PS**

Aylesworth, Jim, *The Completed Hickory Dickory Dock.* **Ill. by Eileen Christelow. Aladdin, 1990. ISBN 0689316062.**
    Additional verses to the traditional nursery rhyme go through twelve o'clock. **PS, K**

Baker, Alan, *Gray Rabbit's 1, 2, 3.* **Kingfisher, 1994. ISBN 0753452529 (pbk).**
    Gray Rabbit makes animals from clay. 1 to 10. **T, PS**

Barrett, Judi, *I Knew Two Who Said Moo: A Counting and Rhyming Book.* **Ill. by Daniel Moreton. Atheneum, 2000. ISBN 0689821042.**
    Sentences rhyme with each number from one to ten. **PS, K**

Behrman, Carol H., *The Ding Dong Clock.* **Ill. by Hideko Takahashi. Holt, 1999. ISBN 0805058044.**
    From 1 a.m. to 12 noon, a clock strikes the time on the hour. **PS, K**

Beil, Karen Magnuson, *A Cake All for Me!* **Ill. by Paul Meisel. Holiday House, 1998. ISBN 0823413683.**
    A pig counts to 20 as he bakes a cake. **PS**

Bourke, Linda, *Eye Count: A Book of Counting Puzzles*. Chronicle, 1995. ISBN 0811807320.
: Each page illustrates a number (1 to 12) of different meanings for a word: for example, page 3 has a baseball diamond, a diamond ring, and a jack of diamonds. Numerals shown. **K, Pr**

Brett, Jan, *Comet's Nine Lives*. Putnam, 1996. ISBN 0399229310.
: A cat on Nantucket Island loses eight of his nine lives. **PS, K, Pr**

Brimner, Larry Dane, *Firehouse Sal*. Ill. by Ethel Gold. Children's Press, 1996. ISBN 0516200100.
: Fire companies 1 through 4 rush to firehouse #5, where the dog has had 5 puppies. Simple text includes counting from 1 to 5, with numerals. **T, PS**

Brown, Margaret Wise, *Another Important Book*. Ill. by Chris Raschka. Joanna Cotler Books/HarperCollins, 1999. ISBN 0060262834.
: Children from ages one to six show what they can do. **PS**

Coats, Lucy, *One Smiling Sister*. Ill. by Emily Bolam. DK, 2000. ISBN 0789456222 (pbk).
: Using numbers one through ten (not numerals), this story shows a child's day at preschool. **PS**

Cole, Norma, *Blast Off! A Space Counting Book*. Ill. by Marshall Peck III. Charlesbridge, 1994. ISBN 0881064998.
: Facts about space travel introduce numerals 0 to 20. Large numbers (to one trillion) are mentioned, and then there is a countdown from 10 to 0. **K, Pr**

Cousins, Lucy, *Maisy Drives the Bus*. Candlewick, 2000. ISBN 0763610836.
: Maisy drives the bus from stop number 1 to stop number 5. **T, PS**

de Regniers, Beatrice Schenk, *So Many Cats!* Ill. by Ellen Weiss. Houghton Mifflin, 1988. ISBN 0899197000 (pbk).
: One or a few at a time a family acquires a dozen cats. **PS, K**

deRubertis, Barbara, *Count on Pablo*. Ill. by Rebecca Thornburgh. Kane, 1999. ISBN 1575650908 (pbk).
: When helping at the market, Pablo counts by ones, by twos, by fives and by tens. **K, Pr**

Elya, Susan Middleton, *Eight Animals on the Town*. Ill. by Lee Chapman. Putnam, 2000. ISBN 0399234373.
: Eight animals go to a market, each looking for the appropriate food. Numerals are shown in the corners of the pages. Text is mainly in English, but includes Spanish words. **PS, K**

Feelings, Muriel, *Moja Means One: A Swahili Counting Book.* **Ill. by Tom Feelings. Puffin, 1992. ISBN 0140546626 (pbk).**
Numerals and Swahili words 1 to 10 showing ten African scenes. **PS, K**

Fleming, Candace, *Who Invited You?* **Ill. by George Booth. Atheneum, 2000. ISBN 0689831536.**
Poling her boat through the swamp, a girl is joined by eight unwelcome critters. Then Gator shows up. Uses numbers (not numerals) one to ten. **K, Pr**

Fleming, Denise, *Count!* **Henry Holt, 1992. ISBN 0805015957.**
Animals are counted by ones to 10 and then by 10s to 50. Numerals. **PS, K**

Harley, Bill, *Sitting Down to Eat.* **Ill. by Kitty Harvill. August House Little Folk, 1996. ISBN 0874834600.**
One by one, ten animals join a boy at his meal. **PS, K**

Hoban, Tana, *26 Letters and 99 Cents.* **Greenwillow, 1987. ISBN 0688063616.**
Double book. One direction shows coins that add up to amounts from 1 to 30 cents, then 35, 40, 45, 50, 60, 70, 80, 90, and 99 cents. **PS, K, Pr**

Inkpen, Mick, *The Great Pet Sale.* **Orchard, 1999. ISBN 0531301303.**
A boy looks at animals for sale in a pet shop, costing from 1 cent to 25 cents, then determines that he can buy everything for $1.00. **PS, K, Pr**

Larios, Julie Hofstrand, *On the Stairs.* **Ill. by Mary Hofstrand Cornish. Front Street, 1999. ISBN 1886910340.**
A little mouse girl gives a special name to each of the 12 steps on her staircase. Numerals. **PS, K**

Martin, Bill, Jr., and Michael Sampson, *Rock It, Sock It, Number Line.* **Ill. by Heather Cahoon. Henry Holt, 2001. ISBN 0805063048.**
Numerals 1 through 10 take part in a dance. **PS, K**

Moss, Lloyd, *Zin! Zin! Zin! A Violin.* **Ill. by Marjorie Priceman. Simon & Schuster, 1995. ISBN 0671882392.**
One musical instrument at a time is introduced, making a solo, a duo, a trio, and up to a chamber group of ten. No numerals. **Pr**

Mozelle, Shirley, *The Pig Is in the Pantry, The Cat Is on the Shelf.* **Ill. by Jennifer Plecas. Clarion, 2000. ISBN 0395786274.**
Eight farm animals make a mess when they enter an unlocked house. **PS, K, Pr**

Slater, Teddy, . . . *98, 99, 100! Ready or Not, Here I Come.* **Ill. by Gioia Fiammenghi. Scholastic, 1999. ISBN 0590120093 (pbk).**
Some girls play hide-and-seek, counting to 100 by ones, by fives, by tens and by 20s. **K, Pr**

Smith, Maggie, *Counting Our Way to Maine.* **Orchard, 1995. ISBN 0531068846.**
   A vacation in Maine is described with things from 1 to 20. Not all items are easily countable, though numerals are presented. **PS, K**

Walsh, Ellen Stoll, *Mouse Count.* **Harcourt Brace Jovanovich, 1991. ISBN 0152560238.**
   A snake finds ten mice, counting them as he catches them, but they cleverly get away. **T, PS**

Walton, Rick, *So Many Bunnies: A Bedtime ABC and Counting Book.* **Ill. by Paige Miglio. Lothrop, Lee & Shepard, 1998. ISBN 0688136567.**
   Old Mother Rabbit lived in a shoe with her 26 children, whose names each begin with a different letter of the alphabet (shown in upper case). **PS, K**

Wells, Rosemary, *Emily's First 100 Days of School.* **Hyperion, 2000. ISBN 0786805072.**
   Emily relates what happens on each of the 100 days, demonstrating other uses of numbers as well. Numerals. **PS, K, Pr**

Counting Down *[Books that give numerals in order from larger to smaller, with or without things to count]*

Alda, Arlene, *Arlene Alda's 123.* **Tricycle, 1998. ISBN 1883672716.**
   Photos of things that resemble numerals 1 to 10 and 10 to 1. **PS, K**

Appelt, Kathi, *Bat Jamboree.* **Ill. by Melissa Sweet. Morrow, 1996. ISBN 0688138829.**
   Bats from 1 to 10 and down again (55 in all) perform in a show. Numerals shown. **PS, K**

Appelt, Kathi, *Toddler Two-Step.* **Ill. by Ward Schumaker. Harper, 2000. ISBN 0694012440.**
   Counting up to ten and down again as children do dance steps. No numerals. **T, PS**

Arnold, Tedd, *Five Ugly Monsters.* **Cartwheel, 1995. ISBN 0590222260.**
   Five monsters jump on the bed, and one by one they fall off. **PS**

Bang, Molly, *Ten, Nine, Eight.* **Greenwillow, 1989. ISBN 0688009069.**
   Counting down from 10 toes to 1 big girl all ready for bed. Numerals. **T, PS**

Boynton, Sandra, *Doggies: A Counting and Barking Book.* **Little Simon, 1995. ISBN 0671493183.**
   Noisy dogs from 1 to 10, with numerals. Board. **T, PS**

Boynton, Sandra, *Hippos Go Berserk!* **Simon & Schuster, 1996. ISBN 0689808542.**
>Groups of hippos from 1 to 9 arrive at a party, then leave again in the morning. Numerals shown. **PS**

Brisson, Pat, *Benny's Pennies***. Ill. by Bob Barner. Pearson, 1995. ISBN 0440410169.**
>With his five pennies, Benny buys five different things. **PS, K**

Brown, Ruth, *Ten Seeds.* **Knopf, 2001. ISBN 0375806970.**
>There are ten seeds to start with, but due to many things only one flower results, though it produces ten seeds. **PS**

Brusca, Maria Cristina, and Tona Wilson, *Three Friends/Tres Amigos: A Counting Book/Un Cuento para Contar***. Ill. by Maria Cristina Brusca. Henry Holt, 1995. ISBN 0805037071.**
>Scenes of cowboys in the Southwest (without numerals) illustrate a story using numbers one to ten and ten to one. In Spanish and English. **PS, K**

Carlstrom, Nancy White, *Let's Count It Out, Jesse Bear***. Ill. by Bruce Degen. Simon & Schuster, 1996. ISBN 0689804784.**
>Rhymes about each number 1 to 10, plus numerals through 20, and explanation of adding one each time. Also, counting backwards from 10. **PS, K, Pr**

Christelow, Eileen, *Five Little Monkeys Jumping on the Bed.* **Clarion, 1989. ISBN 0899197698.**
>An expanded version of the familiar rhyme in which five monkeys fall off the bed one by one. See also the author's *Five Little Monkeys with Nothing to Do* [1996: ISBN 0395758300] and *Five Little Monkeys Sitting in a Tree* [1991: ISBN 0395544343]. **PS, K**

Cole, Norma, *Blast Off! A Space Counting Book.* **Ill. by Marshall Peck III. Charlesbridge, 1994. ISBN 0881064998.**
>Facts about space travel introduce numerals 0 to 20. Large numbers (to one trillion) are mentioned, and then there is a countdown from 10 to 0. **K, Pr**

Dale, Penny, *Ten in the Bed.* **Candlewick, 2001. ISBN 0763615757.**
>Nine stuffed animals fall out of bed one by one, leaving a little boy all alone. No numerals. Board book, also older edition in hardcover. **PS**

Dale, Penny, *Ten out of Bed.* **Candlewick, 1996. ISBN 1564023222.**
>A little boy and his nine stuffed animals play until they fall asleep one by one. **PS**

Enderle, Judith Ross, and Stephanie Gordon Tessler, *Six Sandy Sheep.* **Ill. by John O'Brien. Boyds Mills, 1997. ISBN 1563975823.**
>One by one, six sheep on the beach enter the water. No numerals. **PS, K**

Falwell, Catherine, *Turtle Splash! Countdown at the Pond.* **Greenwillow, 2001. ISBN 0060294839.**
> One by one, ten turtles jump off a log into the pond. Large numerals. **PS, K**

Flather, Lisa, *Ten Silly Dogs: A Countdown Story.* **Orchard, 1999. ISBN 0531301923.**
> Ten dogs are playing in the park, but one by one they find other things to do. Using numerals, subtracts one at a time from 10 to 1. **PS, K**

Geddes, Anne, *10 in the Bed.* **Cedco, 2000. ISBN 0768322839.**
> Ten babies climb out of bed one by one. Story can be read with book right side up or upside down, so the reader can see how many babies are in or out of the bed at one time. Numerals. **PS, K**

Greenstein, Elaine, *Dreaming: A Countdown to Sleep.* **Arthur Levine Books, 2000. ISBN 0439063027.**
> Items from 10 to 1 are shown with numerals, as a boy goes to sleep. **PS**

Hague, Kathleen, *Ten Little Bears: A Counting Rhyme.* **Ill. by Michael Hague. Morrow, 1999. ISBN 0688163831.**
> Ten bears play, and one by one go away until only one is left. **PS**

Hayes, Sarah, *Nine Ducks Nine.* **Candlewick, 1996. ISBN 1564028305 (pbk).**
> A fox chases nine ducks who go away one by one. **PS, K**

Hutchins, Pat, *1 Hunter.* **Morrow, 1982. ISBN 0688006140.**
> A hunter is observed by animals in groups of 2 through 10. No words other than numerals and names of animals. **T, PS**

Hutchins, Pat, *Ten Red Apples.* **Greenwillow, 2000. ISBN 0688167977.**
> Ten red apples on a tree are eaten one by one, down to zero. Numerals are used. **PS, K**

Jackson, Woody, *Counting Cows.* **Harcourt Brace, 1995. ISBN 0152201653.**
> Numerals 10 to 0, plus paintings of the right number of cows. **T, PS, K**

Jahn-Clough, Lisa, *123 Yippie.* **Houghton Mifflin, 1998. ISBN 0395870038.**
> A party happens with one house, two children, and other groups of animals up to ten. Then each group leaves, ten to one. **T, PS**

Katz, Karen, *Counting Kisses.* **Margaret K. McElderry, 2001. ISBN 0689834705.**
> A tired baby needs kisses, starting with 10 on his toes and ending with 1 on his head. Includes numerals. **T, PS**

Kohn, Rita, *Celebrating Summer.* **Ill. by Kevin Warren Smith. Children's, 1995. ISBN 0516052012.**

Ten dancers gather to begin preparing for a powwow, and one by one they leave. Numerals 10 to 1 shown. **PS**

Maccarone, Grace, *Monster Math.* **Ill. by Marge Hartelius. Scholastic, 1995. ISBN 0590227122 (pbk).**

Twelve monsters wake up together but during the day they go away one by one, until there's zero. No numerals. **PS, K**

Martin, Bill, Jr., and Michael Sampson, *Rock It, Sock It, Number Line.* **Ill. by Heather Cahoon. Henry Holt, 2001. ISBN 0805063048.**

Numerals 1 through 10 take part in a dance. **PS, K**

Masurel, Claire, *Ten Dogs in the Window: A Countdown Book.* **Ill. by Pamela Paparone. North-South, 1997. ISBN 1558587543.**

Ten dogs in the window are purchased one by one by people who resemble them. **PS, K**

Merriam, Eve, *Ten Rosy Roses.* **Ill. by Julia Gorton. HarperCollins, 1999. ISBN 0060278870.**

Ten red roses are picked one by one by a different children. **T, PS**

O'Donnell, Elizabeth Lee, *Winter Visitors.* **Ill. by Carol Schwartz. Morrow, 1997. ISBN 0688130631.**

When a girl and her cat go outdoors in the snow, their home is invaded by animals in groups of ten to one. Awkward rhymes, but great pictures. **PS, K**

Paparone, Pamela, *Five Little Ducks: An Old Rhyme.* **North-South, 1995. ISBN 1558584730.**

Five little ducks go out, but only four come back, then three, two, one, and zero, but finally all return. No numerals. **PS, K**

Rathmann, Peggy, *10 Minutes Till Bedtime.* **Putnam, 1998. ISBN 039923103X.**

As a boy's father counts the minutes (10 to 1) till bedtime, a large group of hamsters takes a tour of his home. **PS, K**

Samton, Sheila White, *Ten Tiny Monsters: A Superbly Scary Story of Subtraction.* **Crown, 1997. ISBN 0517709414.**

One by one, ten little monsters are bumped from the monster team for not being scary enough. Subtraction facts are shown as 10-1=9 and so on, down to 1-1=0. **PS, K**

Sendak, Maurice, *One Was Johnny: A Counting Book.* **Harper & Row, 1991. ISBN 0064432513 (pbk).**

Johnny's house is invaded by others, one by one up to 10, but he rids himself of them, one by one from 10 to 1. Numerals. Small format. **PS, K**

Sierra, Judy, *Counting Crocodiles.* **Ill. by Will Hillenbrand. Harcourt Brace, 1997. ISBN 0152001921.**

A monkey persuades some crocodiles to line up and be counted, so that he can use them as a bridge to get across the sea. The crocs are counted both up and down in groups of one to ten, without numerals. **PS, K, Pr**

Stickland, Paul, *Ten Terrible Dinosaurs.* **Dutton, 1997. ISBN 0525459057.**

Ten dinosaurs count down one by one. Numerals. **PS, K**

Sturges, Philemon, *Ten Flashing Fireflies.* **Ill. by Anna Vojtech. North-South, 1995. ISBN 155858420X.**

Ten fireflies are captured one by one. Rhymes without numerals show how many of the ten are free and how many are in the jar. **PS, K, Pr**

Wallace, Nancy Elizabeth, *Count Down to Clean Up!* **Houghton Mifflin, 2001. ISBN 0618101306.**

Ten bunnies disperse one by one to gather what they need, then meet to clean up a park. **PS**

Walsh, Ellen Stoll, *Mouse Count.* **Harcourt Brace Jovanovich, 1991. ISBN 0152560238.**

A snake finds ten mice, counting them as he catches them, but they cleverly get away. **T, PS**

Wise, William, *Ten Sly Piranhas: A Counting Story in Reverse.* **Ill. by Victoria Chess. Dial, 1993. ISBN 0803712006.**

Ten piranhas eat each other one by one, until the last is eaten by a crocodile. No numerals. **K**

Counting by 2

Curry, Don L., *How Many Birds?* **A Books/Capstone, 2000. ISBN 0736870393.**

Using photographs of birds, this title explains how to count by twos and threes and how to add to get the total. **K, Pr**

Dee, Ruby, *Two Ways to Count to Ten: A Liberian Folktale.* **Ill. by Susan Meddaugh. Holt, 1990. ISBN 0805013148 (pbk).**

An antelope wins the leopard king's contest by counting by twos instead of by ones. **K, Pr**

deRubertis, Barbara, *Count on Pablo.* **Ill. by Rebecca Thornburgh. Kane, 1999. ISBN 1575650908 (pbk).**

When helping at the market, Pablo counts by ones, by twos, by fives, and by tens. **K, Pr**

Friedman, Aileen, *The King's Commissioners.* Ill. by Susan Guevara. Scholastic, 1995. ISBN 0590489895.
> The king and his advisors count the commissioners in different ways—by twos, by fives, and by tens. **K, Pr**

Glass, Julie, *Counting Sheep.* Ill. by Mike Wohnoutka. Scholastic, 2000. ISBN 0375906193.
> As he tries to go to sleep, a boy counts animals by ones, twos, threes, fours, and fives. No numerals. **PS, K**

Hamm, Diane Johnston, *How Many Feet in the Bed?* Ill. by Kate Salley Palmer. Aladdin, 1994. ISBN 0671899031 (pbk).
> There are different numbers of feet in the bed as a family of five jumps in and out. **PS, K**

Murphy, Stuart J., *Spunky Monkeys on Parade.* Ill. by Lynne Cravath. HarperCollins, 1999. ISBN 006028014X.
> Monkeys march in a parade in groups of two, three, and four. **PS, K, Pr**

Pallotta, Jerry, *Underwater Counting: Even Numbers.* Ill. by David Biedrzycki. Charlesbridge, 2001. ISBN 0881069523.
> Underwater creatures are described and counted by twos from 0 to 50. **K, Pr**

Ryan, Pat Muñoz, and Jerry Pallotta, *The Crayon Counting Book.* Ill. by Frank Mazzola, Jr. Charlesbridge, 1996. ISBN 088106954X.
> Colorful crayons are counted by twos from 0 to 24 and from 1 to 23, illustrating even and odd numbers. **PS, K**

Counting by 5

deRubertis, Barbara, *Count on Pablo.* Ill. by Rebecca Thornburgh. Kane, 1999. ISBN 1575650908 (pbk).
> When helping at the market, Pablo counts by ones, by twos, by fives, and by tens. **K, Pr**

Glass, Julie, *Counting Sheep.* Ill. by Mike Wohnoutka. Scholastic, 2000. ISBN 0375906193.
> As he tries to go to sleep, a boy counts animals by ones, twos, threes, fours, and fives. No numerals. **PS, K**

Hassett, John, and Ann Hassett, *Cats up a Tree.* Houghton Mifflin, 1998. ISBN 0395884152.
> Nana Quimby tries to get various city departments to help get a cat out of a tree. One cat becomes 5, then 10 and so on up to 40. **K, Pr**

Pinczes, Elinor J., *Arctic Fives Arrive*. Ill. by Holly Berry. Houghton Mifflin, 1996. ISBN 0395735777.

Animals arrive in groups of five to watch the northern lights. **K, Pr**

Slater, Teddy, *. . . 98, 99, 100! Ready or Not, Here I Come*. Ill. by Gioia Fiammenghi. Scholastic, 1999. ISBN 0590120093 (pbk).

Some girls play hide-and-seek, counting to 100 by ones, by fives, by tens, and by 20s. **K, Pr**

Counting by 10

Brimner, Larry Dane, *How Many Ants?* Ill. by Joan Cottle. Children's Press, 1997. ISBN 0516203983.

Ants are counted by tens, from 10 to 100. **PS, K**

Cuyler, Margery, *100th Day Worries*. Ill. by Arthur Howard. Simon & Schuster, 2000. ISBN 080503191X.

Jessica can't find 100 things to take to school for the hundredth day, but she does come up with 10 groups of 10 things. **K, Pr**

deRubertis, Barbara, *Count on Pablo*. Ill. by Rebecca Thornburgh. Kane, 1999. ISBN 1575650908 (pbk).

When helping at the market, Pablo counts by ones, by twos, by fives, and by tens. **K, Pr**

Fleming, Denise, *Count!* Henry Holt, 1992. ISBN 0805015957.

Animals are counted by ones to 10 and then by 10s to 50. Numerals. **PS, K**

Friedman, Aileen, *The King's Commissioners*. Ill. by Susan Guevara. Scholastic, 1995. ISBN 0590489895.

The king and his advisors count the commissioners in different ways—by twos, by fives, and by tens. **K, Pr**

King, Dave, *Counting Book*. DK, 1998. ISBN 0789434482.

Pictures of things 1-20, 30, 40, and so on to 100, plus 1,000. Numerals are hidden in the pictures, and other counting activities are included for each picture. **PS, K**

McGrath, Barbara Barbieri, *The Cheerios Counting Book*. Ill. by Rob Bolster and Frank Mazzola, Jr. Scholastic, 1998. ISBN 0590683578.

Counting Cheerios and fruit from 1 to 20, then by 10s from 10 to 100. Also introduces zero. Numerals. **PS, K**

Miranda, Anne, *Monster Math*. Ill. by Polly Powell. Harcourt Brace, 1999. ISBN 0152018352.

Monsters arrive for a party, one by one to ten, then in tens up to fifty. Mother shoos them away in groups. No numerals. **PS, K**

Rockwell, Anne, *100 School Days*. Ill. by Lizzie Rockwell. HarperCollins, 2002. ISBN 0060291443.
> On the way to the hundredth day of school, a class celebrates days 10, 20, 30, and so on. **K, Pr**

Ryan, Pam Muñoz, *One Hundred Is a Family*. Ill. by Benrei Huang. Hyperion, 1996. ISBN 078681120X (pbk).
> Shows different kinds of families, which number from one to ten, then by tens to a hundred. Numerals not shown. **PS, K**

Slater, Teddy, . . . *98, 99, 100! Ready or Not, Here I Come*. Ill. by Gioia Fiammenghi. Scholastic, 1999. ISBN 0590120093 (pbk).
> Some girls play hide-and-seek, counting to 100 by ones, by fives, by 10s and by 20s. **K, Pr**

Sloat, Teri, *From One to One Hundred*. Scott Foresman, 1995. ISBN 0140556435 (pbk).
> Each illustration includes several groups of things of the featured number 1 to 10, then by 10s from 20 to 100. Numerals are used. **PS, K, Pr**

Even, Odd

Cristaldi, Kathryn, *Even Steven and Odd Todd*. Ill. by Henry B. Morehouse. Scholastic, 1996. ISBN 0590227157 (pbk).
> Steven always does things in even numbers, while his cousin Todd likes to be odd. Activities relating to even and odd are included. **K, Pr**

Murphy, Stuart J., *Missing Mittens*. Ill. by G. Brian Karas. HarperCollins, 2001. ISBN 0060280263.
> Farmer Bill tries to find pairs of mittens, but keeps finding odd numbers of them. **PS, K**

Pallotta, Jerry, *Underwater Counting: Even Numbers*. Ill. by David Biedrzycki. Charlesbridge, 2001. ISBN 0881069523.
> Underwater creatures are described and counted by 2s from 0 to 50. **K, Pr**

Ryan, Pat Muñoz, and Jerry Pallotta, *The Crayon Counting Book*. Ill. by Frank Mazzola, Jr. Charlesbridge, 1996. ISBN 088106954X.
> Colorful crayons are counted by 2s from 0 to 24 and from 1 to 23, illustrating even and odd numbers. **PS, K**

Turner, Priscilla, *Among the Odds and Evens: A Tale of Adventure*. Ill. by Whitney Turner. Scholastic, 1999. ISBN 0374303436.
> X and Y land in the village of Wontoo and discover the differences between the Odds and the Evens. **Pr**

Ziefert, Harriet, *Bears Odd, Bears Even*. Ill. by Andrea Baruffi. Puffin, 1997. ISBN 0140385398.
Bears illustrate odd and even numbers. **K**

Ordinals *[First, second, third, and so on]*

Anno, Mitsumasa, *Anno's Magic Seeds*. Philomel, 1995. ISBN 0399225382.
First Jack eats one seed and plants the other, which produces two more, but then he experiments with planting more and giving some away. **Pr**

Bishop, Claire Huchet, *The Five Chinese Brothers*. Ill. by Kurt Wiese. Putnam, 1996. ISBN 0698113587 (pbk).
Five identical brothers pose as each other and use their magic powers to escape an unjust execution. **PS, K, Pr**

Brown, Margaret Wise, *The Little Scarecrow Boy*. Ill. by David Diaz. Joanna Cotler Books/HarperCollins, 1998. ISBN 0060262842.
A little scarecrow boy has to make six fierce faces (first through sixth) to scare away the crows. **PS**

Elya, Susan Middleton, *Eight Animals on the Town*. Ill. by Lee Chapman. Putnam, 2000. ISBN 0399234373.
Eight animals go to a market, each looking for the appropriate food. Numerals are shown in the corners of the pages. Text is mainly in English, but includes Spanish words. **PS, K**

Floca, Brian, *Five Trucks*. DK, 1999. ISBN 0789425610.
Five trucks work at an airport. **PS**

Herman, Gail, *The Littlest Duckling*. Ill. by Ann Schweninger. Viking, 1996. ISBN 0670851132.
Four ducklings, first, second, third, and last, go swimming, and the last one almost gets lost. **PS**

Kohn, Rita, *Winter Storytime*. Ill. by Dorothy Sullivan. Children's, 1995. ISBN 0516052047.
A Lenape grandmother tells two children the story of how the first rabbit-tail game was made. **T, PS**

Lanteigne, Helen, *The Seven Chairs*. Ill. by Maryann Kovalski. Orchard, 1998. ISBN 0531301109.
Tells what happens to each of the seven different chairs made by one man. **PS, K, Pr**

Larios, Julie Hofstrand, *On the Stairs.* Ill. by Mary Hofstrand Cornish. Front Street, 1999. ISBN 1886910340.
  A little mouse girl gives a special name to each of the twelve steps on her staircase. Numerals. **PS, K**

Murphy, Stuart J., *Henry the Fourth.* Ill. by Scott Nash. HarperCollins, 1999. ISBN 006027610X.
  Four dogs at a dog show introduce ordinal numbers first through fourth. **PS, K**

Addition [Concept of addition, not math facts]

Anno, Mitsumasa, *Anno's Magic Seeds.* Philomel, 1995. ISBN 0399225382.
  First Jack eats one seed and plants the other, which produces two more, but then he experiments with planting more and giving some away. **Pr**

Axelrod, Amy, *Pigs at Odds: Fun with Math and Games.* Ill. by Sharon McGinley-Nally. Simon & Schuster, 2000. ISBN 0689815662.
  The pigs play carnival games. Includes explanations of odds and probabilities; asks the reader to add up what the pigs spent. **Pr**

Axelrod, Amy, *Pigs on a Blanket: Fun with Math and Time.* Ill. by Sharon McGinley-Nally. Simon & Schuster, 1996. ISBN 0689805055.
  The pig family encounters many delays on their trip to the beach. Adding up different amounts of time. **K, Pr**

Axelrod, Amy, *Pigs Will Be Pigs: Fun with Math and Money.* Ill. by Sharon McGinley-Nally. Simon & Schuster, 1994. ISBN 002765415X.
  In order to go out to eat, the Pig family hunts around the house for money. The reader can add up the value of the coins and bills found, determine how much the pigs spend and how much they have left, and figure out other possible meals the pigs could afford. **Pr**

Baker, Keith, *Quack and Count.* Harcourt Brace, 1999. ISBN 0152928588.
  Seven ducks divide themselves into different groupings, such as 6 and 1 and 2 and 5. **PS, K, Pr**

Boynton, Sandra, *Doggies: A Counting and Barking Book.* Little Simon, 1995. ISBN 0671493183.
  Noisy dogs from 1 to 10, with numerals. Board. **T, PS**

Boynton, Sandra, *Hippos Go Berserk!* Simon & Schuster, 1996. ISBN 0689808542.
  Groups of hippos from one to nine arrive at a party, then leave again in the morning. Numerals shown. **PS**

Brimner, Larry Dane, *How Many Ants?* Ill. by Joan Cottle. Children's Press, 1997. ISBN 0516203983.
  Ants are counted by 10s, from 10 to 100. **PS, K**

Capucilli, Alyssa Satin, *Mrs. McTats and Her Houseful of Cats*. Ill. by Joan Rankin. Margaret K. McElderry, 2001. ISBN 0689831854.
Mrs. McTats has one cat named Abner. She then adds 24 more, in groups of two to six, which she names in alphabetical order, plus a dog she names Zoom. **PS, K**

Carlstrom, Nancy White, *Let's Count It Out, Jesse Bear*. Ill. by Bruce Degen. Simon & Schuster, 1996. ISBN 0689804784.
Rhymes about each number 1 to 10, plus numerals through 20, and explanation of adding one each time. Also, counting backwards from 10. **PS, K, Pr**

Chorao, Kay, *Number One Number Fun*. Holiday House, 1995. ISBN 0823411427.
Animals in a circus invite the reader to add and subtract as they do their tricks. **PS, K**

Cobb, Annie, *The Long Wait*. Ill. by Liza Woodruff. Kane, 2000. ISBN 1575670940 (pbk).
While waiting in line at an amusement park, two boys estimate various things using addition and multiplication. **Pr**

Curry, Don L., *How Many Birds?* A Books/Capstone, 2000. ISBN 0736870393.
Using photographs of birds, this title explains how to count by twos and threes and how to add to get the total. **K, Pr**

de Regniers, Beatrice Schenk, *So Many Cats!* Ill. by Ellen Weiss. Houghton Mifflin, 1988. ISBN 0899197000 (pbk).
One or a few at a time a family acquires a dozen cats. **PS, K**

deRubertis, Barbara, *A Collection for Kate*. Ill. by Gioia Fiammenghi. Kane, 1999. ISBN 1575650894 (pbk).
Kate's classmates all seem to have larger collections than she does. Uses addition to determine number of items in the collections. **K, Pr**

Duke, Kate, *One Guinea Pig Is Not Enough*. Dutton, 1998. ISBN 0525459189.
One guinea pig plus one makes two. One more is added each time to make 10, then 10 more to make 20. Large numerals. **PS, K**

Giganti, Paul, Jr., *Each Orange Had 8 Slices: A Counting Book*. Ill. by Donald Crews. Greenwillow, 1992. ISBN 0688104282.
Many things to count and add or multiply: for example, two oranges with eight slices and two seeds in each slice. **K, Pr**

Goldstone, Bruce, *Ten Friends.* Ill. by Heather Cahoon. Henry Holt, 2001. ISBN 0805062491.
> Describes the different combinations that could make 10 friends: 5 shepherds and 5 sheep, or 4 scuba divers, 3 chauffeurs and 3 bus drivers, for example. Numerals are used. **K, Pr**

Harris, Trudy, *100 Days of School.* Ill. by Beth Griffis Johnson. Millbrook, 1999. ISBN 0761312714.
> Different ways of arriving at the number 100. **K, Pr**

Hulme, Joy N., *Sea Sums.* Ill. by Carol Schwartz. Hyperion, 1996. ISBN 0786801700.
> Animals in a coral reef introduce addition and subtraction facts. **Pr**

Inkpen, Mick, *The Great Pet Sale.* Orchard, 1999. ISBN 0531301303.
> A boy looks at animals for sale in a pet shop, costing from 1 cent to 25 cents, then determines that he can buy everything for $1.00. **PS, K, Pr**

Keenan, Sheila, *Lizzy's Dizzy Day.* Ill. by Jackie Snider. Scholastic, 2001. ISBN 0439059631 (pbk).
> Lizzy tries to help set up a birthday party, but her addition, subtraction, and problem-solving skills are faulty. **K, Pr**

Koller, Jackie French, *One Monkey Too Many.* Ill. by Lynn Munsinger. Harcourt Brace, 1999. ISBN 0152000062.
> A bike for one ends up with two monkeys, a golf cart for two ends up with three, and so on up to seven, with disastrous results. **PS, K**

Leedy, Loreen, *Mission: Addition.* Holiday House, 1997. ISBN 0823413071.
> Animal children use addition in everyday situations. **Pr**

Maccarone, Grace, *Monster Math Picnic.* Ill. by Marge Hartelius. Scholastic, 1998. ISBN 0590371274 (pbk).
> Ten monsters divide up in different groups to do different activities. **PS, K, Pr**

Merriam, Eve, *12 Ways to Get to 11.* Ill. by Bernie Karlin. Aladdin, 1996. ISBN 0689808925 (pbk).
> Shows different groups of things that add up to 11. **K, Pr**

Murphy, Stuart J., *Animals on Board.* Ill. by R. W. Alley. HarperCollins, 1998. ISBN 0060274433.
> Truckloads of animals are added up. **K, Pr**

Murphy Stuart J., *A Fair Bear Share.* Ill. by John Speirs. HarperCollins, 1998. ISBN 0060274387.
> Four bears gather ingredients for a pie. Each bear's contribution is added to the others, with illustrations showing regrouping. **K, Pr**

Murphy, Stuart J., *Get Up and Go!* Ill. by Diane Greenseid. HarperCollins, 1996. ISBN 0060258810.
A girl adds up how long it takes her to get ready for school by using a time line. **PS, K, Pr**

Murphy, Stuart J., *Ready, Set, Hop!* Ill. by Jon Buller. HarperCollins, 1996. ISBN 0060258772.
Two frogs have a contest to see who can take fewer hops to get places. **Pr**

Murphy, Stuart J., *Safari Park.* Ill. by Steve Bjorkman. HarperCollins, 2002. ISBN 0060289147.
At an amusement park, a group of children must decide how many tickets it will take to go on all the rides they want. **Pr**

Murphy, Stuart J., *Too Many Kangaroo Things to Do!* Ill. by Kevin O'Malley. HarperCollins, 1996. ISBN 0060258837.
The story of a birthday illustrates simple multiplication and addition facts. **K, Pr**

Ochiltree, Dianne, *Cats Add Up!* Ill. by Marcy Dunn-Ramsey. Scholastic, 1998. ISBN 0590120050 (pbk).
A girl keeps getting more and more cats, then gives all but one away. **PS, K, Pr**

Ochiltree, Dianne, *Ten Monkey Jamboree.* Ill. by Anne-Sophie Lanquetin. Margaret K. McElderry/Simon & Schuster, 2001. ISBN 0689834020.
Ten monkeys divide themselves up in many different combinations. **PS, K, Pr**

Slater, Teddy, *Stay in Line.* Ill. by Gioia Fiammenghi. Scholastic, 1996. ISBN 0590227130 (pbk).
Twelve children on a trip to the zoo arrange themselves in different groups. **K, Pr**

Walton, Rick, *One More Bunny: Adding from One to Ten.* Ill. by Paige Miglio. Lothrop, Lee & Shepard, 2000. ISBN 0688168477.
Demonstrates adding one bunny at a time, from 1 to 10. Numerals shown. **PS, K, Pr**

Subtraction [Concept of subtraction, not math facts]

Anno, Mitsumasa, *Anno's Magic Seeds.* Philomel, 1995. ISBN 0399225382.
First Jack eats one seed and plants the other, which produces two more, but then he experiments with planting more and giving some away. **Pr**

Arnold, Tedd, *Five Ugly Monsters.* Cartwheel, 1995. ISBN 0590222260.
Five monsters jump on the bed, and one by one they fall off. **PS**

Axelrod, Amy, *Pigs Will Be Pigs: Fun with Math and Money*. Ill. by Sharon McGinley-Nally. Simon & Schuster, 1994. ISBN 002765415X.

In order to go out to eat, the Pig family hunts around the house for money. The reader can add up the value of the coins and bills found, determine how much the pigs spend and how much they have left, and figure out other possible meals the pigs could afford. **Pr**

Chorao, Kay, *Number One Number Fun*. Holiday House, 1995. ISBN 0823411427.

Animals in a circus invite the reader to add and subtract as they do their tricks. **PS, K**

Duke, Kate, *Twenty Is Too Many*. Dutton, 2000. ISBN 0525420266.

Subtracts ten guinea pigs from 20, then one at a time from ten to one. **PS, K, Pr**

Geddes, Anne, *10 in the Bed*. Cedco, 2000. ISBN 0768322839.

Ten babies climb out of bed one by one. Story can be read with book right side up or upside down, so the reader can see how many babies are in or out of the bed at one time. Numerals. **PS, K**

Hulme, Joy N., *Sea Sums*. Ill. by Carol Schwartz. Hyperion, 1996. ISBN 0786801700.

Animals in a coral reef introduce addition and subtraction facts. **Pr**

Keenan, Sheila, *Lizzy's Dizzy Day*. Ill. by Jackie Snider. Scholastic, 2001. ISBN 0439059631 (pbk).

Lizzy tries to help set up a birthday party, but her addition, subtraction, and problem-solving skills are faulty. **K, Pr**

Leedy, Loreen, *Subtraction Action*. Holiday House, 2000. ISBN 082341454X.

The animal children in Miss Prime's class learn about subtraction. **K, Pr**

Miranda, Anne, *Monster Math*. Ill. by Polly Powell. Harcourt Brace, 1999. ISBN 0152018352.

Monsters arrive for a party, one by one to ten, then in tens up to fifty. Mother shoos them away in groups. No numerals. **PS, K**

Murphy, Stuart J., *Elevator Magic*. Ill. by G. Brian Karas. HarperCollins, 1997. ISBN 0060267755.

Going down in an elevator helps to demonstrate subtraction. **K, Pr**

Murphy, Stuart J., *Monster Musical Chairs*. Ill. by Scott Nash. HarperCollins, 2000. ISBN 0060280204.

Five monsters play musical chairs and are eliminated one by one. Numerals are not used. **PS, K**

Murphy, Stuart J., *Ready, Set, Hop!* Ill. by Jon Buller. HarperCollins, 1996. ISBN 0060258772.

Two frogs have a contest to see who can take fewer hops to get places. **Pr**

Murphy, Stuart J., *Shark Swimathon*. Ill. by Lynne Cravath. HarperCollins, 2001. ISBN 00620280301.
> The coach uses subtraction of two-digit numbers to determine how many laps are left to go in the swimathon. **Pr**

Ochiltree, Dianne, *Cats Add Up!* Ill. by Marcy Dunn-Ramsey. Scholastic, 1998. ISBN 0590120050 (pbk).
> A girl keeps getting more and more cats, then gives all but one away. **PS, K, Pr**

Penner, Lucille Recht, *Lights Out!* Ill. by Jerry Smath. Kane, 2000. ISBN 1575650924 (pbk).
> A girl watches the lights go out in the apartment building next door, using subtraction to figure out how many are left. **K, Pr**

Samton, Sheila White, *Ten Tiny Monsters: A Superbly Scary Story of Subtraction*. Crown, 1997. ISBN 0517709414.
> One by one, ten little monsters are bumped from the monster team for not being scary enough. Subtraction facts are shown as 10-1=9 and so on, down to 1-1=0. **PS, K**

Sturges, Philemon, *Ten Flashing Fireflies*. Ill. by Anna Vojtech. North-South, 1995. ISBN 155858420X.
> Ten fireflies are captured one by one. Rhymes without numerals show how many of the ten are free and how many are in the jar. **PS, K, Pr**

Multiplication [Concept of multiplication, not math facts]

Anno, Masaichiro, and Mitsumasa Anno, *Anno's Mysterious Multiplying Jar*. Ill. by Mitsumasa Anno. Putnam, 1983. ISBN 0399209514.
> One island has two countries, each country has three mountains and so on up to ten. Explains factorials. Includes numerals. **Pr**

Anno, Mitsumasa, *Anno's Magic Seeds*. Philomel, 1995. ISBN 0399225382.
> First Jack eats one seed and plants the other, which produces two more, but then he experiments with planting more and giving some away. **Pr**

Appelt, Kathi, *Bats on Parade*. Ill. by Melissa Sweet. Morrow, 1999. ISBN 0688156657.
> The marching bat band has one drum major, four piccolos (marching two by two), nine flute players (marching three by three), and so on up to 100 sousaphones marching 10 by 10. **Pr**

Axelrod, Amy, *Pigs Go to Market: Fun with Math and Shopping.* Ill. by Sharon McGinley-Nally. Simon & Schuster, 1997. ISBN 0689810695.
On Halloween Mrs. Pig wins a five-minute shopping spree in the supermarket. The reader is invited to count, multiply, and measure. **Pr**

Birch, David, *The King's Chessboard.* Ill. by Devis Grebu. Puffin, 1993. ISBN 0140548807 (pbk).
A wise man, forced to accept a reward from an Indian king, asks for one grain of rice on the first square of a chessboard, to be doubled on each following square. **K, Pr**

Buckless, Andrea, *Too Many Cooks!* Ill. by K. A. Jacobs. Scholastic, 2000. ISBN 0439169666 (pbk).
Cara and her brothers try to make soup. They use correct multiplication to determine ingredients, but something is still wrong with the soup! **Pr**

Burns, Marilyn, *Spaghetti and Meatballs for All! A Mathematical Story.* Ill. by Debbie Tilley. Scholastic, 1997. ISBN 0590944592.
For a family reunion of 32 people, Mrs. Comfort sets eight square tables with four places each. People rearrange the tables, in different groupings, so that there are not enough place settings for all. Introduces concepts of area and perimeter. **Pr**

Cobb, Annie, *The Long Wait.* Ill. by Liza Woodruff. Kane, 2000. ISBN 1575670940 (pbk).
While waiting in line at an amusement park, two boys estimate various things using addition and multiplication. **Pr**

Friedman, Aileen, *The King's Commissioners.* Ill. by Susan Guevara. Scholastic, 1995. ISBN 0590489895.
The king and his advisors count the commissioners in different ways—by twos, by fives, and by tens. **K, Pr**

Giganti, Paul, Jr., *Each Orange Had 8 Slices: A Counting Book.* Ill. by Donald Crews. Greenwillow, 1992. ISBN 0688104282.
Many things to count and add or multiply: for example, two oranges with eight slices and two seeds in each slice. **K, Pr**

Glass, Julie, *Counting Sheep.* Ill. by Mike Wohnoutka. Scholastic, 2000. ISBN 0375906193.
As he tries to go to sleep, a boy counts animals by ones, twos, threes, fours, and fives. No numerals. **PS, K**

Hulme, Joy N., *Sea Squares.* Ill. by Carol Schwartz. Hyperion, 1993. ISBN 1562825208 (pbk).
From one to ten sea animals provide examples of square numbers, such as four seals with four flippers each and eight octopuses with eight legs each. **PS, K, Pr**

Leedy, Loreen, *2 X 2=Boo! A Set of Spooky Multiplication Stories.* **Holiday House, 1995. ISBN 0823411907.**
Halloween-inspired vignettes use multiplication. **Pr**

Michelson, Richard, *Ten Times Better.* **Ill. by Leonard Baskin. Marshall Cavendish, 2000. ISBN 076145070X.**
Poems about animals introduce numbers one to ten, and those ten times as much, 10 to 100. **Pr**

Murphy, Stuart J., *Safari Park.* **Ill. by Steve Bjorkman. HarperCollins, 2002. ISBN 0060289147.**
At an amusement park, a group of children must decide how many tickets it will take to go on all the rides they want. **Pr**

Murphy, Stuart J., *Spunky Monkeys on Parade.* **Ill. by Lynne Cravath. HarperCollins, 1999. ISBN 006028014X.**
Monkeys march in a parade in groups of two, three, and four. **PS, K, Pr**

Murphy, Stuart J., *Too Many Kangaroo Things to Do!* **Ill. by Kevin O'Malley. HarperCollins, 1996. ISBN 0060258837.**
The story of a birthday illustrates simple multiplication and addition facts. **K, Pr**

Neuschwander, Cindy, *Amanda Bean's Amazing Dream: A Mathematical Story.* **Ill. by Liza Woodruff. Scholastic, 1998. ISBN 0590300121.**
Amanda's dream makes her understand that sometimes multiplication is faster than counting as a way to find out how many. **Pr**

Rocklin, Joanne, *Just Add Fun!* **Ill. by Martin Lemelman. Scholastic, 1999. ISBN 0590643991 (pbk).**
In this book's four short chapters, Frank and Hank use multiplication to plan a party. **Pr**

Division *[Concept of division, not math facts]*

Dodds, Dayle Ann, *The Great Divide.* **Ill. by Tracy Mitchell. Candlewick, 1999. ISBN 0763604429.**
There are eighty racers to start, but various challenges keep dividing the group in half. **K, Pr**

Hutchins, Pat, *The Doorbell Rang.* **Greenwillow, 1986. ISBN 0688052517.**
Twelve cookies are divided up, first for two people, then for four, six and twelve. **K**

Murphy, Stuart J., *Divide and Ride.* **Ill. by George Ulrich. HarperCollins, 1997. ISBN 0060267763.**
A group of 11 friends goes to an amusement park and must divide up in groups to go on the rides. **Pr**

Murphy, Stuart J., *Jump, Kangaroo, Jump!* Ill. by Kevin O'Malley. HarperCollins, 1999. ISBN 0060276142.
> Different groupings of animal teams at a field day demonstrate fractions and division. **Pr**

Napoli, Donna Jo, and Richard Tchen, *How Hungry Are You?* Ill. by Amy Walrod. Atheneum, 2001. ISBN 068983389X.
> As more and more animals join in the picnic, they must figure out ways to divide up the food each brings. **K, Pr**

Penner, Lucille Recht, *Clean-Sweep Campers*. Ill. by Paige Billin-Frye. Kane, 2000. ISBN 1575650967 (pbk).
> The eight girls in a bunk at sleep-away camp try to divide into teams to make cleaning more fun. **K, Pr**

Pinczes, Elinor J., *One Hundred Hungry Ants*. Ill. by Bonnie MacKain. Houghton Mifflin, 1993. ISBN 0395631165.
> One hundred ants line up in rows of two, four, five and ten, but still arrive too late for the picnic. **PS, K, Pr**

Pinczes, Elinor J., *A Remainder of One*. Ill. by Bonnie MacKain. Houghton Mifflin, 1995. ISBN 0395694558.
> One ant is always left out when his 25-member troop is divided into rows of two, three, or four, but finally the troop divides evenly into fives. **Pr**

Rocklin, Joanna, *One Hungry Cat*. Ill. by Rowan Barnes-Murphy. Scholastic, 1997. ISBN 0590939726 (pbk).
> Tom the Cat bakes a dozen cookies, then a cake, then two blueberry muffins, and tries to divide each three ways. **K, Pr**

Fractions

Leedy, Loreen, *Fraction Action*. Holiday House, 1994. ISBN 0823411095.
> Animal children use sharing, money, shapes, and sets to explore fractions. **Pr**

McMillan, Bruce, *Eating Fractions*. Scholastic, 1991. ISBN 0590437704.
> Two boys make various foods that they divide into halves, thirds, and fourths. Photos, very few words. **PS, K**

Murphy, Stuart J., *Give Me Half!* Ill. by G. Brian Karas. HarperCollins, 1996. ISBN 006025873X.
> A brother and sister who don't like to share food argue about dividing things in half. **K, Pr**

Murphy, Stuart J., *Jump, Kangaroo, Jump!* Ill. by Kevin O'Malley. HarperCollins, 1999. ISBN 0060276142.
   Different groupings of animal teams at a field day demonstrate fractions and division. **Pr**

Penner, Lucille Recht, *Clean-Sweep Campers*. Ill. by Paige Billin-Frye. Kane, 2000. ISBN 1575650967 (pbk).
   The eight girls in a bunk at sleep-away camp try to divide into teams to make cleaning more fun. **K, Pr**

Pinczes, Elinor J., *Inchworm and a Half*. Ill. by Randall Enos. Houghton Mifflin, 2001. ISBN 039582849X.
   An inchworm meets worms that are one-half, one-third, and one-quarter his size, who help him measure garden vegetables. **K, Pr**

Ziefert, Harriet, *Rabbit and Hare Divide an Apple*. Ill. by Emily Bolam. Viking 1998. ISBN 0670877905.
   Two friends try to divide a mushroom and then an apple in half. **PS, K**

Money

Axelrod, Amy, *Pigs at Odds: Fun with Math and Games*. Ill. by Sharon McGinley-Nally. Simon & Schuster, 2000. ISBN 0689815662.
   The pigs play carnival games. Includes explanations of odds and probabilities; asks the reader to add up what the pigs spent. **Pr**

Axelrod, Amy, *Pigs Go to Market: Fun with Math and Shopping*. Ill. by Sharon McGinley-Nally. Simon & Schuster, 1997. ISBN 0689810695.
   On Halloween Mrs. Pig wins a five-minute shopping spree in the supermarket. The reader is invited to count, multiply, and measure. **Pr**

Axelrod, Amy, *Pigs Will Be Pigs: Fun with Math and Money*. Ill. by Sharon McGinley-Nally. Simon & Schuster, 1994. ISBN 002765415X.
   In order to go out to eat, the Pig family hunts around the house for money. The reader can add up the value of the coins and bills found, determine how much the pigs spend and how much they have left, and figure out other possible meals the pigs could afford. **Pr**

Brisson, Pat, *Benny's Pennies*. Ill. by Bob Barner. Pearson, 1995. ISBN 0440410169.
   With his five pennies, Benny buys five different things. **PS, K**

deRubertis, Barbara, *Deena's Lucky Penny*. Ill. by Joan Holub and Cynthia Fisher. Kane, 1999. ISBN 1575650916 (pbk).
   Deena finds a penny, and helpful friends and relatives give her more, changing it to a nickel, dimes, quarters, and a dollar. Shows how much each coin is worth, what it looks like, and what other coins it is equivalent to. **K, Pr**

Glass, Julie, *A Dollar for Penny.* Ill. by Joy Allen. Random, 2000. ISBN 0679989730.
    The price of lemonade at Penny's stand changes from one cent to two cents, and on up to fifty cents. **K, Pr**

Hoban, Tana, *26 Letters and 99 Cents.* Greenwillow, 1987. ISBN 0688063616.
    Double book. One direction shows coins that add up to amounts from 1 to 30 cents, then 35, 40, 45, 50, 60, 70, 80, 90 and 99 cents. For example, 40 is represented by a quarter, a dime and a nickel. **PS, K, Pr**

Holtzman, Caren, *A Quarter from the Tooth Fairy.* Ill. by Betsy Day. Scholastic, 1995. ISBN 0590265989 (pbk).
    With his quarter from the tooth fairy, a boy buys and returns several items, getting his 25 cents back in different coinage each time. **K, Pr**

Inkpen, Mick, *The Great Pet Sale.* Orchard, 1999. ISBN 0531301303.
    A boy looks at animals for sale in a pet shop, costing from 1 cent to 25 cents, then determines that he can buy everything for $1.00. **PS, K, Pr**

Maccarone, Grace, *Monster Money.* Ill. by Marge Hartelius. Scholastic, 1998. ISBN 0590120077 (pbk).
    Several monsters each buy a pet for 10 cents, using different combinations of coins. **PS, K**

McMillan, Bruce, *Jelly Beans for Sale.* Scholastic, 1996. ISBN 0590865846.
    Photographs show children buying (and eating) jelly beans at a penny a piece, using different coin combinations. **PS, K, Pr**

Murphy, Stuart J., *The Penny Pot.* Ill. by Lynne Cravath. HarperCollins, 1998. ISBN 0060276061.
    Coins are counted at the face-painting booth at the fair. **K, Pr**

Nagel, Karen, *The Lunch Line.* Ill. by Jerry Zimmerman. Scholastic, 1996. ISBN 0590602462 (pbk).
    Kim needs to figure out what to buy at the school cafeteria for two quarters and five dimes. **Pr**

Rocklin, Joanne, *The Case of the Shrunken Allowance.* Ill. by Cornelius Van Wright and Ying-Hwa Hu. Scholastic, 1998. ISBN 0590120069.
    Because it takes up less room in the jar than before, PB thinks some of his allowance is missing, but someone has replaced some coins with bills and put what was left into a bigger jar. **Pr**

Rocklin, Joanne, *How Much Is That Guinea Pig in the Window?* Ill. by Meredith Johnson. Scholastic, 1995. ISBN 0590227165.
    Four short chapters tell about a class earning money to buy a guinea pig. **Pr**

Schwartz, David M., *If You Made a Million*. Ill. by Steven Kellogg. Morrow, 1989. ISBN 0688070175.
   Shows how one penny can grow to a million. Explains interest and checks, gives examples of how big a pile of money would be. **Pr**

Slater, Teddy, *Max's Money*. Ill. by Anthony Lewis. Scholastic, 1998. ISBN 0590120107.
   Short chapter book tells of Max trying to get money for a birthday present for his mother. **Pr**

Viorst, Judith, *Alexander, Who Used to Be Rich Last Sunday*. Ill. by Ray Cruz. Atheneum, 1978. ISBN 0689306024.
   Alexander has a dollar, and spends it bit by bit on many things. **K, Pr**

Williams, Rozanne Lanczak, *The Coin Counting Book*. Charlesbridge, 2001. ISBN 0881063258.
   Shows how much various combinations of coins add up to. **K, Pr**

Zimelman, Nathan, *How the Second Grade Got $8,205.50 to Visit the Statue of Liberty*. Ill. by Bill Slavin. Whitman, 1992. ISBN 0807534315.
   A "treasurer's report" of moneymaking schemes, with hilarious expenses and profits. **K, Pr**

Powers of 2

Anno, Mitsumasa, *Anno's Magic Seeds*. Philomel, 1995. ISBN 0399225382.
   First Jack eats one seed and plants the other, which produces two more, but then he experiments with planting more and giving some away. **Pr**

Birch, David, *The King's Chessboard*. Ill. by Devis Grebu. Puffin, 1993. ISBN 0140548807 (pbk).
   A wise man, forced to accept a reward from an Indian king, asks for one grain of rice on the first square of a chessboard, to be doubled on each following square. **K, Pr**

Demi, *One Grain of Rice: A Mathematical Folktale*. Scholastic, 1997. ISBN 059093998X.
   The raja rewards the rani with one grain of rice to be doubled each day for 30 days, which soon adds up to much more than the raja bargained for. Shows how the total reaches one billion. **Pr**

Losi, Carol A., *The 512 Ants on Sullivan Street*. Ill. by Patrick Merrell. Scholastic, 1997. ISBN 0590308769 (pbk).
   One ant, then two, then four, doubling each time, comes to steal food from a picnic. **Pr**

Powers of 10

Schwartz, David M., *On Beyond a Million: An Amazing Math Journey.* Ill. by Paul Meisel. Doubleday, 1999. ISBN 0385322178.
While trying to count popcorn kernels, a group of children learns about counting by powers of 10 all the way to googolplex. **Pr**

Wells, Robert E., *Can You Count to a Googol?* Albert Whitman, 2000. ISBN 0807510602.
Starting with one, and multiplying each time by 10 up to a googol, this book gives humorous examples of that amount. **Pr**

Chapter Five

Time Concepts

Time [Books with general facts about time]

Llewellyn, Claire, *My First Book of Time.* **DK, 1992. ISBN 1879431785.**
Oversized book illustrates concepts of time of day, days of the week, months, seasons, as well as telling time by analog and digital clocks. **K, Pr**

Schuett, Stacey, *Somewhere in the World Right Now.* **Knopf, 1995. ISBN 0679865373.**
Shows that while it is night somewhere on Earth, at other places it is morning or afternoon. **K, Pr**

Sweeney, Joan, *Me Counting Time: From Seconds to Centuries.* **Ill. by Annette Cable. Crown, 2000. ISBN 0517800551.**
A girl describes the relationship between measurements of time: seconds, minutes, hours, days, weeks, months, years, decades, centuries, millennia. **K, Pr**

Time Sense [Understanding the passage of time]

Aliki, *The Two of Them.* **Morrow, 1987. ISBN 0688073379 (pbk).**
Describes the relationship of a little girl and her grandfather from the girl's birth to her grandfather's death. **PS, K**

Anderson, Laurie Halse, *No Time for Mother's Day.* **Whitman, 1999. ISBN 080754955X.**
Charity gives her mother the gift of time for Mother's Day, by unplugging clocks and other things that claim her attention. **PS, K, Pr**

Anderson, Lena, *Tick-Tock.* **R & S, 1998. ISBN 9129640741.**
>From one o'clock to 12 o'clock, four animal friends play in the park and go to bed. **PS, K**

Anno, Mitsumasa, *All in a Day.* **Paper Star, 1999. ISBN 0698117727 (pbk).**
>Pictures by different illustrators show what is happening around the world at the same moment on one day. **K, Pr**

Axelrod, Amy, *Pigs on a Blanket: Fun with Math and Time.* **Ill. by Sharon McGinley-Nally. Simon & Schuster, 1996. ISBN 0689805055.**
>The pig family encounters many delays on their trip to the beach. Adding up different amounts of time. **K, Pr**

Baker, Jeannie, *Window.* **Greenwillow, 1991. ISBN 0688089186.**
>Collage construction illustrations chronicle the changes in a boy's neighborhood as he grows up. Wordless. **PS, K, Pr**

Banks, Sara Harrell, *A Net to Catch Time.* **Ill. by Scott Cook. Knopf, 1997. ISBN 0679866736.**
>A boy's day on a Georgia sea island, introducing Gullah names for different times of day. **K, Pr**

Borgese, Paul, *A Sunday Stroll.* **Ill. by Jane Arimoto. Laugh & Learn, 1996. ISBN 1886489084.**
>It takes Centipede so long to put on all of his shoes that he and LadyBug don't get started on their Sunday stroll until Monday night. **PS, K**

Burton, Virginia Lee, *The Little House.* **Houghton Mifflin, 1978. ISBN 0395181569.**
>Over the years, a little house, built out in the country, is gradually surrounded by the city. **PS, K, Pr**

Dale, Elizabeth, *How Long?* **Ill. by Alan Marks. Orchard, 1998. ISBN 053130101X.**
>Caroline Mouse learns how long a minute, 10 minutes and other lengths of time are by seeing how much she can do in each of those time spans. **PS**

Dunbar, James, *When I Was Young.* **Ill. by Martin Remphry. Carolrhoda, 1999. ISBN 1575053594.**
>Seven generations of memories briefly tell what life was like back into the 1600s. **K, Pr**

Fruisen, Catherine Myler, *My Mother's Pearls.* **Cedco, 2000. ISBN 0768321778.**
>A girl learns the history of her mother's pearls, all the way back to her great-great-great-great-great-great-Grandma in 1788. **PS, K, Pr**

Grunwald, Lisa, *Now Soon Later.* **Ill. by Jane Johnson. Greenwillow, 1996. ISBN 0688139469.**
>Pictures of realistic situations demonstrate the concepts of now, soon, and later. **T, PS**

Howard, Elizabeth Fitzgerald, *When Will Sarah Come?* Ill. by Nina Crews. Greenwillow, 1999. ISBN 0688161804.
> A little boy waits all day for his sister to come home from school. Illustrated with photographs. **PS**

Inkpen, Mick, *Kipper's Birthday.* Red Wagon, 2000. ISBN 0152023976.
> Invitations saying Kipper's party is "tomorrow" are delivered late, so the guests arrive the next day. Text describes Kipper's wait and discusses "yesterday," "today," and "tomorrow." **T, PS**

Murphy, Stuart J., *Game Time!* Ill. by Cynthia Jabar. HarperCollins, 2000. ISBN 0060280247.
> This story of a soccer game explains many divisions of time. **K, Pr**

Murphy, Stuart J., *Get Up and Go!* Ill. by Diane Greenseid. HarperCollins, 1996. ISBN 0060258810.
> A girl adds up how long it takes her to get ready for school by using a time line. **PS, K, Pr**

Murphy, Stuart J., *Pepper's Journal: A Kitten's First Year.* Ill. by Marsha Winborn. HarperCollins, 2000. ISBN 0060276185.
> A girl keeps a diary of her cat's first year. Entries are made at irregular times. Shows the cat's development. **PS, K, Pr**

Sharratt, Nick, *The Time It Took Tom.* Ill. by Stephen Tucker. Little Tiger, 1999. ISBN 1888444630.
> Tom paints everything in the living room red, and then he and his mother redo it. The story uses units of time from seconds to years. **PS, K**

Singer, Marilyn, *Nine O'Clock Lullaby.* Ill. by Frané Lessac. HarperCollins, 1993. ISBN 0064433196 (pbk).
> When it's 9 p.m. in Brooklyn, it is different times in different places around the world. **K, Pr**

Slater, Teddy, *Just a Minute!* Ill. by Dana Regan. Scholastic, 1996. ISBN 0590540823 (pbk).
> Fred's family gives him a false idea of how long a minute is by saying "just a minute," but then taking much longer. Fred then learns the true duration of a minute. **PS, K**

Thornhill, Jan, *Before & After: A Book of Nature Timescapes.* National Geographic, 1997. ISBN 0792270932.
> Detailed pictures of various natural areas are shown at one time and then a few seconds or up to a year later. **PS, K, Pr**

Vizurraga, Susan, *Our Old House.* **Ill. by Leslie Baker. Henry Holt, 1997. ISBN 0805039112.**

Looking around her old house, a girl finds out about its history and the people who used to live there. **K, Pr**

Time of Day

Ackerman, Karen, *By the Dawn's Early Light.* **Ill. by Catherine Stock. Atheneum, 1994. ISBN 0689317883.**

Two children stay with their grandmother while their mother works the night shift at a factory. Shows the different things mother and children are doing at the same time. **K, Pr**

Agell, Charlotte, *To the Island.* **DK, 1998. ISBN 078942505X.**

Four animals leave in the early morning for a boat trip to an island and return at night. See also *Up the Mountain* [2000: ISBN 0789426102]. **T, PS**

Aliki, *All by Myself!* **HarperCollins, 2000. ISBN 0060289295.**

A child's busy day, simple words showing all he can do by himself. **PS, K**

Armstrong, Jennifer, *Sunshine, Moonshine.* **Ill. by Lucia Washburn. Random, 1997. ISBN 0679964428.**

Easy-reader text shows a boy's seaside day, from morning to night. **PS, K**

Asch, Frank, *The Sun Is My Favorite Star.* **Gulliver/Harcourt, 2000. ISBN 0152021272.**

A child enjoys the sun from sunrise to sunset, and even at night, in its reflected light from the moon. **T, PS, K**

Baker, Alan, *Brown Rabbit's Day.* **Kingfisher, 1995. ISBN 1856975843.**

Brown Rabbit spends his day making some gelatin molds for his friends in yellow, green, red, and purple. **T, PS**

Banks, Kate, *The Bird, the Monkey, and the Snake in the Jungle.* **Ill. by Tomek Bogacki. Farrar, Straus & Giroux, 1999. ISBN 0374307296.**

One day the tree in which three animals live falls over, so they search together for a new home. Rebuses are substituted for most nouns in the story. **PS, K, Pr**

Banks, Sara Harrell, *A Net to Catch Time.* **Ill. by Scott Cook. Knopf, 1997. ISBN 0679866736.**

A boy's day on a Georgia sea island, introducing Gullah names for different times of day. **K, Pr**

Barrett, Mary Brigid, *Day Care Days.* **Ill. by Patti Beling Murphy. Little, Brown, 1999. ISBN 0316084565.**

A little boy gets ready with his family, then spends his day at day care and returns home in the evening. **PS**

Bour, Daniele, *The House from Morning to Night.* **Kane/Miller, 1998. ISBN 0916291014.**
> Shows what is going on in a large multifamily house at many different times of day. Detailed pictures, minimal text. **PS, K**

Carle, Eric, *The Grouchy Ladybug.* **HarperCollins, 1996. ISBN 006027087X.**
> From 5 a.m. through 6 p.m. (on the hours and at 5:15, 5:30, and 5:45), the grouchy ladybug tries to pick a fight with increasingly larger animals. Also shows the sun's position at each hour. **PS, K, Pr**

Carlstrom, Nancy White, *Jesse Bear, What Will You Wear?* **Ill. by Bruce Degen. Simon & Schuster, 1986. ISBN 002717350X.**
> Jesse wears different things each time of day, morning, noon, and night. **PS**

Ford, Miela, *What Color Was the Sky Today?* **Ill. by Sally Noll. Greenwillow, 1997. ISBN 0688145582.**
> The sky changes color as the weather changes during the course of a day. Simple text. **PS**

George, Jean Craighead, *Morning, Noon, and Night.* **Ill. by Wendell Minor. HarperCollins, 1999. ISBN 0060236280.**
> Paintings of animals illustrate each time of day from dawn to dawn. **PS, K**

Lavis, Steve, *Little Mouse Has a Busy Day.* **Ragged Bears, 2000. ISBN 192992710X.**
> Little Mouse does many things throughout his day, with on-the-hour times shown. **PS**

London, Jonathan, *Like Butter on Pancakes.* **Ill. by G. Brian Karas. Viking, 1995. ISBN 0670851302.**
> Poetic description of a day, from early morning through evening. **PS, K, Pr**

Ormerod, Jan, *Miss Mouse's Day.* **Lothrop Lee & Shepard, 2000. ISBN 0688163335.**
> A girl and her mouse doll are busy from morning to night. **PS, K**

Schuett, Stacey, *Somewhere in the World Right Now.* **Knopf, 1995. ISBN 0679865373.**
> Shows that while it is night somewhere on Earth, at other places it is morning or afternoon. **K, Pr**

Siddals, Mary McKenna, *Tell Me a Season.* **Ill. by Petra Mathers. Clarion, 1997. ISBN 0395710219.**
> In this book with very simple text, each season and time of day is represented by a different color. **T, PS**

Stow, Jenny, *Following the Sun.* **Carolrhoda, 1996. ISBN 157505048X.**
> Starting with just one animal and reaching ten, animals follow the sun as it goes across the sky. Numerals. **PS, K**

Tafuri, Nancy, *What the Sun Sees/What the Moon Sees.* **Greenwillow, 1997. ISBN 0688144934.**
    Double-sided book shows things in the daytime and things in the nighttime. **T, PS**

Tyers, Jenny, *When It Is Night, When It Is Day.* **Houghton Mifflin, 1996. ISBN 0395715466.**
    Shows different animals' activities in the nighttime and in the daytime. **PS, K**

Zolotow, Charlotte, *Wake Up and Goodnight.* **Ill. by Pamela Paparone. Harper Festival, 1998. ISBN 0694010324.**
    Short, simple text shows waking up in the morning and going to bed at night. *Wake Up* starts in one direction; book is turned upside down to read *Goodnight*. **T, PS**

Morning

Aylesworth, Jim, *Wake up, Little Children: A Rise-and-Shine Rhyme.* **Ill. by Walter Lyon Krudop. Atheneum, 1996. ISBN 068931857X.**
    Rhyming text encourages a child to get up, telling all the things she can do on a summer day. **PS**

Chall, Marsha Wilson, *Rupa Raises the Sun.* **Ill. by Rosanne Litzinger. DK, 1998. ISBN 0789424967.**
    Rupa gets up very early each morning to make the sun rise, but when she finally sleeps in, the sun rises on its own. **K**

Edwards, Pamela Duncan, *The Grumpy Morning.* **Ill. by Darcia Labrosse. Hyperion, 1998. ISBN 0786803312.**
    When the farmer oversleeps, the animals make noises to let her know she needs to get up and feed them. **PS**

Maitland, Barbara, *Moo in the Morning.* **Ill. by Andrew Kulman. Farrar, Straus & Giroux, 2000. ISBN 0374350388.**
    A mother and child leave the noisy city for the country, but find that it is just as noisy in the morning in its own way. **PS, K**

Meeker, Clare Hodgson, *Who Wakes Rooster?* **Ill. by Megan Halsey. Simon & Schuster, 1996. ISBN 0689805411.**
    The sun wakes rooster, who wakes everyone else on the farm. **PS**

Whitman, Candace, *Now It Is Morning.* **Farrar, Straus & Giroux, 1999. ISBN 0374355274.**
    Shows morning routines for families on a farm, in the town and in the city. **PS**

Wong, Janet S., *Buzz.* Ill. by Margaret Chodos-Irvine. Harcourt, 2000. ISBN 0152019235.
A child observes his parents getting up and leaving for work in the morning. **PS, K**

Night

Banks, Kate, *And If the Moon Could Talk.* Ill. by Georg Hallensleben. Farrar, Straus & Giroux, 1998. ISBN 0374302995.
Nighttime scenes around the world. **T, PS**

Banks, Kate, *The Night Worker.* Ill. by Georg Hallensleben. Farrar, Straus & Giroux, 2000. ISBN 0374355207.
A boy goes to work with his father one night at a construction site. **PS, K**

Bogacki, Tomek, *Cat and Mouse in the Night.* Farrar, Straus & Giroux, 1998. ISBN 0374311900.
Cat and Mouse stay out too late and are afraid of the dark until an owl shows them the beauty of the night. **PS**

Bradbury, Ray, *Switch on the Night.* Ill. by Leo and Diane Dillon. Knopf, 1993. ISBN 0394804864.
A boy who doesn't like the night makes friends with a little girl who teaches him to appreciate it. **PS, K, Pr**

Coy, John, *Night Driving.* Ill. by Peter McCarty. Henry Holt, 1996. ISBN 0805029311.
A boy and his father drive all night. **K, Pr**

Day, Alexandra, *Boswell Wide Awake.* Farrar, Straus & Giroux, 1999. ISBN 0374399735.
Young Boswell the bear is awake in the middle of the night and enjoys being all alone. **PS, K**

Derby, Sally, *Taiko on a Windy Night.* Ill. by Kate Kiesler. Henry Holt, 2001. ISBN 080506401X.
A cat goes out for a walk in the nighttime. **PS, K**

Dowling, Paul, *The Night Journey.* Doubleday, 1996. ISBN 0385322879.
Nicky and Dad take a trip in the dark to the fireworks and see other things along the way. Pull-tabs reveal sights hidden by the darkness. **PS**

Duncan, Lois, *I Walk at Night.* Ill. by Steve Johnson and Lou Fancher. Viking, 2000. ISBN 0670875139.
A cat describes how he spends his time. **PS, K**

Garelick, May, *Look at the Moon.* Ill. by Barbara Garrison. Mondo, 1996. ISBN 1572551429.
Different things happen around the world at night. **PS, K**

Rylant, Cynthia, *Night in the Country.* Ill. by Mary Szilagyi. Atheneum, 1986. ISBN 0027772101.
Describes the animals' behavior and the sounds in the country at night. **PS, K**

Wellington, Monica, and Andrew Kupfer, *Night City.* Dutton, 1998. ISBN 0525459480.
Describes a different job being done at each hour from 7 p.m. to 7 a.m., from firemen to jazz musicians to bakers. **PS, K, Pr**

Wormell, Mary, *Hilda Hen's Scary Night.* Harcourt Brace, 1995. ISBN 0152009906.
In the farmyard at night, Hilda Hen is frightened by ordinary things that seem to be something else. **PS, K**

Yolen, Jane, *Owl Moon.* Ill. by John Schoenherr. Philomel, 1987. ISBN 0399214577.
In the depths of winter, a girl and her father look for owls under a full moon. **PS, K, Pr**

Seasons

Alexander, Sue, *One More Time, Mama.* Ill. by David Soman. Marshall Cavendish, 1999. ISBN 0761450513.
A mother recounts how the seasons changed, winter through early autumn, as she waited for her child to be born. **PS, K, Pr**

Bishop, Gavin, *Stay Awake, Bear!* Orchard, 2000. ISBN 0531302490.
Two bears decide not to sleep all winter—and end up sleeping in the summer instead. **PS, K**

Borden, Louise, *Caps, Hats, Socks, and Mittens: A Book about the Four Seasons.* Ill. by Lillian Hoban. Scholastic, 1992. ISBN 0590448722 (pbk).
Short descriptions of things and activities characteristic of each season. **T, PS**

Bowen, Betsy, *Gathering: A Northwoods Counting Book.* Little, Brown, 1995. ISBN 0395981336.
Colored woodcuts illustrate numerals 0 through 12 as well as seasons spring through winter. **K**

Brown, Margaret Wise, *Love Songs of the Little Bear.* Ill. by Susan Jeffers. Hyperion, 2001. ISBN 0786805099.
A little bear takes a walk in each season of the year. **PS**

Bunting, Eve, *Moonstick: The Seasons of the Sioux.* Ill. by John Sandford. Joanna Cotler Books, 1997. ISBN 0060248041.
: A Dakota Sioux boy describes the 13 moons of his people's year. **Pr**

Burrowes, Adjoa J., *Grandma's Purple Flowers.* Lee & Low, 2000. ISBN 1880000733.
: A little girl visits her grandmother in the summer and fall. Grandmother dies in the winter, but spring flowers remind the girl of her. **PS, K, Pr**

Carlstrom, Nancy White, *I Love You, Mama, Any Time of Year.* Ill. by Bruce Degen. Little Simon, 1997. ISBN 0689807295.
: Jesse Bear loves his mother winter through spring. Board. **T, PS**

Chorao, Kay, *Little Farm by the Sea.* Henry Holt, 1998. ISBN 0805050531.
: Seasons from winter through fall on a small farm. **K, Pr**

dePaola, Tomie, *Charlie Needs a Cloak!* Simon & Schuster, 1988. ISBN 0671664670 (pbk).
: Charlie the shepherd takes an entire year to make himself a red cloak, starting by shearing the sheep in the spring, spinning and dyeing in the summer, and weaving and sewing in the fall, so that the cloak is ready for winter. **PS, K**

Drawson, Blair, *Mary Margaret's Tree.* Orchard, 1996. ISBN 0531095215.
: A little girl spends an imaginary year observing nature from the perspective of a tree. **K, Pr**

Edwards, Richard, *Copy Me, Copycub.* Ill. by Susan Winter. HarperCollins, 1999. ISBN 0060285702.
: A bear cub follows his mother all through the year, spring through winter. **PS**

Fuchs, Diane Marcial, *A Bear for All Seasons.* Ill. by Kathryn Brown. Henry Holt, 1995. ISBN 0805021396.
: Fox and Bear try to determine their favorite seasons. **PS, K**

Geisert, Bonnie, and Arthur Geisert, *Mountain Town.* Houghton Mifflin, 2000. ISBN 0395953901.
: In detailed pictures of everyday life, a western mountain town is shown in all seasons, from winter to winter. **K, Pr**

Gibbons, Gail, *The Seasons of Arnold's Apple Tree.* Harcourt Brace, 1984. ISBN 0152712461.
: From spring to winter Arnold observes the way the changing seasons affect his apple tree. **PS, K**

Hall, Zoë, *The Apple Pie Tree.* Ill. by Shari Halpern. BlueSky/Scholastic, 1996. ISBN 0590623826.
: Two girls watch the changes from winter through fall in their apple tree and the robin family that nests in it. **PS, K**

Kelley, Marty, *Fall Is Not Easy.* **Zino, 1998. ISBN 1559332344 (pbk).**
> A tree tells about what happens to it in each season and how much trouble it has when it's time for leaves to change color. **PS, K**

Kindley, Jeff, *Scamper's Year.* **Ill. by Laura Rader. Bantam, 1997. ISBN 0553375822 (pbk).**
> A squirrel enjoys the seasons from one spring through the next. **PS, K**

Lionni, Leo, *Frederick.* **Knopf, 1990. ISBN 0394810406.**
> While the other mice gather food for winter, Frederick gathers words and impressions, which he turns into poetry to revive them in the depths of winter. **PS, K, Pr**

Lobel, Arnold, *Frog and Toad All Year.* **HarperCollins, 1976. ISBN 0060239506.**
> Frog and Toad do things together in each season. Separate story for each season, plus a Christmas Eve story. **PS, K**

London, Jonathan, *Park Beat: Rhymin' Through the Seasons.* **Ill. by Woodleigh Marx Hubbard. HarperCollins, 2001. ISBN 0688139949.**
> Seasons in a park are described in rap-like rhymes. **PS, K**

Marzollo, Jean, *Once upon a Springtime.* **Ill. by Jacqueline Rogers. Scholastic, 1997. ISBN 059046017X (pbk).**
> A deer describes its first year of life, observing the seasons and the activities of the children, playing, and observing Christmas. **PS, K**

Muller, Gerda, *Circle of Seasons.* **Dutton, 1995. ISBN 0525453946.**
> Illustrates different things that happen in each season, ending with Christmas and Chanukah. **PS, K**

Murphy, Mary, *Here Comes Spring and Summer and Fall and Winter.* **DK, 1999. ISBN 0789434839.**
> Simple introduction to the seasons. **T, PS**

Provensen, Alice, and Martin Provensen, *The Year at Maple Hill Farm.* **Aladdin, 2001. ISBN 0689845006 (pbk).**
> A detailed description of each season on an old-fashioned farm. **PS, K, Pr**

Rogers, Alan, *Green Bear.* **World Book/Two-Can, 1997. ISBN 0716644053.**
> Green Bear likes green best, but paints his house to match the seasons. **T, PS**

Rucki, Ani, *When the Earth Wakes.* **Scholastic, 1998. ISBN 0590059513.**
> Simple descriptions and pictures of a bear mother and cub illustrate the seasons. **PS, K**

Siddals, Mary McKenna, *Tell Me a Season.* **Ill. by Petra Mathers. Clarion, 1997. ISBN 0395710219.**

In this book with very simple text, each season and time of day is represented by a different color. **T, PS**

Spring

Bornstein, Ruth, *Rabbit's Good News.* **Clarion, 1995. ISBN 0395687004.**

Rabbit wakes up and discovers spring. **PS, K**

Carlstrom, Nancy White, *Raven and River.* **Ill. by Jon Van Zyle. Little, Brown, 1997. ISBN 0316128945.**

Animals notice the ice breaking up on the river in the Alaskan spring. **PS, K, Pr**

Carr, Jan, *Splish, Splash, Spring.* **Ill. by Dorothy Donohue. Holiday, 2001. ISBN 0823415783.**

Short, bouncy rhymes and collage pictures illustrate spring. **PS, K**

Good, Elaine W., *That's What Happens When It's Spring.* **Ill. by Susie Shenk. Good Books, 1996. ISBN 1561481459.**

A boy learns about the weather, new activities and nature in the spring. **PS, K**

Lee, Huy Voun, *In the Park.* **Henry Holt, 1998. ISBN 0805041281.**

Xiao Ming and his mother go to the park on a spring day and learn many Chinese characters. **K, Pr**

Lindbergh, Reeve, *North Country Spring.* **Ill. by Liz Sivertson. Houghton Mifflin, 1997. ISBN 0395828198.**

Paintings and rhymes show animals in the northern woods getting ready for spring. **PS, K, Pr**

Lobel, Arnold, *Frog and Toad Are Friends.* **HarperCollins, 1970. ISBN 0060239573.**

Five stories. In "Spring," Frog tries to wake Toad up to greet the new season. **PS, K**

Maass, Robert, *When Spring Comes.* **Henry Holt, 1996. ISBN 0805047050 (pbk).**

Photographs show weather and activities in the spring. **PS, K**

Peters, Lisa Westberg, *Cold Little Duck, Duck, Duck.* **Ill. by Sam Williams. Greenwillow, 2000. ISBN 0688161782.**

Little duck tries to land on the pond early in spring, but it is still frozen. **PS**

Pitcher, Caroline, *Are You Spring?* **Ill. by Cliff Wright. DK, 2000. ISBN 0789463504.**

A little bear leaves his den at the end of winter, looking for spring. **PS**

Rockwell, Anne, *My Spring Robin.* Ill. by Harlow Rockwell and Lizzy Rockwell. Aladdin, 1996. ISBN 0689804474 (pbk).
A girl looks for signs of spring, especially the robin. **T, PS**

Schnur, Steven, *Spring: An Alphabet Acrostic.* Ill. by Leslie Evans. Clarion, 1999. ISBN 0395822696.
Short acrostic rhymes about spring topics, one for each letter of the alphabet, shown in upper case. **K, Pr**

Schnur, Steven, *Spring Thaw.* Ill. by Stacey Schuett. Viking, 2000. ISBN 0670879614.
Slowly the snow melts and signs of spring are seen around the farm. **PS, K, Pr**

Seuling, Barbara, *Spring Song.* Ill. by Greg Newbold. Gulliver/Harcourt, 2001. ISBN 0152023178.
Questions and rhyming answers about what many animals will do now that spring has come. **PS, K**

Walters, Catherine, *When Will It Be Spring?* Dutton, 1998. ISBN 0525458816.
A little bear keeps waking up during hibernation to see if spring has arrived. **PS, K**

Summer

Aylesworth, Jim, *Wake up, Little Children: A Rise-and-Shine Rhyme.* Ill. by Walter Lyon Krudop. Atheneum, 1996. ISBN 068931857X.
Rhyming text encourages a child to get up, telling all the things she can do on a summer day. **PS**

Boelts, Maribeth, *Summer's End.* Ill. by Ellen Kandoian. Houghton Mifflin, 1995. ISBN 0395705592.
A little girl prepares to go back to school, remembering what she did in the summer. **K, Pr**

Brennan, Linda Crotta, *Marshmallow Kisses.* Ill. by Mari Takabayashi. Houghton Mifflin, 2000. ISBN 0395738724.
Two children do simple things at home in the summertime. **PS, K**

Crews, Nina, *One Hot Summer Day.* Greenwillow, 1995. ISBN 0688133932.
Photo collage pictures show a little girl on a hot day in the city. **PS, K**

Ehrlich, H. M., *Louie's Goose.* Ill. by Emily Bolam. Houghton Mifflin, 2000. ISBN 0618030239.
A little boy's toy goose suffers many mishaps during a vacation at the shore. **T, PS**

Enderle, Judith Ross, and Stephanie Gordon Tessler, *Six Sandy Sheep*. Ill. by John O'Brien. Boyds Mills, 1997. ISBN 1563975823.
: One by one, six sheep on the beach enter the water. Many words begin with S. **PS, K**

George, Lindsay Barrett, *Around the Pond: Who's Been Here?* Greenwillow, 1996. ISBN 0688143768.
: While picking blueberries, two children discover signs of many animals around the pond. **PS, K, Pr**

Gershwin, George, DuBose and Dorothy Heyward and Ira Gershwin, *Summertime: From Porgy and Bess*. Ill. by Mike Wimmer. Simon & Schuster, 1999. ISBN 0689807198.
: The words to the song from *Porgy and Bess* are illustrated with appropriate paintings. Music to the song is also included. **PS, K, Pr**

Kelley, Marty. *Summer Stinks: An Alphabetical Lexicon for the Estivally Dispirited*. Zino, 2001. ISBN 1559332913.
: An alphabet (upper and lower case) of unpleasant things about summer. **PS, K, Pr**

London, Jonathan, *Sun Dance Water Dance*. Ill. by Greg Couch. Dutton, 2001. ISBN 0525466827.
: A hot summer day at the water's edge. **PS, K**

Lyon, George Ella, *A Day at Damp Camp*. Ill. by Peter Catalanotto. Orchard, 1996. ISBN 0531095045.
: Pairs of rhyming words such as "green screen" and "hot cot" describe a day at summer camp. **PS, K, Pr**

Maass, Robert, *When Summer Comes*. Henry Holt, 1996. ISBN 0805047069 (pbk).
: Photographs show activities and weather in summertime. **PS, K**

Potter, Tessa, *Grayfur: The Story of a Rabbit in Summer*. Ill. by Ken Lilly. Raintree Steck-Vaughn, 1997. ISBN 0817246215.
: Realistic story of a young rabbit outdoors in the summertime. **PS, K**

Schnur, Steven, *Summer: An Alphabet Acrostic*. Ill. by Leslie Evans. Clarion, 2001. ISBN 0618023720.
: Each letter of the alphabet (upper case) is illustrated by an acrostic poem relating to summer. **K, Pr**

Spetter, Jung-Hee, *Lily and Trooper's Summer*. Front Street/Lemniscaat, 1998. ISBN 1886910375.
: A girl and her dog go to the beach in the summer. **PS**

Fall

Arnosky, Jim, *Every Autumn Comes the Bear.* **Putnam, 1996. ISBN 0698114051 (pbk).**
The routine of a bear as he prepares for winter. **T, PS, K**

Carr, Jan, *Dappled Apples.* **Ill. by Dorothy Donohue. Holiday, 2001. ISBN 082341583X.**
Collage pictures illustrate autumn, jumping in leaves, picking apples, and going trick-or-treating. **PS**

Glaser, Linda, *It's Fall!* **Ill. by Susan Swan. Mllbrook, 2001. ISBN 0761317589.**
Colorful cut-paper illustrations plus text show what happens in the autumn. **PS, K**

Hall, Zoë, *Fall Leaves Fall!* **Ill. by Shari Halpern. Scholastic 2000. ISBN 0590100793.**
Two children look at different kinds of leaves in the fall. **PS, K**

Harshman, Marc, and Cheryl Ryan, *Red Are the Apples.* **Ill. by Wade Zahares. Gulliver/Harcourt, 2001. ISBN 0152019170.**
A garden in the fall is described in terms of many colorful things. **PS, K**

Hunter, Anne, *Possum's Harvest Moon.* **Houghton Mifflin, 1996. ISBN 0395735750.**
Possum has a party under the harvest moon. **PS, K, Pr**

Kelley, Marty, *Fall Is Not Easy.* **Zino, 1998. ISBN 1559332344 (pbk).**
A tree tells about what happens to it in each season and how much trouble it has when it's time for leaves to change color. **PS, K**

Kellogg, Steven, *The Mystery of the Flying Orange Pumpkin.* **Dutton, 1983. ISBN 0140546707.**
Children plant a pumpkin for Halloween, but the new owner of the property claims the pumpkin is his. A cheerful trick provides a way for the children to have a jack-o'-lantern and the man to have a pie. **PS, K, Pr**

Maass, Robert, *When Autumn Comes.* **Henry Holt, 1992. ISBN 0805023496.**
Photographs show weather and activities in the fall. **PS, K**

Rockwell, Anne, *Apples and Pumpkins.* **Ill. by Lizzy Rockwell. Simon & Schuster, 1989. ISBN 0027772705.**
A girl and her family go to a farm in the fall, picking apples and a pumpkin for Halloween. **T, PS**

Schnur, Steven, *Autumn: An Alphabet Acrostic.* **Ill. by Leslie Evans. Clarion, 1997. ISBN 0395770432.**
Each letter of the alphabet (shown in upper case) is the first letter of an acrostic poem about fall. **K, Pr**

Wellington, Monica, *Bunny's First Snowflake.* **Dutton, 2000. ISBN 0525464646.**
Simple board book story shows animals getting ready for winter. **T, PS**

Winter

Bliss, Corinne Demas, *Snow Day.* **Ill. by Nancy Poylar. Random, 1998. ISBN 0679882227 (pbk).**
Easy-reader text describes Emily's day off from school because of snow. **PS, K**

Bogacki, Tomek, *Cat and Mouse in the Snow.* **Farrar, Straus & Giroux, 1999. ISBN 0374311927.**
Cat and mouse friends play in the snow. **T, PS**

Brennan, Linda Crotta, *Flannel Kisses.* **Ill. by Mari Takabayashi. Houghton Mifflin, 1997. ISBN 0395736811.**
Simple words tell of a winter day. **T, PS**

Brett, Jan, *The Mitten: A Ukrainian Folktale.* **Putnam, 1989. ISBN 039921920X.**
Lush, detailed pictures tell the story of a lost mitten that becomes home to increasingly larger animals. **PS, K, Pr**

Burton, Virginia Lee, *Katy and the Big Snow.* **Houghton Mifflin, 1973. ISBN 0395181550.**
When the city is covered with snow, Katy the tractor plows everything out with her snowplow. **K, Pr**

Chaconas, Dori, *On a Wintry Morning.* **Ill. by Stephen T. Johnson. Viking, 2000. ISBN 0670892459.**
A man takes his baby daughter out to play on a winter morning. **PS**

Coleman, Michael, *Ridiculous!* **Ill. by Gwyneth Williamson. Little Tiger Press, 1996. ISBN 1888444045.**
Shelley the Tortoise goes outdoors on a winter's day, which is ridiculous for a tortoise. **PS, K**

Crews, Nina, *Snowball.* **Greenwillow, 1997. ISBN 0688149286.**
Photo collages tell of a little girl playing in the snow in the city. **T, PS**

Cuyler, Margery, *The Biggest, Best Snowman.* **Ill. by Will Hillenbrand. Scholastic, 1998. ISBN 0590139223.**
Nell's family says she's too little to do anything, but with the help of some woodland animals she builds a big snowman. **PS, K, Pr**

Evans, Lezlie, *Snow Dance.* **Ill. by Cynthia Jabar. Houghton Mifflin, 1997. ISBN 039578492.**
Children have fun playing in the snow. **PS**

Fleming, Denise, *Time to Sleep.* **Henry Holt, 1997. ISBN 0805037624.**
Animals share with each other the news that winter is on the way. **PS**

Ford, Christine, *Snow!* **Ill. by Candace Whitman. Harper Festival, 1999. ISBN 0694011991. ISBN**
Simple text describes playing in the snow. **T**

Gammell, Stephen, *Is That You, Winter?* **Harcourt Brace, 1997. ISBN 0152014152.**
Old Man Winter is a grouchy fellow in a rattly truck. **PS, K**

Gay, Marie-Louise, *Stella, Queen of the Snow.* **Douglas & McIntyre, 2000. ISBN 0888994044.**
Outdoors, big sister Stella explains all about snow and cold weather to her brother Sam. **PS, K**

George, Lindsay Barrett, *In the Snow: Who's Been Here?* **Greenwillow, 1995. ISBN 0688123201.**
From tracks and other signs in the snow, two children discover which animals have been around. **PS, K, Pr**

Gershator, Phillis, *When It Starts to Snow.* **Ill. by Martin Matje. Scholastic, 1998. ISBN 0805054049.**
Shows what different animals do when it snows. **PS, K**

Henkes, Kevin, *Oh!* **Ill. by Laura Dronzek. Greenwillow, 1999. ISBN 0688170536.**
Animals and children play in the snow. **T, PS**

Hines, Anna Grossnickle, *What Can You Do in the Snow?* **Ill. by Thea Kliros. Greenwillow, 1999. ISBN 0688160786.**
Brief descriptions of things to do in the snow. Board. **T**

Hiscock, Bruce, *When Will It Snow?* **Atheneum, 1995. ISBN 0689319391.**
A boy waits for the first snowfall, while animals prepare for winter. Long text. **K, Pr**

Inkpen, Mick, *Kipper's Snowy Day.* **Red Wagon, 1999. ISBN 0152023038.**
Kipper and his friend Tiger play in the snow. **PS**

Joosse, Barbara M., *Snow Day!* **Ill. by Jennifer Plecas. Clarion, 1995. ISBN 0395665884.**
Everyone in Robby's family has fun on a snowy day. **PS, K**

Keats, Ezra Jack, *The Snowy Day.* **Viking, 1962. ISBN 0670654000.**
A city boy plays in a new snowfall. **T, PS**

Kellogg, Steven, *The Missing Mitten Mystery.* **Dial, 2000. ISBN 0803725663.**
A girl loses her red mitten in the snow and imagines what could have happened to it. **PS, K**

Kohn, Rita, *Winter Storytime.* **Ill. by Dorothy Sullivan. Children's, 1995. ISBN 0516052047.**
A Lenape grandmother tells two children the story of how the first rabbit-tail game was made. **T, PS**

Lasky, Kathryn, *Lucille's Snowsuit.* **Ill. by Marilyn Hafner. Crown, 2000. ISBN 0517800373.**
Lucille rebels against wearing her snowsuit, but finds that it keeps her nice and warm. **PS**

Lawson, Julie, *Midnight in the Mountains.* **Ill. by Sheena Lott. Orca, 1998. ISBN 1551431130.**
A girl and her family spend some time at a remote cabin in the mountains in the wintertime. **PS, K, Pr**

Lewis, Kim, *First Snow.* **Candlewick, 1996. ISBN 1564029638 (pbk).**
A girl and her mother go to feed the sheep in the first snowfall of the year. **PS**

Maass, Robert, *When Winter Comes.* **Henry Holt, 1996. ISBN 0805049266 (pbk).**
Photographs show weather and activities in winter. Chanukah and Christmas are both mentioned. **PS, K**

Neitzel, Shirley, *The Jacket I Wear in the Snow.* **Ill. by Nancy Winslow Parker. Greenwillow, 1989. ISBN 0688080286.**
A girl names all the clothes she must wear to play in the snow, as she puts them on and as she takes them off. **PS, K**

O'Donnell, Elizabeth Lee, *Winter Visitors.* **Ill. by Carol Schwartz. Morrow, 1997. ISBN 0688130631.**
When a girl and her cat go outdoors in the snow, their home is invaded by animals in groups of ten to one. Awkward rhymes, but great pictures. **PS, K**

Rockwell, Anne, and Harlow Rockwell, *The First Snowfall.* **Aladdin, 1992. ISBN 0689716141 (pbk).**
A little girl goes out to play in the snow. **T, PS**

Root, Phyllis, *Grandmother Winter.* **Ill. by Beth Krommes. Houghton Mifflin, 1999. ISBN 0395883997.**
Grandmother Winter shakes her goose-feather quilt to make it snow. **PS, K**

Seuling, Barbara, *Winter Lullaby.* **Ill. by Greg Newbold. Browndeer/Harcourt Brace, 1998. ISBN 0152014039.**
Questions and rhyming answers about what many animals do at the onset of winter. **PS, K**

Siddals, Mary McKenna, *Millions of Snowflakes.* **Ill. by Elizabeth Sayles. Scholastic, 1998. ISBN 0395715318.**
A child sees one snowflake, then two, three, four, five, and millions. No numerals. **T, PS**

Simmonds, Posy, *F-freezing ABC.* **Knopf, 1995. ISBN 0679879153.**
In this story that uses letters A to Z, four friends try to find a warm place to stay. **PS, K**

Simmons, Jane, *Little Fern's First Winter.* **Little, Brown, 2001. ISBN 0316796670.**
Two young rabbits observe other animals preparing for the first snowfall. **PS, K**

Spetter, Jung-Hee, *Lily and Trooper's Winter.* **Front Street/ Lemniscaat, 1998. ISBN 1886910391.**
A girl and her dog make a snowman and go skiing and skating. **PS**

Stewart, Paul, *A Little Bit of Winter.* **Ill. by Chris Riddell. HarperCollins, 1998. ISBN 0060282789.**
Hedgehog asks Rabbit to save a little bit of winter for him to see after his hibernation. **PS, K**

Tafuri, Nancy, *Where Did Bunny Go?* **Scholastic, 2001. ISBN 0439169593.**
Bird and Bunny play hide-and-seek with their friends in the snow. **T, PS**

Tripp, Nathaniel, *Snow Comes to the Farm.* **Ill. by Kate Kiesler. Candlewick, 2001. ISBN 1564024261.**
Two boys go into the woods to watch the coming of the snow. **K, Pr**

Wallace, Nancy Elizabeth, *Snow.* **Artists & Writers Guild/Golden, 1999. ISBN 0307102289.**
A grown rabbit remembers playing in the snow with his brother and mother. **PS, K**

Walters, Catherine, *When Will It Be Spring?* **Dutton, 1998. ISBN 0525458816.**
A little bear keeps waking up during hibernation to see if spring has arrived. **PS, K**

Wellington, Monica, *Bunny's First Snowflake.* **Dutton, 2000. ISBN 0525464646.**
Simple board book story shows animals getting ready for winter. **T, PS**

Yolen, Jane, *Owl Moon.* **Ill. by John Schoenherr. Philomel, 1987. ISBN 0399214577.**
In the depths of winter, a girl and her father look for owls under a full moon. **PS, K, Pr**

Days of the Week

Blackstone, Stella, *Bear about Town.* **Ill. by Debbie Harter. Barefoot Books, 2000. ISBN 1902283570.**
Bear does a different thing each day on his trip to town. Simple text. **T, PS**

Butterworth, Nick, and Mick Inkpen, *Jasper's Beanstalk.* **Simon & Schuster, 1993. ISBN 0027162311.**
From Monday through Sunday, Jasper waits for his bean to grow. **T, PS**

Carle, Eric, *Today Is Monday.* **Philomel, 1993. ISBN 0399219668.**
A different food is named from Monday through Sunday, when the hungry children arrive to eat it up. **T, PS**

Carle, Eric, *The Very Hungry Caterpillar.* **Putnam, 1983. ISBN 0399208534.**
A caterpillar eats his way through the days of the week, then changes into a butterfly. **T, PS**

Carlstrom, Nancy White, *Guess Who's Coming, Jesse Bear.* **Ill. by Bruce Degen. Simon & Schuster, 1998. ISBN 0689807023.**
Jesse's older cousin Sara comes to visit from Monday through Sunday, and they both have more fun then they expected. **PS**

Santos, Rosa, *Play Date.* **Ill. by Gioia Fiammenghi. Kane, 2001. ISBN 157565105X (pbk).**
Two girls try to schedule a play date, but circumstances keep moving it from one day to the next. **K, Pr**

Shields, Carol Diggory, *Day by Day a Week Goes Round.* **Ill. by True Kelley. Dutton, 1998. ISBN 0525454578.**
Shows different things a family does from Monday through Sunday. **PS, K**

Ward, Cindy, *Cookie's Week.* **Ill. by Tomie dePaola. Paper Star, 1997. ISBN 0698114353 (pbk).**
A cat gets into trouble on each day of the week. **T, PS**

Months of the Year

Anno, Mitsumasa, *Anno's Counting Book.* **Harper Trophy, 1986. ISBN 0064431231 (pbk).**
Detailed pictures depict things for numerals 1 through 12 as a village grows and moves through the months of the year (not named). **K, Pr**

Appelt, Kathi, *A Red Wagon Year.* Ill. by Laura McGee Kvasnosky. Red Wagon Books, 1996. ISBN 0152779914.
: A wagon has a different use each month of the year. **PS, K, Pr**

Bacon, Ethel, *To See the Moon.* Ill. by David Ray. BridgeWater, 1996. ISBN 081673822X.
: A girl adopts a sled dog puppy and, month by month through the year, trains him for a sled dog race. Shows the changing seasons as well as the dog's growth and maturity. **K, Pr**

Carlstrom, Nancy White, *How Do You Say It Today, Jesse Bear?* Ill. by Bruce Degen. Simon & Schuster, 1992. ISBN 0027172767.
: A short rhyme shows what Jesse does each month of the year. **PS, K**

Clifton, Lucille, *Everett Anderson's Year.* Ill. by Ann Grifalconi. Holt, 1992. ISBN 0805022473.
: A poem for each month of the year celebrates the life of a small boy. **PS, K**

Day, Nancy Raines, *A Kitten's Year.* Ill. by Anne Mortimer. HarperCollins, 2000. ISBN 0060272317.
: A kitten does something different each month of the year, while growing into a cat. **PS, K**

Dragonwagon, Crescent, *Alligators and Others All Year Long! A Book of Months.* Ill. by Jose Aruego and Ariane Dewey. Atheneum, 1993. ISBN 0027330915.
: A humorous rhyme for each month of the year. **PS, K, Pr**

Hague, Kathleen, *Calendarbears: A Book of Months.* Ill. by Michael Hague. Henry Holt, 1997. ISBN 0805038183.
: A teddy bear's activity for each month of the year. **PS**

Henderson, Kathy, *A Year in the City.* Ill. by Paul Howard. Candlewick, 1996. ISBN 1564028720.
: Long descriptions and detailed pictures show each month in a large city. **PS, K, Pr**

Lasky, Kathryn, *Pond Year.* Ill. by Mike Bostock. Candlewick, 1995. ISBN 1564021874.
: Two girls play in a small pond throughout the year, from April through March. Every month but October is named. **PS, K, Pr**

Martin, Bill, Jr., *The Turning of the Year.* Ill. by Greg Shed. Harcourt Brace, 1998. ISBN 0152010858.
: A rhyme introduces each month of the year. **PS, K**

Otten, Charlotte F., *January Rides the Wind: A Book of Months.* Ill. by Todd L. W. Doney. Lothrop, Lee & Shepard, 1997. ISBN 06888125565.
: A poem describes the weather and nature in each month. **PS, K, Pr**

Peters, Lisa Westberg, *October Smiled Back.* **Ill. by Ed Young. Henry Holt, 1996. ISBN 0805017763.**
Starting with October, short rhymes give a personality to each month of the year. **K, Pr**

Pollock, Penny, *When the Moon Is Full: A Lunar Year.* **Ill. by Mary Azarian. Little, Brown, 2001. ISBN 0316713171.**
A poem for each month of the year reflects the way they were seen by Native Americans. **PS, K, Pr**

Prelutsky, Jack, *Dog Days: Rhymes Around the World.* **Ill. by Dyanna Wolcott. Knopf, 1999. ISBN 0395801049.**
In short rhymes, a dog describes what he does each month of the year. **PS, K**

Sendak, Maurice, *Chicken Soup with Rice.* **HarperCollins, 1992. ISBN 0060255358.**
A nonsense rhyme about months. Small format. December is represented by a Christmas theme. **PS, K, Pr**

Shields, Carol Diggory, *Month by Month a Year Goes Round.* **Ill. by True Kelley. Dutton, 1998. ISBN 0525454586.**
A rhyme that goes through the year's activities month by month, ending with Christmas scenes. **PS**

Spinelli, Eileen, *Here Comes the Year.* **Ill. by Keiko Narahashi. Henry Holt, 2002. ISBN 0805066853.**
A poem about nature and weather for each month of the year, not referring to any holidays. **PS, K, Pr**

Tafuri, Nancy, *Snowy Flowy Blowy: A Twelve Months Rhyme.* **Scholastic, 1999. ISBN 0590189735.**
Large pictures and a single word represent each month. **T, PS**

Updike, John, *A Child's Calendar.* **Ill. by Trina Schart Hyman. Holiday, 1999. ISBN 0823414450.**
An illustrated poem for each month. Halloween, Christmas, and other holidays are included. **Pr**

Wolff, Freida, *A Year for Kiko.* **Ill. by Joung Un Kim. Houghton Mifflin, 1997. ISBN 0395773962.**
A short rhyme shows what a girl does each month of the year. **PS**

March

Singer, Marilyn, *On the Same Day in March.* **Ill. by Frané Lessac. HarperCollins, 2000. ISBN 0060281871.**
Shows the weather at different places in the world on the same day in March. **K, Pr**

November

Rylant, Cynthia, *In November.* **Ill. by Jill Kastner. Harcourt, 2000. ISBN 0152010769.**
Describes things and activities that make November unique. **PS**

Telling Time [Using a clock]

Anderson, Lena, *Tick-Tock.* **R & S, 1998. ISBN 9129640741.**
From one o'clock to 12 o'clock, four animal friends play in the park and go to bed. **PS, K**

Appelt, Kathi, *Bats Around the Clock.* **Ill. by Melissa Sweet. HarperCollins, 2000. ISBN 0688164692.**
Click Dark hosts American Batstand, 12 hours of dancing. Time shown on each hour. **K, Pr**

Axelrod, Amy, *Pigs on a Blanket: Fun with Math and Time.* **Ill. by Sharon McGinley-Nally. Simon & Schuster, 1996. ISBN 0689805055.**
The pig family encounters many delays on their trip to the beach. Adding up different amounts of time. **K, Pr**

Aylesworth, Jim, *The Completed Hickory Dickory Dock.* **Ill. by Eileen Christelow. Aladdin, 1990. ISBN 0689316062.**
Additional verses to the traditional nursery rhyme go through 12 o'clock. Times on the hour only. **PS, K**

Baker, Alan, *Little Rabbit's First Time Book.* **Kingfisher, 1999. ISBN 0753452200.**
Little Rabbit has fun from 8 a.m. to 7 p.m. Digital and analog time-telling, plus a clock with hands to move. **PS, K**

Behrman, Carol H., *The Ding Dong Clock.* **Ill. by Hideko Takahashi. Holt, 1999. ISBN 0805058044.**
From 1 a.m. to 12 noon, a clock strikes the time on the hour. **PS, K**

Berenstain, Stan, and Jan Berenstain, *The Berenstain Bears Catch the Bus.* **Random House, 1999. ISBN 0679892273.**
From 6:59 to 8:00, chronicles the young bears' attempts to get up and catch the school bus. Partial hours on digital and analog clocks. **K, Pr**

Carle, Eric, *The Grouchy Ladybug.* **HarperCollins, 1996. ISBN 006027087X.**
From 5 a.m. through 6 p.m. (on the hours and at 5:15, 5:30 and 5:45), the grouchy ladybug tries to pick a fight with increasingly larger animals. Also shows the sun's position at each hour. **PS, K, Pr**

Conboy, Fiona, *Forgetful Ted.* **Ill. by Jonathan Lambert. Barron's, 1997. ISBN 0764150324.**
A bear who is usually late gets a present of an alarm clock and learns to tell time, half hours as well as on-the-hour times. An included clock also shows minutes. **PS, K, Pr**

Harper, Dan, *Telling Time with Big Mama Cat.* **Ill. by Barry Moser and Cara Moser. Harcourt Brace, 1998. ISBN 0152017380.**
A cat tells what time she does things during the day, mostly on the hour but including a few in between. Includes a clock with movable hands. **K, Pr**

Hutchins, Pat, *Clocks and More Clocks.* **Aladdin, 1994. ISBN 0689717695 (pbk).**
Mr. Higgins' four clocks seem to keep different time, until he learns that by running from one to another, he is looking at them at different times. Shows many in-between-hours times. **K, Pr**

Lavis, Steve, *Little Mouse Has a Busy Day.* **Ragged Bears, 2000. ISBN 192992710X.**
Little Mouse does many things throughout his day, with on-the-hour times shown. **PS**

Lewis, Paul Owen, *You Are Cordially Invited to P. Bear's New Year's Party!* **Tricycle, 1999. ISBN 1883672996 (pbk)**
A polar bear invites only black and white animals to his party. One arrives at one o'clock, two at two o'clock, and so on through twelve midnight. **PS, K**

Maccarone, Grace, *Monster Math School Time.* **Ill. by Marge Hartelius. Scholastic, 1997. ISBN 0590308599 (pbk).**
Tells what the monsters do at each hour from waking at 6 a.m., through schooltime, and bedtime at 8 p.m. **PS, K**

Mozelle, Shirley, *The Pig Is in the Pantry, the Cat Is on the Shelf.* **Ill. by Jennifer Plecas. Clarion, 2000. ISBN 0395786274.**
Eight farm animals make a mess when they enter an unlocked house. Clocks show the time on some of the hours from 8 a.m. to 6 p.m. **PS, K, Pr**

Murphy, Stuart J., *Game Time!* **Ill. by Cynthia Jabar. HarperCollins, 2000. ISBN 0060280247.**
This story of a soccer game explains many divisions of time. **K, Pr**

Richards, Kitty, *It's about Time, Max!* **Ill. by Gioia Fiammenghi. Kane, 2000. ISBN 1575650886 (pbk).**
After being late for school and missing things he wants to attend, Max learns to tell time. Includes partial hours. **Pr**

Wellington, Monica, and Andrew Kupfer, *Night City.* **Dutton, 1998. ISBN 0525459480.**
Describes a different job being done at each hour from 7 p.m. to 7 a.m., from firemen to jazz musicians to bakers. **PS, K, Pr**

Chapter Six

Measurement and Perspective

Measurement *[How, why, when to measure; see also specific types of measurement]*

Aber, Linda Williams, *Carrie Measures Up*. Ill. by Joy Allen. Kane, 2001. ISBN 1575651009 (pbk).
Using a tape measure, Carrie helps her grandmother measure things to be knitted. **K, Pr**

Hightower, Susan, *Twelve Snails to One Lizard: A Tale of Mischief and Measurement*. Ill. by Matt Novak. Simon & Schuster, 1997. ISBN 0689804520.
Bullfrog suggests that Beaver use snails, iguanas, and a boa to measure his dam. **K, Pr**

Keenan, Sheila, *What's Up with That Cup?* Ill. by Jackie Snider. Scholastic, 2000. ISBN 0439099544 (pbk).
A girl tries many different sizes of cups when trying to measure something, finally realizing what a measuring cup is. **PS, K**

Leedy, Loreen, *Measuring Penny*. Henry Holt, 1997. ISBN 0805053603.
Lisa uses standard and nonstandard measurements to measure many different things about her dog. **K, Pr**

Ling, Bettina, *The Fattest, Tallest, Biggest Snowman Ever*. Ill. by Michael Rex. Scholastic, 1997. ISBN 0590972847 (pbk).
Jeff and Maria measure their snowman using string, sticks, and paperclip chains. **K, Pr**

Murphy, Stuart J., *Super Sand Castle Saturday.* **Ill. by Julia Gorton. HarperCollins, 1999. ISBN 0060276126.**
>Children vie to build the tallest sand castle, deepest moat, and longest wall, but measuring with shovels, spoons, and feet turns out to be inaccurate. **K, Pr**

Myller, Rolf, *How Big Is a Foot?* **Dell, 1991. ISBN 0440404959 (pbk).**
>The carpenter's apprentice can't make a bed for the queen three feet wide and six feet long until he knows how big the king's foot is. **Pr**

Stevens, Janet, and Susan Stevens Crummel, *Cook-a-Doodle-Doo!* **Ill. by Janet Stevens. Harcourt Brace, 1999. ISBN 0152019243.**
>With Pig, Turtle, and Iguana as helpers, Big Brown Rooster bakes a strawberry shortcake. **K, Pr**

Size [Bigger and smaller; comparisons]

Alborough, Jez, *My Friend Bear.* **Candlewick, 1998. ISBN 0763605832.**
>Eddie and his teddy bear meet a very big bear and his teddy. **T, PS**

Alborough, Jez, *Watch Out! Big Bro's Coming!* **Candlewick, 1997. ISBN 0763601306.**
>When mouse says Big Bro is coming, each animal imagines a creature larger than himself. **PS, K**

Alborough, Jez, *Where's My Teddy?* **Candlewick, 1994. ISBN 1564022803 (pbk).**
>A small boy and a big bear each lose a teddy bear, and each finds the other's. **T, PS, K**

Barnes, Laura T., *Teeny Tiny Ernest.* **Ill. by Carol A. Camburn. Barnesyard Books, 2000. ISBN 0967468116.**
>Ernest the miniature donkey compares himself to other animals, who are all bigger. **PS, K**

Barrett, Judi, *Cloudy with a Chance of Meatballs.* **Ill. by Ron Barrett. Atheneum, 1978. ISBN 0689306474.**
>Grandpa tells the story of a town where giant food falls from the sky. There is a sequel, *Pickles to Pittsburgh* [1997: ISBN 0689801041]. **K, Pr**

Bartlett, Alison, *Cat Among the Cabbages.* **Dutton, 1997. ISBN 0525457550.**
>A cat wanders around a colorful garden, looking at things of different sizes. **T, PS**

Berenstain, Stan, and Jan Berenstain, *The Berenstain Bears Big Bear Small Bear.* **Random House, 1998. ISBN 0679887172.**
>Shows a big bear and a small bear choosing things of the appropriate size. **T, PS**

Bliss, Corinne Demas, *The Shortest Kid in the World.* **Ill. by Nancy Poydar. Random, 1994. ISBN 0679858091(pbk).**
Emily doesn't like being the shortest one in her class—until another girl, who's even shorter, joins the class. **K**

Bogacki, Tomek, *My First Garden.* **Farrar, Straus & Giroux, 2000. ISBN 0374325189.**
A man remembers the house he grew up in—a large house in a small town. He tells how he discovered the wider world and planted a garden. **PS, K, Pr**

Bornstein, Ruth, *Little Gorilla.* **Houghton Mifflin, 1979. ISBN 0395287731.**
Little Gorilla grows very big—but everyone still loves him. **T, PS**

Bowman, Peter, *I Wish I Were Big.* **Hutchinson, 1998. ISBN 0091765889.**
A tiny teddy bear wishes to be as big as other animals until he learns that an elephant is afraid of a mouse. **T, PS**

Brett, Jan, *The Mitten: A Ukrainian Folktale.* **Putnam, 1989. ISBN 039921920X.**
Lush, detailed pictures tell the story of a lost mitten that becomes home to increasingly larger animals. **PS, K, Pr**

Carle, Eric, *The Grouchy Ladybug.* **HarperCollins, 1996. ISBN 006027087X.**
From 5 a.m. through 6 p.m., the grouchy ladybug tries to pick a fight with increasingly larger animals. **PS, K, Pr**

Cuyler, Margery, *The Biggest, Best Snowman.* **Ill. by Will Hillenbrand. Scholastic, 1998. ISBN 0590139223.**
Nell's family says she's too little to do anything, but with the help of some woodland animals she builds a big snowman. **PS, K, Pr**

Donohue, Dorothy, *Big and Little on the Farm.* **Golden, 1999. ISBN 0307102254.**
Adult and baby farm animals are identified. **T, PS**

Dunbar, Joyce, *The Very Small.* **Ill. by Debi Gliori. Harcourt, 2000. ISBN 0152023461.**
Giant Baby Bear finds a very small creature in the woods and takes it home to meet his family. **PS, K**

Florian, Douglas, *A Pig Is Big.* **Greenwillow, 2000. ISBN 0688171257.**
This story shows things increasingly larger than a pig, up to the universe. **PS, K**

Haring, Keith, *Big.* **Hyperion, 1998. ISBN 0786803908.**
Large-size board book shows funny pictures of oversized clothes in different colors. **T, PS**

Chapter 6: Measurement and Perspective

Hoban, Tana, *Is It Larger? Is It Smaller?* **Greenwillow, 1997. ISBN 0688152872 (pbk).**
Photos of everyday things include larger and smaller items. **PS, K**

Hutchins, Pat, *You'll Soon Grow into Them, Titch.* **Mulberry, 1992. ISBN 0688115071 (pbk).**
Titch inherits oversized hand-me-downs from his older siblings. When he finally gets clothes that fit, he passes on his outgrown clothes to the new baby. **PS, K**

Jenkins, Steve, *Big & Little.* **Houghton Mifflin, 1996. ISBN 0395726646.**
Shows pairs of related animals that are very different in size. **PS, K**

Jenkins, Steve, *Biggest, Strongest, Fastest.* **Ticknor & Fields, 1995. ISBN 0395697018.**
Shows animals that are the biggest, strongest, fastest, and so on. Diagrams show how they compare to humans. **PS, K, Pr**

Jonell, Lynne, *Mommy Go Away!* **Ill. by Petra Mathers. Putnam, 1997. ISBN 0399230017.**
Christopher's mother becomes small and he has to take care of her. **PS**

Kalan, Robert, *Blue Sea.* **Ill. by Donald Crews. Greenwillow, 1992. ISBN 0688115098 (pbk).**
A little fish, a big fish, a bigger fish and the biggest fish follow each other through progressively smaller holes, leaving only the little one to fit through them all. Very simple text. **T, PS**

Keenan, Sheila, *The Biggest Fish.* **Ill. by Holly Hannon. Scholastic, 1996. ISBN 0590266004 (pbk).**
Many people bring big fish, to try to win the biggest fish contest. The fish are compared in size to other familiar objects. **PS, K**

Lacome, Julie, *Ruthie's Big Old Coat.* **Candlewick, 2000. ISBN 0763609692.**
Ruthie's red hand-me-down coat is too big for her, so she and her friend Fiona wear it together and play in it. Contains a scene where one girl uses the toilet. **PS, K**

MacKinnon, Debbie, *What Size?* **Ill. by Anthea Sieveking. Dial, 1995. ISBN 0803717458.**
Photographs of children playing illustrate things of different sizes, including long and short, thick and thin, high and low, wide and narrow. **PS**

Masurel, Claire, *Too Big!* **Ill. by Hanako Wakiyama. Chronicle, 1999. ISBN 0811820914.**
Charlie's stuffed dinosaur is too big to take most places, but he's just right as a companion to the doctor's. **PS**

Miller, Margaret, *Big and Little.* **Greenwillow, 1998. ISBN 0688147488.**
Photographs introduce common items in big and little sizes. **T, PS**

Mitchell, Adrian, *Twice My Size.* **Ill. by Daniel Pudles. Millbrook, 1999. ISBN 0761314237.**
From a ladybug to the sun, each one has a friend bigger than he. **PS, K**

Murphy, Stuart J., *The Best Bug Parade.* **Ill. by Holly Keller. HarperCollins, 1996. ISBN 0060258713.**
In a parade, bugs compare their sizes: small, smaller, smallest; long, longer, longest; and so on. **PS, K**

Peck, Jan, *The Giant Carrot.* **Ill. by Barry Root. Dial, 1998. ISBN 0803718233.**
A family grows a carrot so huge that they have trouble getting it out of the ground. **K, Pr**

Rotner, Shelley, and Richard Olivo, *Close, Closer, Closest.* **Atheneum, 1997. ISBN 0689807627.**
Photographs show things from three different distances. **PS, K, Pr**

Wells, Robert E., *Is a Blue Whale the Biggest Thing There Is?* **Albert Whitman, 1993. ISBN 0807536555.**
Illustrations show how sizes compare, from a blue whale to Mt. Everest, to the sun and the universe. See also *What's Smaller Than a Pygmy Shrew?* [1995: ISBN 0807588385] **PS, K, Pr**

More & Less

Hoban, Tana, *More, Fewer, Less.* **Greenwillow, 1998. ISBN 0688156932.**
Color photographs with no words show things that are more and less. **PS, K**

Murphy, Stuart J., *Just Enough Carrots.* **Ill. by Frank Remkiewicz. HarperCollins, 1997. ISBN 006026778X.**
As Bunny and his mother shop for food, he compares the amounts of things that they buy. **PS, K**

Murphy, Stuart J., *Ready, Set, Hop!* **Ill. by Jon Buller. HarperCollins, 1996. ISBN 0060258772.**
Two frogs have a contest to see who can take fewer hops to get places. **Pr**

Skinner, Daphne, *Henry Keeps Score.* **Ill. by Page Eastburn O'Rourke. Kane, 2001. ISBN 1575651025 (pbk).**
Henry always wants to have the same number of everything that his sister does. **PS, K**

Weight [Concept of weight, comparison, weight measurements]

Allen, Pamela, *Who Sank the Boat?* **Paper Star, 1996. ISBN 069811373X (pbk).**
A cow, a donkey, a sheep, and a pig get into the boat—but it is when the mouse gets in that it sinks. **PS, K**

Axelrod, Amy, *Pigs Go to Market: Fun with Math and Shopping.* **Ill. by Sharon McGinley-Nally. Simon & Schuster, 1997. ISBN 0689810695.**
On Halloween Mrs. Pig wins a five-minute shopping spree in the supermarket. The reader is invited to count, multiply, and measure. **Pr**

Dussling, Jennifer, *The 100-Pound Problem.* **Ill. by Rebecca Thornburgh. Kane, 2000. ISBN 1575650959 (pbk).**
Because his boat can only carry one hundred pounds, a boy must figure out how much he, his dog, and his gear weigh. He makes a simple balance scale to compare things. **K, Pr**

Tompert, Ann, *Just a Little Bit.* **Ill. by Lynn Munsinger. Houghton Mifflin, 1993. ISBN 0395515270.**
Many animals get on the seesaw to balance Elephant, but it is the addition of a small beetle that makes the difference. **PS, K**

Length & Height

Aber, Linda Williams, *Carrie Measures Up.* **Ill. by Joy Allen. Kane, 2001. ISBN 1575651009 (pbk).**
Using a tape measure, Carrie helps her grandmother measure things to be knitted. **K, Pr**

Hightower, Susan, *Twelve Snails to One Lizard: A Tale of Mischief and Measurement.* **Ill. by Matt Novak. Simon & Schuster, 1997. ISBN 0689804520.**
Bullfrog suggests that Beaver use snails, iguanas, and a boa to measure his dam. **K, Pr**

Lionni, Leo, *Inch by Inch.* **Greenwillow, 1995. ISBN 0688132839 (pbk).**
An inchworm escapes being eaten by measuring birds' beaks, and finally gets away entirely while measuring the nightingale's song. **K**

Myller, Rolf, *How Big Is a Foot?* **Dell, 1991. ISBN 0440404959 (pbk).**
The carpenter's apprentice can't make a bed for the queen three feet wide and six feet long until he knows how big the king's foot is. **Pr**

Pinczes, Elinor J., *Inchworm and a Half.* Ill. by Randall Enos. Houghton Mifflin, 2001. ISBN 039582849X.

An inchworm meets worms that are one-half, one-third, and one-quarter his size, who help him measure garden vegetables. **K, Pr**

Distance

Baer, Gene, *Thump, Thump, Rat-a-Tat-Tat.* Ill. by Lois Ehlert. HarperCollins, 1991. ISBN 0064432653 (pbk).

A marching band comes closer, sounding louder and looking bigger, then moves away again. **T, PS, K**

Banyai, Istvan, *Zoom.* Viking, 1995. ISBN 0670858048.

A series of pictures shows a scene from farther and farther away. See also the author's similar *Re-zoom* [1995: ISBN 0670863920]. **K, Pr**

Baron, Alan, *Little Pig's Bouncy Ball.* Candlewick, 1996. ISBN 0763601268.

Dan Dog chases a ball and takes a long time to return with it. **T, PS**

Cuyler, Margery, *From Here to There.* Ill. by Yu Cha Pak. Henry Holt, 1999. ISBN 080503191X.

Maria gives her locations, from her family, to her house, to her town, all the way to her place in the universe. **PS, K, Pr**

Herman, Gail, *Keep Your Distance!* Ill. by Jerry Smath. Kane, 2001. ISBN 1575651076 (pbk).

A girl tells her sister exactly how far—in various measurements—she wants her to stay away. **K, Pr**

Lobel, Arnold, *Ming Lo Moves the Mountain.* Mulberry, 1993. ISBN 0688109950 (pbk).

A wise man teaches Ming Lo to "move" the mountain that is too near their home. They are to dismantle their house and do a dance that consists of walking backwards. **K, Pr**

Murphy, Stuart J., *Racing Around.* Ill. by Mike Reed. HarperCollins, 2002. ISBN 0060289139.

Mike practices riding his bike around different perimeters in preparation for the big race. **Pr**

Volume [Including cooking measurements]

Axelrod, Amy, *Pigs in the Pantry: Fun with Math and Cooking.* Ill. by Sharon McGinley-Nally. Aladdin, 1997. ISBN 0689806655.
Mr. Pig and the piglets try to make chili. Includes information about cooking measurements. **K, Pr**

Beil, Karen Magnuson, *A Cake All for Me!* Ill. by Paul Meisel. Holiday House, 1998. ISBN 0823413683.
A pig counts to 20 as he bakes a cake. Also includes information about cooking measurements (separate from story). **PS**

deRubertis, Barbara, *Lulu's Lemonade.* Ill. by Paige Billin-Frye. Kane, 2000. ISBN 1575650932 (pbk).
Three children make lemonade with a variety of ingredients. **K, Pr**

Murphy, Stuart J., *Room for Ripley.* Ill. by Sylvie Wickstrom. HarperCollins, 1999. ISBN 0060276207.
Carlos learns about cups, pints, quarts, and gallons as he fills a fishbowl for his new goldfish. **K, Pr**

Rocklin, Joanne, *The Case of the Shrunken Allowance.* Ill. by Cornelius Van Wright and Ying-Hwa Hu. Scholastic, 1998. ISBN 0590120069.
Because it takes up less room in the jar than before, PB thinks some of his allowance is missing, but someone has replaced some coins with bills and put what was left into a bigger jar. **Pr**

Perspective [How things look different from different vantage points; how things appear smaller when they are farther away]

Alborough, Jez, *Watch Out! Big Bro's Coming!* Candlewick, 1997. ISBN 0763601306.
When mouse says Big Bro is coming, each animal imagines a creature larger than himself. **PS, K**

Baer, Gene, *Thump, Thump, Rat-a-Tat-Tat.* Ill. by Lois Ehlert. HarperCollins, 1991. ISBN 0064432653 (pbk).
A marching band comes closer, sounding louder and looking bigger, then moves away again. **T, PS, K**

Banyai, Istvan, *Zoom.* Viking, 1995. ISBN 0670858048.
A series of pictures shows a scene from farther and farther away. See also the author's similar *Re-zoom* [1995: ISBN 0670863920]. **K, Pr**

Bogacki, Tomek, *My First Garden.* **Farrar, Straus & Giroux, 2000. ISBN 0374325189.**
A man remembers the house he grew up in—a large house in a small town. He tells how he discovered the wider world and planted a garden. **PS, K, Pr**

Cohen, Caron Lee, *Where's the Fly?* **Ill. by Nancy Barnet. Greenwillow, 1996. ISBN 0688140440.**
Starting with the fly on the dog's nose, this book shows increasingly distant perspectives, all the way to the ocean on the earth. **PS, K**

Cuyler, Margery, *From Here to There.* **Ill. by Yu Cha Pak. Henry Holt, 1999. ISBN 080503191X.**
Maria gives her locations, from her family, to her house, to her town, all the way to her place in the universe. **PS, K, Pr**

Hoban, Tana, *Just Look.* **Greenwillow, 1996. ISBN 0688140408.**
The reader can look at part of a photograph through a peephole, then see a another view of the same thing from another perspective. See also the author's similar *Look Book* [1997: ISBN 0688149715]. **PS, K**

Hutchins, Pat, *Shrinking Mouse.* **Greenwillow, 1997. ISBN 0688139612.**
Animals notice that when one of them goes away, he appears to get smaller. **PS, K**

Jenkins, Steve, *Looking Down.* **Houghton Mifflin, 1995. ISBN 0395726654.**
Starting with a view of Earth from far out in space, the wordless collage illustrations show progressively closer views, all the way up to a close-up of a ladybug. **PS, K, Pr**

Rotner, Shelley, and Richard Olivo, *Close, Closer, Closest.* **Atheneum, 1997. ISBN 0689807627.**
Photographs show things from three different distances. **PS, K, Pr**

Sweeney, Joan, *Me on the Map.* **Ill. by Annette Cable. Crown, 1996. ISBN 0517700956.**
A girl shows maps of her room, her house, her town, her state, her country, and her world. **PS, K, Pr**

Chapter Seven

Letters, Language, and Words

Letters & Language *[Letters of the alphabet in no particular order; how letters form words]*

Banks, Kate, *Alphabet Soup.* **Ill. by Peter Sis. Knopf, 1994, c1988. ISBN 0679867236 (pbk).**
With his alphabet soup, a boy spells words that turn into the real thing. **K, Pr**

de Vicq de Cumptich, Roberto, *Bembo's Zoo: An Animal ABC Book.* **Henry Holt, 2000. ISBN 080506382X.**
This book presents the alphabet in uppercase and lowercase letters, plus animals for each letter that are formed from the letters in the animal's name. **PS, K**

Falwell, Cathryn, *Word Wizard.* **Clarion, 1998. ISBN 0395855802.**
Anna makes words with the letters in her breakfast cereal and turns them into an anagram adventure. **K, Pr**

Johnson, Stephen T., *Alphabet City.* **Viking, 1995. ISBN 0670856312.**
Photographs of items in a city that resemble letters of the alphabet. **K, Pr**

Lionni, Leo, *The Alphabet Tree.* **Knopf, 1990. ISBN 0679808353 (pbk).**
The letters on the alphabet tree learn to make words and then sentences. **K**

Schnur, Steven, *Autumn: An Alphabet Acrostic.* **Ill. by Leslie Evans. Clarion, 1997. ISBN 0395770432.**
Each letter of the alphabet (shown in upper case) is the first letter of an acrostic poem about fall. Also *Spring: An Alphabet Acrostic* [1999: ISBN 0395822696] and *Summer: An Alphabet Acrostic* [2001: ISBN 0618023720]. **K, Pr**

Turner, Priscilla, *The War between the Vowels and the Consonants.* **Ill. by Whitney Turner. Farrar, Straus & Giroux, 1996. ISBN 0374382360.**
> The vowels and consonants are at war until a mutual enemy in the form of a chaotic scribble forces them to work together and make words. **K, Pr**

Viorst, Judith, *The Alphabet from Z to A (With Much Confusion on the Way).* **Ill. by Richard Hull. Atheneum, 1994. ISBN 0689317689.**
> This reverse alphabet book has rhymes that explore homonyms (such as "in" and "inn") and non-phonetic spelling (C is for Ceiling but not for Seal, F is for Fake but not for Phony). **Pr**

Wilbur, Richard, *The Disappearing Alphabet.* **Ill. by David Diaz. Harcourt Brace, 1998. ISBN 0152014705.**
> Short poems explore the idea of what would happen if a letter of the alphabet disappeared. **Pr**

Wood, Audrey, *Alphabet Adventure.* **Ill. by Bruce Wood. Blue Sky/Scholastic, 2001. ISBN 043908069X.**
> Lowercase i loses its dot and the rest of the alphabet helps to look for it. Uppercase letters are also shown. **K, Pr**

Alphabet Books [Books that show letters in alphabetical order, usually with a representative item for each letter]

Alda, Arlene, *Arlene Alda's ABC.* **Tricycle, 2002. ISBN 1582460736 (pbk).**
> Photos of things that resemble uppercase letters of the alphabet. **PS, K**

Aylesworth, Jim, *Old Black Fly.* **Ill. by Stephen Gammell. Holt, 1992. ISBN 0805014012.**
> Black fly has a busy day, bothering things from A to Z. Uppercase letters are not shown separately from the text. **PS, K**

Azarian, Mary, *A Gardener's Alphabet.* **Houghton Mifflin, 2000. ISBN 0618033807.**
> Woodcuts depict a garden-related word, written all in upper case, for each letter of the alphabet. The author has also written a similar *Farmer's Alphabet* [Godine, 1981: ISBN 087923394X]. **PS, K**

Baker, Alan, *Black and White Rabbit's ABC.* **Kingfisher, 1994. ISBN 1856979512.**
> Black and White Rabbit paints a picture of an apple, in a story featuring the letters A to Z. Upper and lower case shown. **T, PS, K**

Barron, Rex, *Fed Up! A Feast of Frazzled Foods.* **Putnam, 2000. ISBN 0399234500.**
> Short phrases about fruits and vegetables illustrate each uppercase letter. **PS, K**

Bayer, Jane, *A My Name Is Alice.* **Ill. by Steven Kellogg. Dutton, 1984. ISBN 0803701233.**
   Animals with names and things they sell that illustrate each letter. Upper case only. **PS, K**

Beaton, Clare, *Zoë and Her Zebra.* **Barefoot Books, 1999. ISBN 1902283759.**
   Three-D felt pictures illustrate a child and an animal for each letter of the alphabet. Upper and lower case. The animals are identified at the end of the book. **T, PS**

Bender, Robert, *The A to Z Beastly Jamboree.* **Dutton/Lodestar, 1996. ISBN 0525675205.**
   An animal and a verb for each letter. Uppercase and lowercase letters shown. **T, PS, K**

Bond, Michael, *Paddington's ABC.* **Ill. by John Lobban. Puffin, 1996. ISBN 0140557636 (pbk).**
   Pictures featuring Paddington Bear illustrate each letter of the alphabet, which is given in upper and lower case. Includes some alphabet activities. **T, PS**

Boynton, Sandra, *A Is for Angry.* **Workman, 1987. ISBN 089480507X.**
   An animal (or two) and a descriptive adjective illustrate each uppercase letter. **PS, K**

Cahoon, Heather, *Word Play ABC.* **Walker, 1999. ISBN 0802786839.**
   Uppercase and lowercase letters are illustrated by pictures of puns and wordplay, such as a tree full of pans labeled "pantry." **K, Pr**

Capucilli, Alyssa Satin, *Mrs. McTats and Her Houseful of Cats.* **Ill. by Joan Rankin. Margaret K. McElderry, 2001. ISBN 0689831854.**
   Mrs. McTats has one cat named Abner. She then adds 24 more, in groups of two to six, which she names in alphabetical order, plus a dog she names Zoom. **PS, K**

Carlson, Nancy, *ABC I Like Me!* **Viking, 1997. ISBN 0670874582.**
   A pig tells good things about herself from A to Z. **PS, K**

Carter, David A., *Alpha Bugs.* **Little Simon, 1994. ISBN 0671866311.**
   Pop-up and lift-the-flap illustrations show alliterative bugs for each letter, upper and lower case shown. **PS, K**

Chandra, Deborah, *A Is for Amos.* **Ill. by Keiko Narahashi. Farrar, Straus & Giroux, 1999. ISBN 0374300011.**
   The story of a child riding a horse around a farm, using uppercase and lowercase letters from A to Z. **PS, K**

Cleary, Beverly, *Hullabaloo ABC.* **Ill. by Ted Rand. Morrow, 1998. ISBN 0688151825.**
> Sounds on the farm are the words used to illustrate the uppercase and lowercase letters of the alphabet. **PS, K**

Cline-Ransome, Lesa, *Quilt Alphabet.* **Ill. by James E. Ransome. Holiday House, 2001. ISBN 0823414531.**
> Uppercase letters in quilt squares are illustrated by poems and pictures of unnamed countryside things. **PS, K**

Cohen, Izhar, *A B C Discovery! An Alphabet Book of Picture Puzzles.* **Dial, 1998. ISBN 0803723210.**
> Pictures containing many words starting with each letter of the alphabet. Letters are shown in upper and lower case. **PS, K, Pr**

Crosbie, Michael J., *Arches to Zigzags: An Architecture ABC.* **Ill. by Steve and Kit Rosenthal. Henry N. Abrams, 2000. ISBN 0810942186.**
> Clear uppercase and lowercase letters are illustrated by photographs of architectural features. **PS, K, Pr**

de Vicq de Cumptich, Roberto, *Bembo's Zoo: An Animal ABC Book.* **Henry Holt, 2000. ISBN 080506382X.**
> This book presents the alphabet in uppercase and lowercase letters, plus animals for each letter that are formed from the letters in the animal's name. **PS, K**

Demarest, Chris, *The Cowboy ABC.* **DK, 1999. ISBN 0789425092.**
> Uppercase letters are illustrated with things in cowboy country. **PS**

Demarest, Chris L., *Firefighters A to Z.* **Margaret K. McElderry, 2000. ISBN 0689837984.**
> Uppercase letters are illustrated with pictures of things associated with firefighters. **PS, K**

Dena, Anaël, *Letters.* **Ill. by Christel Desmoinaux. Gareth Stevens, 1997. ISBN 0836819853.**
> Uppercase and lowercase letters, as well as letters in lowercase script, are illustrated with several items in a picture. **PS, K**

Dodd, Emma, *Dog's ABC: A Silly Story about the Alphabet.* **Dutton, 2000. ISBN 0525468374.**
> Dog's adventures introduce him to things for each letter, shown in upper and lower case. **PS, K, Pr**

Dodd, Lynley, *The Minister's Cat ABC.* **Gareth Stevens, 1994. ISBN 0836810732.**
> Cats exhibit different qualities for each letter, shown in upper case. **PS, K**

Ehlert, Lois, *Eating the Alphabet: Fruits and Vegetables from A to Z.* **Harcourt Brace, 1989. ISBN 0152244352.**
Uppercase and lowercase letters and bright, clear pictures of fruits and vegetables for each one. **PS**

Eichenberg, Fritz, *Ape in a Cape: An Alphabet of Odd Animals.* **Harcourt Brace, 1980. ISBN 0156078309 (pbk).**
Uppercase letters are illustrated by animals starting with each letter and a rhyme. **PS, K**

Elting, Mary, and Michael Folsom, *Q Is for Duck: An Alphabet Guessing Game.* **Ill. by Jack Kent. Houghton Mifflin, 1985. ISBN 0395300622 (pbk).**
Each uppercase letter of the alphabet introduces an animal riddle, such as "Q is for duck. Why? Because a duck quacks." **PS, K, Pr**

Ernst, Lisa Campbell, *The Letters Are Lost!* **Puffin, 1999. ISBN 014055663X (pbk).**
Each uppercase letter of the alphabet disappears in an appropriate way. **PS, K**

Fain, Kathleen, *Handsigns: A Sign Language Alphabet.* **Chronicle, 1995. ISBN 0811811964 (pbk).**
An animal, lowercase and uppercase letters, and the American Sign Language sign for that letter. **PS, K**

Gaga, *Pass the Celery, Ellery!* **Ill. by Jeffrey Fisher. Stewart, Tabori & Chang, 2000. ISBN 1584790318.**
Different foods beginning with each letter of the alphabet are paired with rhyming names. Letters are shown in various typefaces and cases. **PS, K, Pr**

Gerstein, Mordicai, *The Absolutely Awful Alphabet.* **Harcourt Brace, 1999. ISBN 0152014942.**
Each uppercase letter appears as an unpleasant character in this alliterative tale. **PS, K, Pr**

Girnis, Meg, *A B C For You and Me.* **Ill. by Shirley Leamon Green. Albert Whitman, 2000. ISBN 0807501018.**
Down's syndrome children are featured in photographs in this alphabet book, with uppercase and lowercase letters. **PS, K**

Golding, Kim, *Alphababies.* **DK, 1998. ISBN 0789425297.**
Pictures made of photographs of babies combined with drawings introduce a single word for each large uppercase letter. A simple rhyme connects the words. **T, PS**

Grimes, Nikki, and Pat Cummings, *C Is for City.* **Lothrop, Lee & Shepard, 1994. ISBN 0688118089.**
Colorful pictures and rhymes about things in the city for each letter of the alphabet (shown in upper case). **PS, K**

Grover, Max, *The Accidental Zucchini: An Unexpected Alphabet.* Browndeer/Harcourt Brace, 1993. ISBN 0152776958.
: An unusual combination of words (such as "fork fence") is illustrated for each letter, upper and lower case. **PS, K**

Gustafson, Scott, *Alphabet Soup: A Feast of Letters.* Greenwich Workshop Press, 1996. ISBN 0867130253.
: An alliterative rhyme shows animals arriving with soup ingredients for each letter of the alphabet. Uppercase letters shown. **K, Pr**

Hague, Kathleen, *Alphabears: An ABC Book*. Ill. by Michael Hague. Holt, 1991. ISBN 0805016376 (pbk).
: A rhyme about a bear for each uppercase letter of the alphabet. **PS, K**

Heller, Nicholas, *Goblins in Green*. Ill. by Jos. A. Smith. Greenwillow, 1995. ISBN 0688128025.
: Goblins with names from A to Z try on clothes. Each description includes words starting with that letter, plus one with the next letter. **PS, K**

Heller, Nicholas, *Ogres! Ogres! Ogres! A Feasting Frenzy from A to Z*. Ill. by Jos. A. Smith. Greenwillow, 1999. ISBN 0688169864.
: Creatures illustrate each uppercase letter in an alliterative sentence, which also introduces the next letter, such as "Abednego adores anchovy butter." **K, Pr**

Hepworth, Cathi, *Antics! An Alphabetical Anthology*. Putnam, 1992. ISBN 0399218629.
: Each letter of the alphabet is illustrated by a word containing "ant," such as "chant" and "mutant." Letters are shown in upper case. **K, Pr**

Hoban, Tana, *26 Letters and 99 Cents*. Greenwillow, 1987. ISBN 0688063616.
: Double book. One direction has simple photo-illustrations of each uppercase and lowercase letter. **PS, K, Pr**

Hobbie, Holly, *Puddle's ABC*. Little, Brown, 2000. ISBN 0316365939.
: Puddle creates an alphabet book for his friend, with uppercase and lowercase letters. **PS, K**

Holtz, Lara Tankel, *Alphabet Book*. Ill. by Dave King. DK, 1997. ISBN 0789420538.
: Photographs of many things for each letter of the alphabet. Letters are shown in various cases and styles. Alliterative sentences make comments or ask questions about the pictures. **K, Pr**

Horenstein, Henry, *A Is for. . . ? A Photographer's Alphabet of Animals*. Gulliver, 1999. ISBN 0152015825.
: Uppercase letters provide a clue to the identity of the animals in black-and-white photographs. **PS, K, Pr**

Howland, Naomi, *ABCDrive! A Car Trip Alphabet.* **Clarion, 1994. ISBN 0395664144.**
Something is seen for each letter of the alphabet on a car trip from city to country. Upper and lower case. **PS, K**

Hubbard, Woodleigh, *C is for Curious: An ABC of Feelings.* **Chronicle, 1995. ISBN 081181078X.**
An illustration of an emotion for each uppercase letter. [Bound with *2 Is for Dancing*]. **PS, K**

Hughes, Shirley, *Alfie's ABC.* **Lothrop Lee & Shepard, 1998. ISBN 068816126X.**
Alfie and his sister Annie Rose illustrate letters from A to Z, in upper and lower case. **PS**

Hunt, Judith A., ill. *The Timbertoes ABC Alphabet Book.* **Boyds Mills, 1997. ISBN 1564976048.**
Simple pictures introduce uppercase and lowercase letters. **PS**

Inkpen, Mike, *Kipper's A to Z: An Alphabet Adventure.* **Harcourt, 2001. ISBN 0152035944.**
Uppercase and lowercase letters are illustrated by things that Kipper and his friend Arnold collect. **PS**

Isadora, Rachel, *ABC Pop!* **Viking, 1999. ISBN 0670883298.**
Pop Art-style pictures illustrate each uppercase letter. **PS**

Jahn-Clough, Lisa, *ABC Yummy.* **Houghton Mifflin, 1997. ISBN 0395845424.**
Children's names, an adjective, and a food for each letter of the alphabet, shown in upper case. Small format. **PS**

Jordan, Martin and Tanis Jordan, *Amazon Alphabet.* **Kingfisher, 1996. ISBN 1856976661.**
Uppercase and lowercase letters are illustrated with animals from South America. **PS, K, Pr**

Kalman, Maira, *What Pete Ate from A–Z.* **Putnam, 2001. ISBN 0399233628.**
This story uses letters A through Z (shown in upper case, lower case, and script) to tell about a dog who eats everything but dog food. **PS, K, Pr**

Kelley, Marty. *Summer Stinks: An Alphabetical Lexicon for the Estivally Dispirited.* **Zino, 2001. ISBN 1559332913.**
An alphabet (upper and lower case) of unpleasant things about summer. **PS, K, Pr**

Kirk, David, *Miss Spider's ABC.* **Scholastic, 1998. ISBN 0590282794.**
Bugs and activities from A to Z add up to a birthday party for Miss Spider. Uppercase letters. **PS, K**

Kutner, Merrily, *Z Is for Zombie*. Ill. by John Manders. Albert Whitman, 1999. ISBN 0807594903.
   An alphabet book of creepy things, from "alien" to "ooze" to "zombie." Letters are not shown separately. **K**

Lester, Alison, *Alice and Aldo*. Houghton Mifflin, 1998. ISBN 0039587092.
   The story of a day with Alice and her toy donkey Aldo uses each letter of the alphabet in order. Pictures of many other things for each letter are included. Letters are not shown separately. **K, Pr**

Lester, Mike, *A Is for Salad*. Putnam & Grosset, 2000. ISBN 0399233881.
   A "wrong" item for each letter is named, but an animal starting with that letter is shown too. **PS, K, Pr**

Lindbergh, Reeve, *The Awful Aardvarks Go to School*. Ill. by Tracy Campbell Pearson. Viking, 1997. ISBN 0670859206.
   The aardvarks create havoc from A to Z when they visit a school. The whole alphabet in uppercase and lowercase letters is shown on each page **K, Pr**

Lobel, Anita, *Alison's Zinnia*. Greenwillow, 1990. ISBN 0688088651.
   Beginning with "Alison acquired an amaryllis for Beryl," this book presents a flower for each uppercase letter. **PS, K**

Lobel, Anita, *Away from Home*. Greenwillow, 1994. ISBN 0688103545.
   "Adam arrived in Amsterdam," followed by a boy in a faraway place for each letter. **PS, K**

Lobel, Arnold, *On Market Street*. Ill. by Anita Lobel. Greenwillow, 1981. ISBN 0688803091.
   Uppercase letters are illustrated by figures made up of things that start with that letter. **PS, K**

Lyne, Alice, *A My Name Is. . . .* Ill. by Lynne Cravath. Whispering Coyote, 1997. ISBN 1879085402.
   The familiar game "A my name is Alex, my best friend's name is Angie, we live in Alabama, and we sell alligators." Some rhymes combine two letters. Includes unnamed illustrations of things starting with the featured letters. **PS, K, Pr**

MacDonald, Suse, *Alphabatics*. Simon & Schuster, 1986. ISBN 0027615200.
   Letters of the alphabet (shown in upper and lower case) change into a picture of something starting with that letter. **PS, K**

Magee Doug, and Robert Newman, *All Aboard ABC*. Cobblehill, 1990. ISBN 0525650369.
   Uppercase and lowercase letters are illustrated by pictures of train-related items. See also the authors' *Let's Fly from A to Z* [1992: ISBN 0525651055], which is illustrated with airplane-related things. **PS, K**

Mahurin, Tim, *Jeremy Kooloo.* **Dutton, 1995. ISBN 0525452036.**
> This simple story of a cat has one word for each letter of the alphabet, shown in upper case. **PS, K**

Marshall, Janet, *Look Once Look Twice.* **Ticknor & Fields, 1995. ISBN 0395716446.**
> Each lowercase letter is patterned in a design that is revealed to be part of something starting with that letter. Patterns are stylized and not easy to guess. **PS, K**

Martin, Bill, Jr., and John Archambault, *Chicka Chicka Boom Boom.* **Ill. by Lois Ehlert. Aladdin, 2000. ISBN 068983568X.**
> A rollicking rhyme introduces uppercase and lowercase letters of the alphabet. Does not include pictures of items starting with the letters. **PS, K**

Martin, Mary Jane, *From Anne to Zach.* **Ill. by Michael Grejniec. Boyds Mills, 1996. ISBN 1563975734.**
> A rhyme introduces a child whose name starts with each letter of the alphabet. Letters are shown in upper case. **PS, K**

Maurer, Donna, *Annie, Bea, and Chi Chi Dolores: A School Day Alphabet.* **Ill. by Denys Cazet. Orchard, 1993. ISBN 0531054675.**
> Pictures introduce activities of a schoolday for each letter of the alphabet (upper and lower case shown). **PS**

McDonnell, Flora, *Flora McDonnell's ABC.* **Candlewick, 1997. ISBN 0763601187.**
> Large pages, uppercase and lowercase letters, and two representative items for each letter make up this simple alphabet book. **T, PS**

McMullan, Kate. *I Stink!* **Ill. by Jim McMullan. Joanna Cotler Books, 2002. ISBN 0060298499.**
> A garbage truck brags about its smelly contents, from A to Z. Letters are in upper case. **PS, K, Pr**

Metaxas, Eric, *The Birthday ABC.* **Ill. by Tim Raglin. Simon & Schuster, 1995. ISBN 0671883062.**
> Amusing rhymes about an alphabet of animals who help celebrate a birthday. Uppercase letters. **PS, K**

Miller, Jane, *Farm Alphabet Book.* **Scholastic, 1987. ISBN 0590319914 (pbk).**
> Photographs illustrate each letter of the alphabet (shown in upper and lower case) with something on a farm. **PS**

Miranda, Anne, *Pignic.* **Ill. by Rosekrans Hoffman. Boyds Mills, 1996. ISBN 1563975580.**
> At the annual picnic for pigs, each named pig brings things that start with the same letter as his name. Uppercase and lowercase alphabet presented. **PS, K**

Most, Bernard, *ABC T-Rex.* **Harcourt, 2000. ISBN 0152020071.**
  A dinosaur eats his way through the alphabet. Uppercase letters. **PS, K, Pr**

Moxley, Sheila, *ABCD: An Alphabet Book of Cats and Dogs.* **Little, Brown, 2001. ISBN 0316592404.**
  Uppercase and lowercase letters are illustrated by cats and dogs in alliterative sentences. **PS, K**

Pandell, Karen, *Animal Action ABC.* **Ill. by Art Wolfe and Nancy Sheehan. Dutton, 1996. ISBN 0525454861.**
  Photographs of animals and children illustrate action words from arch through leap and zap. Letters are shown in upper case. **PS, K, Pr**

Paul, Ann Whitford, *Everything to Spend the Night: From A to Z.* **Ill. by Maggie Smith. DK Ink, 1999. ISBN 0789425114.**
  A girl takes a bag full of things from A to Z when visiting her grandparents, but she forgets her pajamas. Uppercase letters are incorporated in the text. **PS, K**

Pelletier, David, *The Graphic Alphabet.* **Orchard, 1996. ISBN 0531360016.**
  Each letter of the alphabet itself becomes the illustration of a word. Letters are shown in various cases and typefaces. **PS, K, Pr**

Penney, Ian, *Ian Penney's ABC.* **Henry N. Abrams, 1998. ISBN 0810943506.**
  Uppercase and lowercase letters are illustrated by a picture with one identified item and many others not named. **PS, K, Pr**

Rankin, Laura, *The Handmade Alphabet.* **Dial, 1991. ISBN 0803709742.**
  Shows uppercase letters plus hands making the American Sign Language signs for each letter and an illustration of a word starting with that letter. **PS, K, Pr**

Rose, Deborah Lee, *Into the A, B, Sea.* **Ill. by Steve Jenkins. Scholastic, 2000. ISBN 0439096960.**
  Uppercase letters of the alphabet are illustrated by various sea creatures. **PS, K**

Rosen, Michael, *Michael Rosen's ABC.* **Ill. by Bee Willey. Millbrook, 1995. ISBN 1562941380.**
  Uppercase and lowercase letters are illustrated by alliterative poems and elaborate pictures with many things for each letter. **K, Pr**

Rosen, Michael J., *Avalanche.* **Ill. by David Butler. Candlewick, 1998. ISBN 0763605891.**
  An avalanche is so big that it fills the universe and then unrolls. Items from A to Z are caught up in this rollicking rhyme. **PS, K, Pr**

Rosenberg, Liz, *A Big and Little Alphabet.* **Ill. by Vera Rosenberry. Orchard, 1997. ISBN 0531300501.**
Animals of the appropriate letter act out things that start with each letter, given in upper and lower case. Other items are also included in the pictures and named at the end of the book. **PS, K, Pr**

Schneider, R. M., *Add It Dip It Fix It: A Book of Verbs.* **Houghton Mifflin, 1995. ISBN 0395727715.**
A verb for each lowercase letter of the alphabet, showing what is done to "it." **PS, K, Pr**

Schnur, Steven, *Autumn: An Alphabet Acrostic.* **Ill. by Leslie Evans. Clarion, 1997. ISBN 0395770432.**
Each letter of the alphabet (shown in upper case) is the first letter of an acrostic poem about fall. See also *Spring: An Alphabet Acrostic* [1999: ISBN 0395822696] and *Summer: An Alphabet Acrostic* [2001: ISBN 0618023720]. **K, Pr**

Schroeder, Pamela J. P., and Jean M. Donisch, *Alphabet.* **Rourke, 1996. ISBN 0866255761.**
Photographs show many things that start with each letter. In most cases, items starting with two consecutive letters are shown in each picture. Uppercase and lowercase letters are shown. **PS, K, Pr**

Sendak, Maurice, *Alligators All Around.* **HarperCollins, 1962. ISBN 0060255307.**
Small-sized book shows an uppercase alphabet of alligators doing unusual things. **PS, K**

Seuss, Dr., *Dr. Seuss's ABC.* **Beginner Books, 1963. ISBN 0394800303.**
Uppercase and lowercase letters of the alphabet are introduced with Seuss's familiar nonsense rhymes. **PS, K, Pr**

Shannon, George, *Tomorrow's Alphabet.* **Ill. by Donald Crews. Greenwillow, 1996. ISBN 0688135048.**
Examples like "D is for puppy—tomorrow's dog." Uppercase letters. **K, Pr**

Simmonds, Posy, *F-freezing ABC.* **Knopf, 1995. ISBN 0679879153.**
In this story that uses letters A to Z, four friends try to find a warm place to stay. Uppercase letters are incorporated into the text. **PS, K**

Slate, Joseph, *Miss Bindergarten Celebrates the 100th Day of Kindergarten.* **Ill. by Ashley Wolff. Dutton, 1998. ISBN 0525460004.**
Children from A to Z and their teacher find many items representing 100. Uppercase letters are part of the text. Other Miss Bindergarten books also use children's names from A to Z. **K**

Sloat, Teri, *Patty's Pumpkin Patch.* **Putnam, 1999. ISBN 0399230106.**
> A girl points out things from A to Z as she grows pumpkins in her pumpkin patch. Both uppercase and lowercase letters are shown. **PS, K**

Stutson, Caroline, *Prairie Primer A to Z.* **Ill. by Susan Condie Lamb. Dutton, 1996. ISBN 0525451633.**
> The alphabet (upper case) is illustrated by rhymes and pictures of Midwestern scenes from around 1900. **PS, K**

Testa, Fulvio, *A Long Trip to Z.* **Harcourt Brace, 1997. ISBN 0152016104.**
> A boy takes an imaginary trip in an airplane, using words that start with each letter of the alphabet. Letters are not shown separate from the text. **K, Pr**

Tudor, Tasha, *A Is for Annabelle.* **Simon & Schuster, 2001. ISBN 0689828454.**
> This alphabet book with uppercase letters is illustrated with things relating to an old-fashioned doll. **PS**

Van Allsburg, Chris, *The Z Was Zapped: A Play in Twenty-Six Acts.* **Houghton Mifflin, 1987. ISBN 0395446120.**
> Each uppercase letter has something happen to it, starting with the appropriate letter. **PS, K**

Viorst, Judith, *The Alphabet from Z to A (With Much Confusion on the Way).* **Ill. by Richard Hull. Atheneum, 1994. ISBN 0689317689.**
> This reverse alphabet book has rhymes that explore homonyms (such as in and inn) and non-phonetic spelling (C is for Ceiling but not for Seal, F is for Fake but not for Phony). **Pr**

Walton, Rick, *So Many Bunnies: A Bedtime ABC and Counting Book.* **Ill. by Paige Miglio. Lothrop, Lee & Shepard, 1998. ISBN 0688136567.**
> Old Mother Rabbit lived in a shoe with her 26 children, whose names each begin with a different letter of the alphabet (shown in upper case). **PS, K**

Wildsmith, Brian, *Brian Wildsmith's ABC.* **Star Bright Books, 1996. ISBN 1887734023.**
> Uppercase letters are illustrated by a single picture. Board pages. **T, PS**

Williams, Laura Ellen, *ABC Kids.* **Philomel, 2000. ISBN 0399233709.**
> Photographs and uppercase letters represent each letter of the alphabet. **T, PS**

Wilson-Max, Ken, *L Is for Loving.* **Hyperion, 1999. ISBN 0786805277.**
> Uppercase and lowercase letters are illustrated by descriptions of feelings from "angelic" to "zippy." **PS, K**

Wojtowycz, David, *Animal ABC.* **David & Charles, 1999. ISBN 1862331073.**
> Uppercase and lowercase letters are illustrated by humorous pictures of alliterative animals, such as a clumsy cow and an itchy iguana. **PS, K**

Yolen, Jane, *All in the Woodland Early: An ABC Book*. Ill. by Jane Breskin Zalben. Boyds Mills, 1997. ISBN 1563976455 (pbk).
: An alphabet of animals is introduced in this poem (with music). Uppercase letters shown. **PS, K**

Alliteration *[Words with the same initial sound]*

Barron, Rex, *Fed Up! A Feast of Frazzled Foods*. Putnam, 2000. ISBN 0399234500.
: Short phrases about fruits and vegetables illustrate each uppercase letter. **PS, K**

Bayer, Jane, *A My Name Is Alice*. Ill. by Steven Kellogg. Dutton, 1984. ISBN 0803701233.
: Animals with names and things they sell that illustrate each letter. Upper case only. **PS, K**

Bender, Robert, *The A to Z Beastly Jamboree*. Dutton/Lodestar, 1996. ISBN 0525675205.
: An animal and a verb for each letter. Uppercase and lowercase letters shown. **T, PS, K**

Carter, David A., *Alpha Bugs*. Little Simon, 1994. ISBN 0671866311.
: Pop-up and lift-the-flap illustrations show alliterative bugs for each letter, upper and lower case shown. **PS, K**

Edwards, Pamela Duncan, *The Wacky Wedding: A Book of Alphabet Antics*. Ill. by Henry Cole. Hyperion, 1999. ISBN 0786803088.
: The story of an ant wedding is told, with each page an alliterative sentence from A to Z. **PS, K, Pr**

Gerstein, Mordicai, *The Absolutely Awful Alphabet*. Harcourt Brace, 1999. ISBN 0152014942.
: Each uppercase letter appears as an unpleasant character in this alliterative tale. **PS, K, Pr**

Grover, Max, *The Accidental Zucchini: An Unexpected Alphabet*. Browndeer/Harcourt Brace, 1993. ISBN 0152776958.
: An unusual combination of words (such as "fork fence") is illustrated for each letter, upper and lower case. **PS, K**

Gustafson, Scott, *Alphabet Soup: A Feast of Letters*. Greenwich Workshop Press, 1996. ISBN 0867130253.
: A alliterative rhyme shows animals arriving with soup ingredients for each letter of the alphabet. Uppercase letters shown. **K, Pr**

Heller, Nicholas, *Ogres! Ogres! Ogres! A Feasting Frenzy from A to Z.* **Ill. by Jos. A. Smith. Greenwillow, 1999. ISBN 0688169864.**

Creatures illustrate each uppercase letter in an alliterative sentence, which also introduces the next letter, such as "Abednego adores anchovy butter." **K, Pr**

Holtz, Lara Tankel, *Alphabet Book.* **Ill. by Dave King. DK, 1997. ISBN 0789420538.**

Photographs of many things for each letter of the alphabet. Letters are shown in various cases and styles. Alliterative sentences make comments or ask questions about the pictures. **K, Pr**

Jahn-Clough, Lisa, *ABC Yummy.* **Houghton Mifflin, 1997. ISBN 0395845424.**

Children's names, an adjective, and a food for each letter of the alphabet, shown in upper case. Small format. **PS**

Lobel, Anita, *Alison's Zinnia.* **Greenwillow, 1990. ISBN 0688088651.**

Beginning with "Alison acquired an amaryllis for Beryl," this book presents a flower for each uppercase letter. **PS, K**

Lobel, Anita, *Away from Home.* **Greenwillow, 1994. ISBN 0688103545.**

"Adam arrived in Amsterdam," followed by a boy in a faraway place for each letter. **PS, K**

Moxley, Sheila, *ABCD: An Alphabet Book of Cats and Dogs.* **Little, Brown, 2001. ISBN 0316592404.**

Uppercase and lowercase letters are illustrated by cats and dogs in alliterative sentences. **PS, K**

Rosen, Michael, *Michael Rosen's ABC.* **Ill. by Bee Willey. Millbrook, 1995. ISBN 1562941380.**

Uppercase and lowercase letters are illustrated by alliterative poems and elaborate pictures with many things for each letter. **K, Pr**

Schwartz, Alvin, *Busy Buzzing Bumblebees and Other Tongue Twisters.* **Ill. by Paul Meisel. HarperCollins, 1992. ISBN 0064440362 (pbk).**

A collection of mostly alliterative tongue twisters. **K, Pr**

Seuss, Dr., *Dr. Seuss's ABC.* **Beginner Books, 1963. ISBN 0394800303.**

Upper and lower case letters of the alphabet are introduced with Seuss's familiar nonsense rhymes. **PS, K, Pr**

Wojtowycz, David, *Animal ABC.* **David & Charles, 1999. ISBN 1862331073.**

Upper and lower case letters are illustrated by humorous pictures of alliterative animals, such as a clumsy cow and an itchy iguana. **PS, K**

Rhyme [Books that emphasize rhyme, not simply stories that rhyme]

Alarcon, Karen Beaumont, *Louella Mae, She's Run Away!* Ill. by Rosanne Litzinger. Henry Holt, 1997. ISBN 080503532X.
Everyone looks for the missing Louella Mae. The reader can supply the rhyming last words. **K, Pr**

Barrett, Judi, *I Knew Two Who Said Moo: A Counting and Rhyming Book*. Ill. by Daniel Moreton. Atheneum, 2000. ISBN 0689821042.
Sentences rhyme with each number from 1 to 10. **PS, K**

Boynton, Sandra, *But Not the Hippopotamus*. Little Simon, rev. ed., 1995. ISBN 0671449044.
Simple rhymes about animals. Board. **T, PS**

Bynum, Janie, *Altoona Baboona*. Harcourt Brace, 1999. ISBN 0152018603.
Altoona Baboona has many activities that rhyme with her name. **PS, K**

Dunn, Carolyn, *A Pie Went By*. Ill. by Christopher Santoro. HarperCollins, 2000. ISBN 0060288086.
On his way to ask Queen Bea to marry him, King Bing carries a cherry pie on his head, and several animals try to get the pie. The story features many rhyming phrases. **K, Pr**

Durant, Alan, *Mouse Party*. Ill. by Sue Heap. Candlewick, 1995. ISBN 1564025845.
Mouse's party in his new, large house, attended by a cat with a mat, a dog with a log, and other rhyming animals, is interrupted when the original owner of the house, an elephant, returns. **PS, K**

Eichenberg, Fritz, *Ape in a Cape: An Alphabet of Odd Animals*. Harcourt Brace, 1980. ISBN 0156078309 (pbk).
Uppercase letters are illustrated by animals starting with each letter and a rhyme. **PS, K**

Gaga, *Pass the Celery, Ellery*! Ill. by Jeffrey Fisher. Stewart, Tabori & Chang, 2000. ISBN 1584790318.
Different foods beginning with each letter of the alphabet are paired with rhyming names. Letters are shown in various typefaces and cases. **PS, K, Pr**

Goldstone, Bruce, *The Beastly Feast*. Ill. by Blair Lent. Henry Holt, 1998. ISBN 0805038671.
The beasts are having a feast, and each animal brings something that rhymes. **PS, K**

Karlin, Nurit, *The Fat Cat Sat on the Mat*. HarperCollins, 1996. ISBN 0060266732.
A rat, a bat, and a hat try to get the cat off the mat, using such lures as a fish on a dish. **PS, K**

Lyon, George Ella, *A Day at Damp Camp.* Ill. by Peter Catalanotto. Orchard, 1996. ISBN 0531095045.
 Pairs of rhyming words such as "green screen" and "hot cot" describe a day at summer camp. **PS, K, Pr**

McCall, Francis, and Patricia Keeler, *A Huge Hog Is a Big Pig: A Rhyming Word Game.* Greenwillow, 2002. ISBN 0060297654.
 Photos of farm animals illustrate rhyming answers to riddles. **K, Pr**

McMillan, Bruce, *Puffins Climb, Penguins Rhyme.* Harcourt Brace, 1995. ISBN 0152003622.
 Photographs of penguins and puffins illustrate pairs of rhyming verbs. **PS, K**

Phonics *[Sounds of the language]*

McGuinness, Diane, *My First Phonics Book.* DK, 1999. ISBN 0789447371.
 Photographs of items that illustrate sounds, not letters. Short and long vowel sounds and vowel blends are illustrated. "Cymbal" is on the S sound page and "giraffe" is on the J sound page. **K, Pr**

Books That Emphasize Individual Letters

B

Berenstain, Stan, and Jan Berenstain, *Berenstains' B Book.* Beginner/Random, 1987. ISBN 0394923243.
 An adventure with Big Brown Bear causes Baby Bird's balloon to break. Most words start with B. **PS, K, Pr**

C

Berenstain, Stan, and Jan Berenstain, *Berenstains' C Book.* Beginner Books/Random, 1997. ISBN 0679988343.
 A clown named Clarence balances many things that start with C. Formerly published as *C is for Clown* [1972]. **PS, K**

Edwards, Pamela Duncan, *Clara Caterpillar.* Ill. by Henry Cole. HarperCollins, 2001. ISBN 0060289953.
 Clara Caterpillar grows into a cream-colored butterfly, and her plain color turns out to be good camouflage. Many words start with the letter C. **PS, K, Pr**

D

Edwards, Pamela Duncan, *Dinorella: A Prehistoric Fairy Tale*. Ill. by Henry Cole. Hyperion, 1997. ISBN 0789803096.
Dinorella—a dinosaur Cinderella—finds true love with the help of Fairydactyl and her own bravery. The story features words starting with D. **PS, K, Pr**

F

Edwards, Pamela Duncan, *Four Famished Foxes and Fosdyke*. Ill. by Henry Cole. HarperCollins, 1995. ISBN 0060249250.
Four foxes don't have much luck hunting, but fortunately their brother fixes a vegetarian meal. Uses many words starting with F. **PS, K, Pr**

P

Atwood, Margaret, *Princess Prunella and the Purple Peanut*. Ill. by Maryann Kovalski. Workman, 1995. ISBN 0761101667.
Prunella is spoiled and selfish until a wise woman curses her with a purple peanut on her nose. Story's words mostly start with P. **K, Pr**

Brooks, Eric, *The Practically Perfect Pajamas*. Winslow, 2000. ISBN 1890817228.
Percy the polar bear likes his pajamas, but the other bears tease him. Many words start with P. **PS, K, Pr**

Pomerantz, Charlotte, *The Piggy in the Puddle*. Ill. by James Marshall. Simon & Schuster, 1974. ISBN 0027749002.
A tongue-twister story of pigs playing in a mud puddle. Uses many words starting with P. **PS, K, Pr**

R

Coxe, Molly, *R Is for Radish*. Random, 1997. ISBN 0679985743.
Four easy-to-read stories about a rabbit named Radish, which emphasize words starting with R. **PS, K**

S

Edwards, Pamela Duncan, *Some Smug Slug*. Ill. by Henry Cole. HarperCollins, 1996. ISBN 0060247894.
A smug slug climbs up a slope—which turns out to be a hungry toad. Many words begin with the letter S. **PS, K, Pr**

Enderle, Judith Ross, and Stephanie Gordon Tessler, *Six Sandy Sheep*. Ill. by John O'Brien. Boyds Mills, 1997. ISBN 1563975823.
One by one, six sheep on the beach enter the water. Many words begin with S. **PS, K**

T

Most, Bernard, *A Trio of Triceratops.* **Harcourt Brace, 1998. ISBN 0152014489.**
Three dinosaurs do many things—from trimming trees to telling tales—that start with T. **PS, K**

U

Haskins, Lori, *Ducks in Muck.* **Ill. by Valeria Petrone. Random, 2000. ISBN 0679891668 (pbk).**
Trucks carrying ducks get stuck in muck. Simple text, mostly words ending in "uck." **PS, K**

W

Edwards, Pamela Duncan, *The Worrywarts.* **Ill. by Henry Cole. HarperCollins, 1999. ISBN 0060281505.**
Wombat, Weasel, and Woodchuck worry about what might happen if they set out to wander the world. Uses many words that start with W. **PS, K, Pr**

Jonas, Ann, *Watch William Walk.* **Greenwillow, 1997. ISBN 0688141722.**
A story about two children, a dog, and a duck, in which all words begin with W. **PS, K, Pr**

Parts of Speech

Nouns

Banks, Kate, *The Bird, the Monkey, and the Snake in the Jungle.* **Ill. by Tomek Bogacki. Farrar, Straus & Giroux, 1999. ISBN 0374307296.**
One day the tree in which three animals live falls over, so they search together for a new home. Rebuses are substituted for most nouns in the story. **PS, K, Pr**

Bender, Robert, *The A to Z Beastly Jamboree.* **Dutton/Lodestar, 1996. ISBN 0525675205.**
An animal and a verb for each letter. **T, PS, K**

Cleary, Brian P., *A Mink, a Fink, a Skating Rink: What Is a Noun?* **Ill. by Jenya Promitsky. Lerner, 2000. ISBN 1575054027.**
Humorous examples of nouns. **K, Pr**

Heller, Ruth, *Merry-Go-Round: A Book about Nouns.* **Grosset & Dunlap, 1990. ISBN 0448400855.**
Colorful pictures illustrate and explain nouns. See also *A Cache of Jewels and Other Collective Nouns* [1987: ISBN 044819211X] and the author's books on other parts of speech. **Pr**

Payne, Nina, *Four in All.* Ill. by Adam Payne. Front Street, 2001. ISBN 1886910162.
Cut-paper illustrations of a girl building a house and inviting animal friends to visit are accompanied by four nouns for each picture, such as "roof window chimney door" and "fork plate knife spoon." **PS, K, Pr**

Verbs

Bender, Robert, *The A to Z Beastly Jamboree.* Dutton/Lodestar, 1996. ISBN 0525675205.
An animal and a verb for each letter. Uppercase and lowercase letters shown. **T, PS, K**

Blackstone, Stella, *Baby Rock, Baby Roll.* Ill. by Denise & Fernando. Holiday House, 1997. ISBN 082341311X.
Three babies do many things. **T, PS**

Brooks, Alan, *Frogs Jump: A Counting Book.* Ill. by Steven Kellogg. Scholastic, 1996. ISBN 0590455281.
Numerals from 1 to 12 are illustrated by animal activities interpreted in unusual ways: for example, monkeys swing golf clubs, not on trees. **PS, K**

Cleary, Brian P., *To Root, to Toot, to Parachute: What Is a Verb?* Ill. by Jenya Promitsky. Carolrhoda, 2001. ISBN 1575054035.
Humorous examples of verbs. **K, Pr**

Davis, Katie, *Who Hops?* Harcourt Brace, 1998. ISBN 0152018395.
Different animals can do different things. **PS, K**

Heller, Ruth, *Kites Sail High: A Book about Verbs.* Paper Star, 1998. ISBN 0698113896 (pbk).
Intriguing illustrations of verbs. **Pr**

Hines-Stephens, Sarah, *Soup's Oops!* Ill. by Anna Grossnickle Hines. Red Wagon, 2000. ISBN 0152021655.
Cat, dog, and baby play, demonstrating verbs. Board. **T**

McMillan, Bruce, *Puffins Climb, Penguins Rhyme.* Harcourt Brace, 1995. ISBN 0152003622.
Photographs of penguins and puffins illustrate pairs of rhyming verbs. **PS, K**

Pandell, Karen, *Animal Action ABC.* Ill. by Art Wolfe and Nancy Sheehan. Dutton, 1996. ISBN 0525454861.
Photographs of animals and children illustrate action words from "arch" through "leap" and "zap." **PS, K, Pr**

Schneider, R. M., *Add It Dip It Fix It: A Book of Verbs.* **Houghton Mifflin, 1995. ISBN 0395727715.**

A verb for each lower case letter of the alphabet, showing what is done to "it." **PS, K, Pr**

Adjectives

Barton, Byron, *The Three Bears.* **HarperCollins, 1991. ISBN 0060204230.**

Goldilocks sneaks into the bears' house, eats some porridge, breaks a rocker and falls asleep, after making comparisons. Simple text. **T, PS**

Berenstain, Stan, and Jan Berenstain, *Old Hat, New Hat.* **Random, 1970. 0394806697.**

A bear tries on many hats, but prefers his old one. Short text is mostly adjectives, preceded by "too." **T, PS**

Bishop, Gavin, *Little Rabbit and the Sea.* **North-South, 1997. ISBN 1558588108.**

Little Rabbit, who longs to go to sea, learns many words to describe it. **PS, K**

Boynton, Sandra, *A Is for Angry.* **Workman, 1987. ISBN 089480507X.**

An animal (or two) and a descriptive adjective illustrate each upper case letter. **PS, K**

Cleary, Brian P., *Hairy, Scary, Ordinary: What Is an Adjective?* **Ill. by Jenya Promitsky. Carolrhoda, 2000. ISBN 1575054019.**

Humorous, rhyming introduction to adjectives. **Pr**

Daniels, Teri, *Just Enough.* **Ill. by Harley Jessup. Viking, 2000. ISBN 0670888737.**

A boy uses many adjectives to describe himself. **PS, K, Pr**

Heller, Ruth, *Many Luscious Lollipops: A Book about Adjectives.* **Paper Star, 1998. ISBN 0698116410 (pbk).**

Colorful pictures depict adjectives. **Pr**

Rex, Michael, *The Pie Is Cherry.* **Henry Holt, 2001. ISBN 0805067175.**

Adjectives describe many foods and other things in a kitchen. **PS, K, Pr**

Walton, Rick, *That's My Dog!* **Ill. by Julia Gorton. Putnam, 2001. ISBN 0399233520.**

A boy describes his big red dog, using many adjectives, including comparative ones. **PS, K**

Comparative Adjectives [Small, smaller, smallest; good, better, best]

Barrett Judi, *Things That Are Most in the World*. Ill. by John Nickle. Atheneum, 1998. ISBN 0689813333.
Funny pictures illustrate statements like "The quietest thing in the world is a worm chewing peanut butter." **PS, K, Pr**

Kalan, Robert, *Blue Sea*. Ill. by Donald Crews. Greenwillow, 1992. ISBN 0688115098 (pbk).
A little fish, a big fish, a bigger fish, and the biggest fish follow each other through progressively smaller holes, leaving only the little one to fit through them all. Very simple text. **T, PS**

Murphy, Stuart J., *The Best Bug Parade*. Ill. by Holly Keller. HarperCollins, 1996. ISBN 0060258713.
In a parade, bugs compare their sizes: small, smaller, smallest; long, longer, longest; and so on. **PS, K**

Schreiber, Anne, *Slower Than a Snail*. Ill. by Larry Daste. Scholastic, 1995. ISBN 0590265997 (pbk).
Accused of being slower than a snail, a girl compares herself to many other things. **PS, K**

Walton, Rick, *Pig Pigger Piggest*. Ill. by Jimmy Holder. Gibbs-Smith, 1997. ISBN 0879058064.
Witch, Witcher, and Witchest want to buy the tall, taller, and tallest castles built by the three pigs, but the pigs love the mud created when the castles are destroyed. **K, Pr**

Walton, Rick, *That's My Dog!* Ill. by Julia Gorton. Putnam, 2001. ISBN 0399233520.
A boy describes his big red dog, using many adjectives, including comparative ones. **PS, K**

Homonyms & Homophones [Words that sound alike but have different meanings or spellings]

Bourke, Linda, *Eye Count: A Book of Counting Puzzles*. Chronicle, 1995. ISBN 0811807320.
Each page illustrates a number (1 to 12) of different meanings for a word: for example, page 3 has a baseball diamond, a diamond ring, and a jack of diamonds. Numerals shown. **K, Pr**

Cahoon, Heather, *Word Play ABC*. Walker, 1999. ISBN 0802786839.
Uppercase and lowercase letters are illustrated by pictures of puns and wordplay, such as a tree full of pans labeled "pantry." **K, Pr**

Gwynne, Fred, *A Little Pigeon Toad.* **Aladdin, 1990. ISBN 0671694448 (pbk).**
Humorous illustrations of homonyms and figures of speech. See also the author's *A Chocolate Moose for Dinner* [1988: ISBN 0671667416] and *The King Who Rained* [1988: ISBN 0671667440]. **K, Pr**

Viorst, Judith, *The Alphabet from Z to A (With Much Confusion on the Way).* **Ill. by Richard Hull. Atheneum, 1994. ISBN 0689317689.**
This reverse alphabet book has rhymes that explore homonyms (such as "in" and "inn") and non-phonetic spelling (C is for Ceiling but not for Seal, F is for Fake but not for Phony). **Pr**

Chapter Eight

Senses, Growth, and Emotions

Senses

Aliki, *My Five Senses.* **Crowell, rev. ed., 1989. ISBN 0690047924.**
Simple introduction to sight, hearing, smell, taste, and touch. **T, PS, K**

Cash, Megan Montague, *I Saw the Sea and the Sea Saw Me.* **Viking, 2001. ISBN 0670899666.**
A little girl uses all her senses on a visit to the sea. **PS, K**

Cole, Joanna, *The Magic School Bus Explores the Senses.* **Ill. by Bruce Degen. Scholastic, 1999. ISBN 0590446975.**
The assistant principal accidentally takes Ms. Frizzle's magic bus on a tour of the sensory organs. Serious information presented in a humorous way. **K, Pr**

Garelli, Cristina, *Forest Friends' Five Senses.* **Ill. by Francesca Chessa. Knopf, 2001. ISBN 037581308X.**
Five animals each tell a story about a different sense. **PS, K**

Miller, Margaret, *My Five Senses.* **Aladdin, 1998. ISBN 0689820097 (pbk).**
Photographs of children illustrate uses of the five senses. **PS, K**

Murphy, Mary, *You Smell and Taste and Feel and See and Hear.* **DK, 1997. ISBN 0789424711.**
A puppy experiences different things with different senses. **T, PS**

Pinkney, Andrea, and Brian Pinkney, *I Smell Honey.* **Gulliver, 1997. ISBN 0152006400.**
A child smells, hears, sees, touches, and tastes while helping make a meal. Board. **T, PS**

Pittman, Helena Clare, *One Quiet Morning.* **Carolrhoda, 1996. ISBN 0876148380.**
The morning seems too noisy for Gerald to write a poem, but when he gets up very early he hears and sees things differently. **K, Pr**

Slater, Teddy, *Busy Bunnies' Five Senses.* **Ill. by Maggie Swanson. Scholastic, 1999. ISBN 0439099102 (pbk).**
A group of bunnies describe what they do with their five senses. **PS**

Stojic, Manya, *Rain.* **Crown, 2000. ISBN 0517800853.**
Animals in Africa use their senses to predict the rain and to enjoy its aftermath. **PS, K**

Strom, Maria Diaz, *Rainbow Joe and Me.* **Lee & Low, 1999. ISBN 1880000938.**
Eloise, who loves to paint with colors, learns how a blind man perceives color. **K, Pr**

Sight

Belk-Moncure, Jane, *My Eyes Are for Seeing.* **Ill. by Viki Woodworth. Child's World, 1998. ISBN 1567662811.**
Tells how our eyes help us see. **PS**

Brown, Marc, *Arthur's Eyes.* **Little, Brown, 1983. ISBN 0316110639.**
Arthur's classmates tease him about his glasses, but when he doesn't wear them, he has trouble seeing. **K, Pr**

Priceman, Marjorie, *It's Me, Marva! A Story about Color and Optical Illusions.* **Knopf, 2001. ISBN 0679889930 (pbk).**
Marva's invention causes her trouble with colors and optical illusions. **K, Pr**

Sound

Auzary-Luton, Sylvie, *1, 2, 3 Music.* **Orchard, 1999. ISBN 0531301885.**
Annie loves to listen to music, then finds some musical instruments to form a band. **PS, K**

Baer, Gene, *Thump, Thump, Rat-a-Tat-Tat.* **Ill. by Lois Ehlert. HarperCollins, 1991. ISBN 0064432653 (pbk).**
A marching band comes closer, sounding louder and looking bigger, then moves away again. **T, PS, K**

Baker, Alan, *I Thought I Heard.* **Copper Beech, 1996. ISBN 0761304606.**
A girl thinks ordinary nighttime noises are something else. **PS, K**

Becker, Bonny, *The Quiet Way Home.* **Ill. by Benrei Huang. Henry Holt, 1995. ISBN 0805035303.**
A man and a girl listen for sounds on the way home from school. **PS, K**

Belk-Moncure, Jane, *Clang, Boom, Bang.* **Ill. by Viki Woodworth. Child's World, 1998. ISBN 1567662854.**
Children describe many different kinds of sounds. **PS**

Bond, Rebecca, *Bravo, Maurice!* **Little, Brown, 2000. ISBN 0316105457.**
His family introduces him to all of their occupations, but what Maurice likes best are the sounds he hears, and singing. **PS, K, Pr**

Bottner, Barbara, *Hurricane Music.* **Ill. by Paul Yalowitz. Putnam, 1995. ISBN 0399225447.**
Aunt Margaret discovers a clarinet and learns to play along with everything—even a hurricane. **PS, K, Pr**

Brown, Margaret Wise, *Bunny's Noisy Book.* **Ill. by Lisa McCue. Hyperion, 2000. ISBN 0786804726.**
A little bunny explores his forest world, listening for many things. **PS**

Cleary, Beverly, *Hullabaloo ABC.* **Ill. by Ted Rand. Morrow, 1998. ISBN 0688151825.**
Sounds on the farm are the words used to illustrate the uppercase and lowercase letters of the alphabet. **PS, K**

Coy, John, *Vroomaloom Zoom.* **Ill. by Joe Cepeda. Crown, 2000. ISBN 0157800098.**
Dad takes Carmela on a wild car ride full of different sounds. **PS, K**

Davol, Marguerite W., *The Loudest, Fastest, Best Drummer in Kansas.* **Ill. by Cat Bowman Smith. Orchard, 2000. ISBN 0531301915.**
Maggie's loud drumming disturbs everyone in town, until she drums away a tornado. **K, Pr**

Hendry, Diana, *The Very Noisy Night.* **Ill. by Jane Chapman. Dutton, 1999. ISBN 0525462619.**
Little Mouse hears many noises at night. **PS, K**

Heo, Yumi, *One Afternoon.* **Orchard, 1994. ISBN 0531068455.**
Minho and his mother hear many sounds as they do errands in their city neighborhood. **PS, K**

Isadora, Rachel, *Listen to the City.* **Putnam, 2000. ISBN 0399230475.**
Pop Art-style pictures illustrate sounds of the city. **PS, K**

Maitland, Barbara, *Moo in the Morning.* **Ill. by Andrew Kulman. Farrar, Straus & Giroux, 2000. ISBN 0374350388.**
A mother and child leave the noisy city for the country, but find that it is just as noisy in the morning in its own way. **PS, K**

Martin, Bill, Jr., *Polar Bear, Polar Bear, What Do You Hear?* **Ill. by Eric Carle. Henry Holt, 1991. ISBN 0805017593.**
Different animals hear each others' sounds at the zoo. Simple text. **T, PS**

Martin, Bill, Jr., and John Archambault, *Listen to the Rain.* **Ill. by James Endicott. Henry Holt, 1988. ISBN 0805006826.**
Describes the different sounds made by rain. **PS, K**

Moss, Lloyd, *Zin! Zin! Zin! A Violin.* **Ill. by Marjorie Priceman. Simon & Schuster, 1995. ISBN 0671882392.**
One musical instrument at a time is introduced, making a solo, a duo, a trio, and up to a chamber group of 10. **Pr**

Murphy, Mary, *Please Be Quiet.* **Houghton Mifflin, 1999. ISBN 0395971136.**
Penguin makes a lot of noise playing, but finds a way to be quiet. **T, PS**

Showers, Paul, *The Listening Walk.* **Ill. by Aliki. HarperCollins, 1991. ISBN 069049663X.**
A girl and her father take a walk without talking and listen for all the different sounds they can hear. **PS, K, Pr**

Tyger, Rory, *Newton.* **Barron's, 2001. ISBN 0764153900.**
A teddy bear reassures his stuffed animal friends about strange noises they hear at night. **PS**

Wundrow, Deanna, *Jungle Drum.* **Ill. by Susan Swan. Millbrook, 1999. ISBN 0761312706.**
There are many sounds in the jungle, quiet ones as well as loud ones. **PS, K**

Touch

Adoff, Arnold, *Touch the Poem.* **Ill. by Lisa Desimmi, Blue Sky, 2000. ISBN 0590479709.**
Poems illustrated with photographs celebrate the sense of touch. **K, Pr**

Becker, Bonny, *Tickly Prickly.* **Ill. by Shari Halpern. HarperCollins, 1999. ISBN 0694012394.**
Describes how it feels to be touched by different animals. **T, PS**

Belk-Moncure, Jane, *My Fingers Are for Touching.* Ill. by Viki Woodworth. Child's World, 1998. ISBN 1567662846.
   An introduction to the sense of touch. **PS**

Young, Ed, *Seven Blind Mice.* Philomel, 1992. ISBN 0399222618.
   Seven blind mice of different colors each feel a different part of an elephant and get a very different idea of what it is like. **PS, K, Pr**

Hot & Cold

Appelbaum, Diana, *Cocoa Ice.* Ill. by Holly Mead. Orchard, 1997. ISBN 0531300404.
   Cocoa is harvested in the tropics, while ice is harvested in Maine. **K**

Taste

Belk-Moncure, Jane, *A Tasting Party.* Ill. by Viki Woodworth. Child's World, 1998. ISBN 1567662838.
   Children and animals have fun tasting different things. **PS**

Smell

Allen, Jonathan, *Mucky Moose.* Demco Turtleback, 1996. ISBN 0606096434 (pbk.).
   Mucky Moose smells so bad that he repels the wolf that tries to eat him. **PS, K**

Belk-Moncure, Jane, *A Whiff and a Sniff.* Ill. by Viki Woodworth. Child's World, 1998. ISBN 156766282X.
   Children describe all the different kinds of things they can smell. **PS**

McMullan, Kate, *I Stink!* Ill. by Jim McMullan. Joanna Cotler Books, 2002. ISBN 0060298499.
   A garbage truck brags about its smelly contents, from A to Z. Letters are in upper case. **PS, K, Pr**

Growth [Growth of living things]

Aliki, *The Two of Them.* Morrow, 1987. ISBN 0688073379 (pbk).
   Describes the relationship of a little girl and her grandfather from the girl's birth to her grandfather's death. **PS, K**

Bacon, Ethel, *To See the Moon.* Ill. by David Ray. BridgeWater, 1996. ISBN 081673822X.
> A girl adopts a sled dog puppy and, month by month through the year, trains him for a sled dog race. We see the changing seasons as well as the dog's growth and maturity. **K, Pr**

Baker, Jeannie, *Window.* Greenwillow, 1991. ISBN 0688089186.
> Collage construction illustrations chronicle the changes in a boy's neighborhood as he grows up. Wordless. **PS, K, Pr**

Bauer, Marion Dane, *Grandmother's Song.* Ill. by Pamela Rossi. Simon & Schuster, 2000. ISBN 0689822723.
> A woman has a baby who grows into a woman who has a baby herself. **PS, K**

Carle, Eric, *The Tiny Seed.* Simon & Schuster, 1987. ISBN 0887080154.
> A tiny seed grows into a large flower, which produces more seeds. **K, Pr**

Day, Nancy Raines, *A Kitten's Year.* Ill. by Anne Mortimer. HarperCollins, 2000. ISBN 0060272317.
> A kitten does something different each month of the year, while growing into a cat. **PS, K**

Gentieu, Penny, *Grow! Babies!* Crown, 2000. ISBN 0517800292.
> Photos show what babies look like and can do as newborns, and at 3, 4, 5, 7, 9, and 12 months. **PS, K, Pr**

Hutchins, Pat, *You'll Soon Grow into Them, Titch.* Mulberry, 1992. ISBN 0688115071 (pbk).
> Titch inherits oversized hand-me-downs from his older siblings. When he finally gets clothes that fit, he passes on his outgrown clothes to the new baby. **PS, K**

Kirk, Daniel, *Bigger.* Putnam, 1998. ISBN 0399231277.
> A boy tells how he began to grow even before he was born, and how he learns and expands his world as he grows. **PS, K, Pr**

McCarty, Peter, *Baby Steps.* Henry Holt, 2000. ISBN 0805059539.
> Realistic pencil drawings show a baby's growth from one day to one year old. **PS, K, Pr**

Murphy, Stuart J., *Pepper's Journal: A Kitten's First Year.* Ill. by Marsha Winborn. HarperCollins, 2000. ISBN 0060276185.
> A girl keeps a diary of her cat's first year. Entries are made at irregular times. Shows the cat's development. **PS, K, Pr**

Peck, Jan, *The Giant Carrot.* Ill. by Barry Root. Dial, 1998. ISBN 0803718233.
> A family grows a carrot so huge that they have trouble getting it out of the ground. **K, Pr**

Rockwell, Anne, *Growing Like Me*. Ill. by Holly Keller. Silver Whistle/Harcourt, 2001. ISBN 0152022023.
A child sees the many things growing and changing in the natural world. **PS, K**

Rylant, Cynthia, *Birthday Presents*. Ill. by Suçie Stevenson. Orchard, 1991. ISBN 0531070263 (pbk).
Parents tell a little girl about each of her birthdays, from when she was born up to her sixth birthday. **PS, K**

Schindel, John, *Frog Face: My Little Sister and Me*. Ill. by Janet Delaney. Holt, 1998. ISBN 0805055460.
A little girl talks about sharing her life with a younger sister. Illustrated with photos. **PS**

Maturity [How older people or animals have learned to do different things]

Bacon, Ethel, *To See the Moon*. Ill. by David Ray. BridgeWater, 1996. ISBN 081673822X.
A girl adopts a sled dog puppy and, month by month through the year, trains him for a sled dog race. We see the changing seasons as well as the dog's growth and maturity. **K, Pr**

Brown, Margaret Wise, *Another Important Book*. Ill. by Chris Raschka. Joanna Cotler Books/HarperCollins, 1999. ISBN 0060262834.
Children from ages one to six show what they can do. **PS**

Buck, Nola, *Hey, Little Baby!* Ill. by R. W. Alley. Harper Festival, 1999. ISBN 0694012009.
An exuberant little girl shows her baby brother all the things she can do. **PS**

Bunting, Eve, *Can You Do This, Old Badger?* Ill. by LeUyen Pham. Harcourt, 2000. ISBN 0152016546.
A young badger shows an old one what he can do, and the old one teaches the young one about finding food and other useful things. **PS, K**

Curtis, Jamie Lee, *When I Was Little: A Four-Year-Old's Memoir of Her Youth*. Ill. by Laura Cornell. HarperCollins, 1993. ISBN 0060210788.
A four-year-old tells how things are different now that she's grown up. **PS**

Dunbar, Joyce, *Tell Me What It's Like to Be Big*. Ill. by Debi Gliori. Harcourt, 2001. ISBN 0152025642.
Willa's big brother Willoughby tells her what it's like to be grown-up. **PS, K**

Gentieu, Penny, *Grow! Babies!* Crown, 2000. ISBN 0517800292.
Photos show what babies look like and can do as newborns, and at 3, 4, 5, 7, 9, and 12 months. **PS, K, Pr**

Hoffman, Don, *Billy Is a Big Boy.* **Ill. by Todd Dakins. Popcorn Press, 2000. ISBN 0970251807.**
Billy demonstrates the things he can do now (such as use the toilet) that are different from what he used to do as a baby. **PS, K**

Kirk, Daniel, *Bigger.* **Putnam, 1998. ISBN 0399231277.**
A boy tells how he began to grow even before he was born, and how he learns and expands his world as he grows. **PS, K, Pr**

McMillan, Bruce, *Step by Step.* **Lothrop, Lee & Shepard, 1987. ISBN 0685351181.**
Photographs of a boy at different stages of learning to walk, from crawling to running. **PS, K**

Miller, Margaret, *Now I'm Big.* **Greenwillow, 1996. ISBN 0688140777.**
Photographs show what some children were like as babies, contrasting with what they can do now. **PS, K**

Palatini, Margie, *Good as Goldie.* **Hyperion, 2000. ISBN 0786805021.**
Goldie explains all the things she can do better than her baby brother. **PS, K**

Emotions

Aliki, *Feelings.* **Greenwillow, 1984. ISBN 068803831X.**
Simple stories and illustrations describe various emotions. **PS, K**

Anholt, Catherine, and Laurence Anholt, *What Makes Me Happy?* **Pearson, 1998. ISBN 1564028283 (pbk).**
Pictures show things that make a child feel a certain way. **PS**

Baker, Keith, *Sometimes.* **Harcourt Brace, 1999. ISBN 0152020020.**
Simple text describes an alligator's different feelings. **PS**

Bowdish, Lynea, *One Glad Man.* **Ill. by Kristin Sorra. Children's, 1999. ISBN 0516215957.**
A lonely man is sad until animals from one to ten move into his house. **PS**

Cain, Janan, *The Way I Feel.* **Parenting Press, 2000. ISBN 1884734715.**
Amusing but right-on illustrations and descriptions of situations give examples of emotions from angry to jealous and proud. **PS, K, Pr**

Carlson, Nancy, *How about a Hug?* **Viking, 2001. ISBN 0670035068.**
A little pig girl discovers that hugs are good for many situations. **PS, K**

Curtis, Jamie Lee, *Today I Feel Silly & Other Moods That Make My Day.* **Ill. by Laura Cornell. HarperCollins, 1998. ISBN 0060245603.**
A girl describes her many moods and the reasons for them. **PS, K**

Emberley, Ed, and Anne Miranda, *Glad Monster, Sad Monster: A Book about Feelings.* **Little, Brown, 1997. ISBN 0316573957.**
Different colored monsters explain different feelings. Lift-the-flap pages make masks for children to use in acting out the feelings. **PS, K**

Evans, Lezlie, *Sometimes I Feel Like a Storm Cloud.* **Mondo, 1999. ISBN 1572556218.**
A little girl tells how different emotions make her feel like a big balloon, a newborn kitten, a peacock, and so on. **PS, K**

Freedman, Claire, *Where's Your Smile, Crocodile?* **Ill. by Sean Julian. Peachtree, 2001. ISBN 1561452513.**
His animal friends try to cheer up little Kyle Crocodile, who has lost his smile. **PS, K**

Freymann, Saxton, and Joost Elffers, *How Are You Peeling? Foods with Moods.* **Arthur A. Levine, 1999. ISBN 0439104319.**
Photographs of vegetables with faces illustrate various moods. **PS, K**

Hobbie, Holly, *Toot & Puddle: You Are My Sunshine.* **Little, Brown, 1999. ISBN 0316365629.**
Toot is moping and all of Puddle's efforts do not cheer him up, until there is a big thunderstorm. **PS, K**

Hubbard, Woodleigh, *C is for Curious: An ABC of Feelings.* **Chronicle, 1995. ISBN 081181078X.**
An illustration of an emotion for each uppercase letter. [Bound with *2 Is for Dancing*]. **PS, K**

Inkpen, Mick, *Wibbly Pig Is Happy!* **Viking, 2000. ISBN 0670892637.**
Simple text on board pages shows Wibbly Pig in various moods. **T, PS**

Jahn-Clough, Lisa, *My Friend and I.* **Houghton Mifflin, 1999. ISBN 0395935458.**
Simple story of two children who are happy being friends, angry at the breaking of a toy, and sad when they are apart. **T, PS**

Jones, Elisabeth, *Sunshine & Storm.* **Ill. by James Coplestone. Ragged Bears, 2001. ISBN 1929927274.**
Sunshine the cat is angry because Storm the dog gets her wet, but the two soon become friends again. **PS, K**

Modesitt, Jeanne, *Sometimes I Feel Like a Mouse: A Book about Feelings.* Ill. by Robin Spowart. Scholastic, 1996. ISBN 0590448366 (pbk).
A child describes his feelings in terms of animals: a horse galloping bravely, a squirrel chittering excitedly, and so on. **PS, K**

Moran, Alex, *Six Silly Foxes.* Ill. by Keith Baker. Green Light/Harcourt, 2000. ISBN 015202560X.
Simple text tells of six fox siblings and their changing emotions. **PS**

Murphy, Joanne Brisson, *Feelings.* Ill. by Heather Collins. Firefly, 1985. ISBN 088753129 (pbk).
A young boy describes many different feelings he has in different situations. **PS, K**

Murphy, Mary, *I Feel Happy and Sad and Angry and Glad.* DK, 2000. ISBN 0789426803.
Two puppies experience a variety of emotions during a day of playing together. **T, PS**

Oram, Hiawyn, *Kiss It Better.* Ill. by Frederic Joos. Dutton, 1999. ISBN 0525463860.
Big Bear kisses away Little Bear's troubles, and later Little Bear tries to kiss away Big Bear's sadness. **PS**

Parr, Todd, *The Feelings Book.* Little, Brown, 2000. ISBN 0316691313.
Small-format book with childlike drawings illustrates various moods. **PS**

Parr, Todd, *Things That Make You Feel Good, Things That Make You Feel Bad.* Little, Brown, 1999. ISBN 0316692700.
Childlike illustrations show simple things that can make a person feel good or bad. **PS**

Proimos, James, *The Loudness of Sam.* Harcourt Brace, 1999. ISBN 015202087X.
In this humorous story, Sam, who always laughs and cries loudly, teaches his aunt to show her emotions. **PS, K, Pr**

Seuss, Dr., *My Many Colored Days.* Ill. by Steve Johnson and Lou Fancher. Knopf, 1996. ISBN 0679875972.
Days are illustrated by different colors, which represent the mood of the day. **PS, K, Pr**

Tuxworth, Nicola, *Funny Faces: A Very First Picture Book.* Gareth Stevens, 1996. ISBN 0836822722.
Photos of baby and toddler faces showing various moods and emotions. **T, PS**

Wilson-Max, Ken, *L Is for Loving.* Hyperion, 1999. ISBN 0786805277.
Uppercase and lowercase letters are illustrated by descriptions of feelings from "angelic" to "zippy." **PS, K**

Zehler, Antonia, *Two Fine Ladies Have a Tiff.* **Random, 2001. ISBN 0375911049.**
  Two sisters argue and make up. **PS, K**

Anger

Aaron, Jean, *When I'm Angry.* **Golden, 1998. ISBN 0307440192.**
  Childlike drawings and descriptions show the feeling of anger. Comes with parent guide. **PS, K**

Everitt, Betsy, *Mean Soup.* **Harcourt Brace, 1992. ISBN 0152531467.**
  After Horace's bad day, he and his mother snarl away their bad moods making Mean Soup. **PS, K, Pr**

French, Vivian, *Tiger and the Temper Tantrum.* **Ill. by Rebecca Elgar. Kingfisher, 1999. ISBN 0753451972.**
  After Tiger throws a temper tantrum in the store, his mother won't take him to the park. **PS**

Jackson, Jean, *Thorndike and Nelson.* **Ill. by Vera Rosenberry. DK, 1997. ISBN 0789424525.**
  Two monster friends get angry at each other, with silly monster consequences. **PS, K**

Lachner, Dorothea, *Andrew's Angry Words.* **Ill. by The Tjong-Khing. North-South, 1995. ISBN 1558584358.**
  When Andrew shouts some angry words, they take on a life of their own, affecting many other people until a woman throws them into the sea and gives Andrew a bundle of nice words. **K, Pr**

Langreuter, Jutta, and Vera Sobat, *Little Bear and the Big Fight.* **Millbrook, 1998. ISBN 0761304037.**
  Two little bears have a fight at kindergarten when they can't share the pink clay. One bear bites the other's ear, but they eventually make up. **PS, K**

Palatini, Margie, *Goldie Is Mad.* **Hyperion, 2001. ISBN 078680565X.**
  A little girl is angry at her baby brother, but begins to think that he's not so bad after all. **PS, K**

Schami, Rafik, *Fatima and the Dream Thief.* **Ill. by Els Cools and Oliver Streich. North-South, 1996. ISBN 1558586539.**
  Hassan and Fatima try to earn money by working for a dream thief who won't pay them if they lose their temper. **Pr**

Spelman, Cornelia Maude, *When I Feel Angry.* **Ill. by Nancy Cote. Albert Whitman, 2000. ISBN 0807588881.**
  A bunny-child tells what makes him angry and what he can do about it. **PS, K**

Udry, Janice May, *Let's Be Enemies.* Ill. by Maurice Sendak. Harper Trophy, 1988. ISBN 0064431886 (pbk).
Small-format book tells the story of two friends who have a falling-out. **PS, K, Pr**

Zolotow, Charlotte, *The Hating Book.* Ill. by Ben Shecter. Harper Trophy, 1989. ISBN 0064431975 (pbk).
Two girls are angry at each other because of a misunderstanding. **PS, K, Pr**

Sadness

Fox, Mem, *Tough Boris.* Ill. by Kathryn Brown. Harcourt Brace, 1994. ISBN 0152896120.
A tough pirate cries when his pet parrot dies. **PS, K**

Oram, Hiawyn, *Kiss It Better.* Ill. by Frederic Joos. Dutton, 1999. ISBN 0525463860.
Big Bear kisses away Little Bear's troubles, and later Little Bear tries to kiss away Big Bear's sadness. **PS**

Paschkis, Julie, *So Happy/So Sad.* Henry Holt, 1995. ISBN 0805038620.
One-half of the book shows happy animals; turning the book around shows sad animals. **T, PS**

Fear

Aaron, Jean, *When I'm Afraid.* Golden, 1998. ISBN 0307440575.
Childlike drawings and descriptions of what it feels like to be afraid. Comes with parents' guide. **PS, K**

Bonsall, Crosby, *Who's Afraid of the Dark?* HarperCollins, 1987. ISBN 0060205997.
A little boy explains to an older girl how his dog is afraid of the dark, and her suggestions help the boy overcome his own fears. Simple text. **PS**

Bowdish, Lynea, *Thunder Doesn't Scare Me.* Ill. by John Wallace. Children's Press, 2001. ISBN 0516221515.
Short, simple text describes how a girl and her dog deal with the noise of thunder. **PS, K**

Bradbury, Ray, *Switch on the Night.* Ill. by Leo and Diane Dillon. Knopf, 1993. ISBN 0394804864.
A boy who doesn't like the night makes friends with a little girl who teaches him to appreciate it. **PS, K, Pr**

Cohen, Miriam, *Jim Meets the Thing.* Ill. by Lillian Hoban. Bantam, 1997. ISBN 044041167X (pbk).
Jim is the only one in his class to be scared by a TV show, but he is also the only one who's not afraid of the praying mantis. **PS, K, Pr**

Curtis, Munzee, *When the Big Dog Barks.* Ill. by Susan Avishai. Greenwillow, 1997. ISBN 0688095399.
A girl tells about frightening things, and how her parents are there to help her. **PS, K**

Gorbachev, Valeri, *Chicken Chickens.* North-South, 2001. ISBN 0735815410.
Two little chickens are afraid of many things at the playground, until Beaver helps them to go down the slide. **PS, K**

Heide, Florence Parry, *Some Things Are Scary.* Ill. by Jules Feiffer. Candlewick, 2000. ISBN 0763612227.
Illustrates many situations—from having your friend move away to getting a shot—that are scary. **PS, K, Pr**

Keller, Holly, *Brave Horace.* Greenwillow, 1998. ISBN 0688154077.
In preparation for his friend's scary monster party, Horace practices being scary and brave. **PS, K, Pr**

Mayer, Mercer, *There's a Nightmare in My Closet.* Dial, 1984. ISBN 0803786824.
A boy learns to deal with the nightmare in his closet by taking it to bed with him. The author has other titles such as *There's an Alligator Under My Bed* [1987: ISBN 0803703740] and *There's Something in My Attic* [1992: ISBN 0140548130]. **PS, K**

Rankin, Joan, *Scaredy Cat.* Margaret K. McElderry Book, 1996. ISBN 0689809484.
A little kitten learns not to be afraid of many things. **PS, K**

Tyger, Rory, *Newton.* Barron's, 2001. ISBN 0764153900.
A teddy bear reassures his stuffed animal friends about strange noises they hear at night. **PS**

Walsh, Ellen Stoll, *Pip's Magic.* Harcourt Brace, 1994. ISBN 0152928502.
In trying to find a wizard to help him with his fear of the dark, a salamander goes through many dark places and learns that he has created his own magic. **PS, K**

Whybrow, Ian, *Little Farmer Joe.* Ill. by Christian Birmingham. Kingfisher, 2001. ISBN 0753452138.
Joe is fearful of things on the farm until he one night when he helps at the birth of a lamb. **PS, K**

Wishinsky, Frieda, *Nothing Scares Us.* Ill. by Neal Layton. Carolrhoda, 2000. ISBN 1575054906.

> Two friends pretend to be fearless, but they find that one is afraid of spiders and the other of scary TV shows **PS, K**

Wormell, Mary, *Hilda Hen's Scary Night.* Harcourt Brace, 1995. ISBN 0152009906.

> In the farmyard at night, Hilda Hen is frightened by ordinary things that seem to be something else. **PS, K**

Zarin, Cynthia, *Rose and Sebastian.* Ill. by Sarah Durham. Houghton Mifflin, 1997. ISBN 039575920X.

> Rose is frightened by the noises coming from the upstairs apartment, until she meets the boy who lives there. **PS, K**

Happiness

Cohen, Caron Lee, *Happy to You!* Ill. by Rosanne Litzinger. Clarion, 2001. ISBN 0618042296.

> A little boy is happy all the rest of the day after a birthday party. **PS, K**

Lloyd, David, *Polly Molly Woof Woof.* Ill. by Charlotte Hard. Candlewick, 2000. ISBN 076360755X.

> Dogs in a park show their owners what it means to be happy. **PS, K**

Paschkis, Julie, *So Happy/So Sad.* Henry Holt, 1995. ISBN 0805038620.

> One-half of the book shows happy animals; turning the book around shows sad animals. **T, PS**

Index by Concept

A
Addition 72
Adjectives 138
Alliteration 131
Alphabet Books 120
Anger 151
Antonyms, *see* Opposites 28
Autumn, *see* Fall 98

B
B (letter) 134
Being Afraid, *see* Fear 152
Bigger and Smaller, *see* Size 110
Billion, *see* Large Numbers 48
Black 18
Blue 16
Brown 19

C
C (letter) 134
Cause and Effect 31
Change 5
Circle 24
Clock, *see* Telling Time 106
Cold, *see* Hot and Cold 145
Color 7
Color Identification 9
Color Mixing 19
Colors, *see* Color Identification 9
    or Books Emphasizing Particular Colors 15
Comparative Adjectives 139
Comparison, *see* Comparative Adjectives 139
    or Same/Different 1
    or More and Less 113
    or Size 110
Consequences, *see* Cause and Effect 31
Cooking Measurements, *see* Volume 116
Counting Books 49
Counting by Two 67
Counting by Five 68
Counting by 10 69
Counting Down 63
Counting Up 60

D
D (letter) 135
Days of the Week 103
Diamond-Shape 25
Different, *see* Same/Different 1
Distance 115
Division 79

E
Eight 45
Eleven 47
Emotions 148
Even Numbers, *see* Even, Odd 70
Even, Odd 70

F
F (letter) 135
Fall 98
Fear 152
Feeling, *see* Touch 144
Feelings, *see* Emotions 148
First, *see* Ordinals 71
Five 43
Four 43
Fractions 80

G
Googol, *see* Large Numbers 48
Green 17
Growing Up, *see* Growth 45
    or Maturity 147
Growth 145

H
Happiness 154
Hearing, *see* Sound 142
Height, *see* Length and Height 114
Homonyms and Homophones 139
Hot and Cold 145
Hundred, *see* One hundred 47

I
In and Out 28

L
Language 119
Large Numbers 48
Left and Right 34
Length and Height 114
Letter Sounds, *see* Phonics 134
    or Books That Emphasize Individual Letters 134
Letters and Language 119
    see also Alphabet Books 120
    or Books That Emphasize Individual Letters 134

M
March 106
Maturity 147
Measurement 109
Million, *see* Large Numbers 48
Money 81
Months of the Year 103
More and Less 113
Morning 90
Multiple Concepts 1
Multiplication 77

N
Night 91
Nine 45
Nouns 136
November 106
Number Concept 40
Numbers 37
    see also Particular Numbers
Numeration, *see* Number Concept 40

O
Odd numbers, *see* Even, Odd 70
One 41

Index by Concept 155

One hundred 47
Opposites. 28
Orange 18
Ordinals 71

P
P (letter). 135
Parts of Speech 136
Patterns 33
Perspective. 116
Phonics 134
Point of View. 34
        see also Perspective. 116
Position 26
Powers of Two 83
Powers of 10 84
Prepositions, *see* Position 26
Pretend, *see* Real/Pretend 6
Primary colors, *see* Color Mixing. 19
Purple 18

R
R (letter) 135
Real/Pretend 6
Red 15
Rhyme 133
Right and Left, *see* Left and Right 34

S
S (letter). 135
Sadness 152
Same/Different 1
Seasons 92
Secondary colors, *see* Color Mixing. 19
Seeing, *see* Sight. 142
Senses 141
Sets 4
Seven 45
Shape 21
Sight. 142
Six 44
Size 110
Smell 145

Solid Shapes 26
Sound. 142
Sound-Alike Words, *see* Homonyms and Homophones 139
Spring 95
Square 25
Subtraction. 75
Summer 96
Symmetry 34

T
T (letter). 136
Taste. 145
Telling Time. 106
Temper, *see* Anger. 151
Ten. 46
Things to Count. 37
Three 42
Time. 85
Time of Day. 88
Time Sense 85
Touch. 144
Triangle 25
Twelve 47
Two 42

U
U (letter) 136
Unhappiness, *see* Sadness. 152

V
Verbs 137
Volume. 116

W
W (letter) 136
Week, *see* Days of the Week 103
Weight 114
White 18
Winter 99

Y
Yellow 16

Index by Title

1 Gaping Wide-Mouthed Hopping Frog (Tryon) 59
1 Hunter (Hutchins) 54, 65
1 Is One (Tudor) 59
1 2 3 (Geddes) 53
1, 2, 3 for You and Me (Girnis) 53
1, 2, 3, Go! (Lee) 55
1, 2, 3 Music (Auzary-Luton) 142
123 Pop! (Isadora) 48, 54
1, 2, 3 to the Zoo: A Counting Book (Carle) 51
1, 2, 3 What Do You See? An Animal Counting Book (Bohdal) .. 50
123 Yippie (Jahn-Clough) 55, 65
2 X 2=Boo! A Set of Spooky Multiplication Stories (Leedy) 79
6 Sticks (Coxe) 44
10 in the Bed (Geddes) 46, 65, 76
10 Minutes Till Bedtime (Rathman) 66
12 Ways to Get to 11 (Merriam) 39, 47, 74
26 Letters and 99 Cents (Hoban) 62, 82, 124
...98, 99, 100! Ready or Not, Here I Come (Slater) 62, 69, 70
100 Days of School (Harris) 39, 47, 74
The 100-Pound Problem (Dussling) 114
100 School Days (Rockwell) 48, 70
The 100th Day of School (Medearis) 47
100th Day Worries (Cuyler) 38, 47, 69
The 512 Ants on Sullivan Street (Losi) 83

A

A B C Discovery! An Alphabet Book of Picture Puzzles (Cohen) 122
A B C For You and Me (Girnis) 123
ABC I Like Me! (Carlson) 121
ABC Kids (Williams) 130
ABC Pop! (Isadora) 125
ABC T-Rex (Most) 128
ABC Yummy (Jahn-Clough) 125, 132
ABCD: An Alphabet Book of Cats and Dogs (Moxley) ... 128, 132
ABCDrive! A Car Trip Alphabet (Howland) 125
A Is for...? A Photographer's Alphabet of Animals (Horenstein) 124
A Is for Amos (Chandra) 121
A Is for Angry (Boynton) 121, 138
A Is for Annabelle (Tudor) 130
A Is for Salad (Lester) 126
A My Name Is... (Lyne) 126
A My Name Is Alice (Bayer) 121, 131
The A to Z Beastly Jamboree (Bender) 121, 131, 136, 137
The Absolutely Awful Alphabet (Gerstein) 123, 131
The Accidental Zucchini: An Unexpected Alphabet (Grover) 124, 131
Add It Dip It Fix It: A Book of Verbs (Schneider) 129, 138
Alexander and the Wind-up Mouse (Lionni) 6
Alexander, Who Used to Be Rich Last Sunday (Viorst) 83
Alfie's 123 (Hughes) 54
Alfie's ABC (Hughes) 125
Alice and Aldo (Lester) 126
Alison's Zinnia (Lobel) 126, 132
All Aboard ABC (Magee) 126
All by Myself! (Aliki) 88
All in a Day (Anno) 1, 86
All in the Woodland Early: An ABC Book (Yolen) 131
Alligators All Around (Sendak) 129
Alligators and Others All Year Long! A Book of Months (Dragonwagon) 104
Alpha Bugs (Carter) 121, 131
Alphababies (Golding) 123
Alphabatics (MacDonald) 126
Alphabears: An ABC Book (Hague) 124
Alphabet (Schroeder) 129
Alphabet Adventure (Wood) 120
Alphabet Book (Holtz) 124, 132
Alphabet City (Johnson) 119
The Alphabet from Z to A (With Much Confusion on the Way) (Viorst) 120, 130, 140
Alphabet Soup (Banks) 119
Alphabet Soup: A Feast of Letters (Gustafson) 124, 131
The Alphabet Tree (Lionni) 119
Altoona Baboona (Bynum) 133
Amanda Bean's Amazing Dream: A Mathematical Story (Neuschwander) 79
Amazing and Incredible Counting Stories: A Number of Tall Tales (Grover) 53
Amazon Alphabet (Jordan) 125
Among the Odds and Evens: A Tale of Adventure (Turner) 70
Anansi the Spider: A Tale from the Ashanti (McDermott) 45
And If the Moon Could Talk (Banks) 91
Andrew's Angry Words (Lachner) 151
Animal ABC (Wojtowycz) 130, 132
Animal Action ABC (Pandell) 3, 128, 137
Animals Antics from 1 to 10 (Wojtowycz) 60
Animals Black and White (Tildes) 19
Animals on Board (Murphy) 39, 74
Annie, Bea, and Chi Chi Dolores: A School Day Alphabet (Maurer) 127
Anno's Counting Book (Anno) 49, 103
Anno's Magic Seeds (Anno) 71, 72, 75, 77, 83
Anno's Mysterious Multiplying Jar (Anno) 49, 77
Another Important Book (Brown) 61, 147
Antics! An Alphabetical Anthology (Hepworth) 124
Ape in a Cape: An Alphabet of Odd Animals (Eichenberg) 123, 133
The Apple Pie Tree (Hall) 93
Apples and Pumpkins (Rockwell) 98
April Wilson's Magpie Magic: A Tale of Colorful Mischief (Wilson) 9
Arches to Zigzags: An Architecture ABC (Crosbie) 122
Arctic Fives Arrive (Pinczes) 69
Are You Spring? (Pitcher) 95
Arlene Alda's 123 (Alda) 60, 63
Arlene Alda's ABC (Alda) 120
Around the Pond: Who's Been Here? (George) 32, 97
Arthur's Eyes (Brown) 142
Aunt Pitty Patty's Pig (Aylesworth) 31
Autumn: An Alphabet Acrostic (Schnur) 98, 119, 129
Avalanche (Rosen) 128
Away from Home (Lobel) 126, 132
The Awful Aardvarks Go to School (Lindbergh) 126

B

Baby Animals Black and White (Tildes) 19
Baby Rock, Baby Roll (Blackstone) 42, 137
Baby Steps (McCarty) 146
Ballerina (Sis) 14
Barn Cat: A Counting Book (Saul) 58
The Baseball Counting Book (McGrath) 56
Bat Jamboree (Appelt) 49, 63
Bats Around the Clock (Appelt) 106
Bats on Parade (Appelt) 77
Bean Soup (Hines-Stephens) 27, 29
Bear about Town (Blackstone) 103

A Bear for All Seasons (Fuchs) 93
Bear in a Square (Blackstone) 21
Bearobics: A Hip-Hop Counting Story (Parker) 57
Bears at the Beach: Counting 10 to 20 (Yektai) 60
Bears in the Night (Berenstain) 26
Bears Odd, Bears Even (Ziefert) 71
The Beastly Feast (Goldstone) 133
Beep Beep, Vroom Vroom! (Murphy) 33
Before and After: A Book of Nature Timescapes (Thornhill) .. 5, 87
Behind the Mask: A Book about Prepositions (Heller) 27
Bembo's Zoo: An Animal ABC Book (de Vicq
 de Cumptich) 119, 122
Benny's Pennies (Brisson) 64, 81
The Berenstain Bears and the Spooky Old Tree
 (Berenstain) 26, 42
The Berenstain Bears Big Bear Small Bear (Berenstain) 110
The Berenstain Bears Catch the Bus (Berenstain) 106
The Berenstain Bears Go Up and Down (Berenstain) 37
Berenstains' B Book (Berenstain) 134
Berenstains' C Book (Berenstain) 134
The Best Bug Parade (Murphy) 113, 139
Big (Haring) 11, 111
Big and Little (Jenkins) 112
Big and Little (Miller) 113
A Big and Little Alphabet (Rosenberg) 129
Big and Little on the Farm (Donohue) 111
The Big Brown Box (Russo) 19
Big Fat Hen (Baker) 49
*Big Numbers and Pictures That Show Just How Big
 They Are* (Packard) 48
The Big Orange Splot (Pinkwater) 4
Bigger (Kirk) 146, 148
The Biggest, Best Snowman (Cuyler) 99, 111
The Biggest Fish (Keenan) 112
Biggest, Strongest, Fastest (Jenkins) 112
Billy Is a Big Boy (Hoffman) 148
The Bird, the Monkey, and the Snake in the Jungle (Banks) .. 88, 136
The Birthday ABC (Metaxas) 127
Birthday Presents (Rylant) 147
Black and White Rabbit's ABC (Baker) 120
Black Cat (Myers) 18
Blast Off! A Space Counting Book (Cole) 61, 64
Blue Hat, Green Hat (Boynton) 10
Blue Sea (Kalan) 112, 139
Blue Tortoise (Rogers) 16
Bob's Vacation (Rau) 13, 19
Bonnie's Blue House (Asbury) 16
Boswell Wide Awake (Day) 91
Brave Horace (Keller) 153
Bravo, Maurice! (Bond) 143
Brian Wildsmith's ABC (Wildsmith) 130
Brown Bear, Brown Bear, What Do You See? (Martin) 13
Brown Cow, Green Grass, Yellow Mellow Sun (Jackson) 12
Brown Rabbit's Day (Baker) 9, 88
Brown Rabbit's Shape Book (Baker) 9, 21, 26
Bug Dance (Murphy) 34
The Bull and the Fire Truck (Johnston) 15
Bunny Party (Wells) 40
Bunny's First Snowflake (Wellington) 99, 102
Bunny's Noisy Book (Brown) 143
Busy Bunnies' Five Senses (Slater) 142
Busy Buzzing Bumblebees and Other Tongue Twisters
 Schwartz) 132
But Not the Hippopotamus (Boynton) 133
The Button Box (Reid) 5
Buzz (Wong) 91
By a Blazing Blue Sea (Garne) 11
By the Dawn's Early Light (Ackerman) 88

C

C Is for City (Grimes) 123
C Is for Curious: An ABC of Feelings (Hubbard) 125, 149
A Cache of Jewels and Other Collective Nouns (Heller) 136
A Cake All for Me! (Beil) 60, 116
Calendarbears: A Book of Months (Hague) 104
*Can You Count Ten Toes? Count to 10 in 10 Different
 Languages* (Evans) 52
Can You Count to a Googol? (Wells) 49, 84
Can You Do This, Old Badger? (Bunting) 147
Can You See the Red Balloon? (Blackstone) 9
*Caps, Hats, Socks, and Mittens: A Book about the
 Four Seasons* (Borden) 92
Captain Invincible and the Space Shapes (Murphy) 26
Carrie Measures Up (Aber) 109, 114
The Case of the Missing Birthday Party (Rocklin) 41
The Case of the Shrunken Allowance (Rocklin) 82, 116
Cat among the Cabbages (Bartlett) 9, 110
Cat and Mouse in the Night (Bogacki) 91
Cat and Mouse in the Snow (Bogacki) 99
Catch That Cat! (Meister) 30
Cats Add Up! (Ochiltree) 75, 77
Cat's Colors (Cabrera) 10
Cats up a Tree (Hassett) 68
Celebrating Summer (Kohn) 66
Charlie Needs a Cloak! (de Paola) 15, 32, 93
The Cheerios Counting Book (McGrath) 56, 69
Chicka Chicka Boom Boom (Martin) 127
Chicken Chickens (Gorbachev) 153
Chicken Chuck (Martin) 16
Chicken Soup with Rice (Sendak) 105
Chidi Only Likes Blue: An African Book of Colors
 (Onyefulu) 13
A Child's Calendar (Updike) 105
A Chocolate Moose for Dinner (Gwynne) 140
Circle City (Rau) 25
Circle Dogs (Henkes) 22
Circle of Seasons (Muller) 94
Circle Song (Engel) 24
Circles and Squares Everywhere! (Grover) 24, 25
Circus 1—2—3 (Halsey) 53
Circus Shapes (Murphy) 23
Clang, Boom, Bang (Belk-Moncure) 143
Clara Caterpillar (Edwards) 134
Clean-Sweep Campers (Penner) 80, 81
A Cloak for the Dreamer (Friedman) 22
Clocks and More Clocks (Hutchins) 107
Close, Closer, Closest (Rotner) 113, 117
Cloudy with a Chance of Meatballs (Barrett) 110
Cock-a-Doodle-Doo: A Farmyard Counting Book (Lavis) 55
Cocoa Ice (Appelbaum) 1, 145
The Coin Counting Book (Williams) 83
Cold Little Duck, Duck, Duck (Peters) 95
A Collection for Kate (deRubertis) 73
The Color Box (Dodds) 11
Color Dance (Jonas) 12, 20
Color Farm (Ehlert) 7, 22
The Color Kittens (Brown) 19
Color Me a Rhyme: Nature Poems for Young People (Yolen) .. 14
A Color of His Own (Lionni) 3, 8
Color Zoo (Ehlert) 7, 22
Colors (Bourgoing) 10, 19
Colors (Dena) 10, 19
Colors: Animagicals (Shields) 14
Colors Around Us (Rotner) 13
Colors Everywhere (Hoban) 12
The Colors of Us (Katz) 2, 19
Comet's Nine Lives (Brett) 45, 61
The Completed Hickory Dickory Dock (Aylesworth) 60, 106

Cook-a-Doodle-Doo! (Stevens) 110
Cookie's Week (Ward) 103
Copy Me, Copycub (Edwards) 93
Count! (Fleming) 62, 69
Count and See (Hoban) 54
Count Down to Clean Up! (Wallace) 59, 67
Count on Pablo (deRubertis) 61, 67, 68, 69
Count with Maisy (Cousins) 51
Counting Book (King) 55, 69
Counting Cows (Jackson) 65
Counting Crocodiles *(Sierra)* 58, 67
Counting Kids (Golding) 53
Counting Kisses (Katz) 65
Counting Kittens (Plummer) 40
Counting Our Way to Maine (Smith) 63
Counting Sheep (Glass) .... 53, 68 [2 entries], 78
Counting Wildflowers (McMillan) 56
The Cowboy ABC (Demarest) 122
The Crayon Box That Talked (DeRolf) 7
The Crayon Counting Book (Ryan) 13, 68, 70
Cubes, Cones, Cylinders, and Spheres (Hoban) 26

D

Dappled Apples (Carr) 98
Dave's Down-to-Earth Rock Shop (Murphy) 4
A Day at Damp Camp (Lyon) 97, 134
Day by Day a Week Goes Round (Shields) 103
Day Care Days (Barrett) 88
The Day Jimmy's Boa Ate the Wash (Noble) 32
Deena's Lucky Penny (deRubertis) 81
Different Just Like Me (Mitchell) 3
The Ding Dong Clock (Behrman) 60, 106
Dinorella: A Prehistoric Fairy Tale (Edwards) 135
Dinosaur (Sis) 17
Dinosaur Deals (Murphy) 41
Dinosaur Roar! (Stickland) 31
The Disappearing Alphabet (Wilbur) 120
Divide and Ride (Murphy) 79
Dog Days: Rhymes Around the World (Prelutsky) 105
Dog's ABC: A Silly Story about the Alphabet (Dodd) . 122
*Dog's Colorful Day: A Messy Story about Colors and
   Counting* (Dodd) 11, 52
Doggies: A Counting and Barking Book (Boynton) .. 50, 63, 72
A Dollar for Penny (Glass) 82
The Doorbell Rang (Hutchins) 79
A Dozen Dogs: A Read-and-Count Story (Ziefert) .. 40, 47
A Dozen Dozens (Ziefert) 45, 47
Dr. Seuss's ABC (Seuss) 129, 132
Dreaming: A Countdown to Sleep (Greenstein) 65
Ducks Disappearing (Naylor) 40
Ducks in Muck (Haskins) 136

E

Each Orange Had 8 Slices: A Counting Book
   (Giganti) 39, 73, 78
Earth, Sky, Wet, Dry: A Book of Nature Opposites
   (Bernhard) 28
Eating Fractions (McMillan) 80
Eating the Alphabet: Fruits and Vegetables from A to Z
   (Ehlert) 123
Ed Emberley's Picture Pie: A Circle Drawing Book
   (Emberley) 24
Eight Animals on the Town (Elya) 45, 61, 71
Elephants Aloft (Appelt) 26
Elevator Magic (Murphy) 76
Elmer (McKee) 3, 8
Elmer's Colors (McKee) 3, 8
Emily's First 100 Days of School (Wells) 48, 63
Even Steven and Odd Todd (Cristaldi) 70
Everett Anderson's Year (Clifton) 104

Every Autumn Comes the Bear (Arnosky) 98
Every Buddy Counts (Murphy) 56
Everybody Bakes Bread (Dooley) 2
Everything to Spend the Night: From A to Z (Paul) .. 128
Exactly the Opposite (Hoban) 30
Eye Count: A Book of Counting Puzzles (Bourke) . 61, 139
Eye Spy Colors (MacKinnon) 12
Eye Spy Shapes (MacKinnon) 23

F

A Fair Bear Share (Murphy) 74
Fall Is Not Easy (Kelley) 94, 98
Fall Leaves Fall (Hall) 98
Farm Alphabet Book (Miller) 127
Farmer's Alphabet (Azarian) 120
The Fat Cat Sat on the Mat (Karlin) 133
The Father Who Had Ten Children (Guettier) 46
Fatima and the Dream Thief (Schami) 151
The Fattest, Tallest, Biggest Snowman Ever (Ling) .. 109
Feast for 10 (Falwell) 52
Fed up! A Feast of Frazzled Foods (Barron) 120, 131
Feelings (Aliki) 148
Feelings (Murphy) 150
The Feelings Book (Parr) 150
F-freezing ABC (Simmonds) 102, 129
Fire Truck (Sis) 16, 58
Firefighters A to Z (Demarest) 122
Firehouse Sal (Brimner) 61
First Snow (Lewis) 101
The First Snowfall (Rockwell) 101
Fish Eyes: A Book You Can Count On (Ehlert) 52
Fish Is Fish (Lionni) 3
The Five Chinese Brothers (Bishop) 43, 71
Five Creatures (Jenkins) 4, 44
The Five Hundred Twelve Ants on Sullivan Street (Losi) .. 83
Five Little Ducks: An Old Rhyme (Paparone) 44, 66
Five Little Kittens (Jewell) 44
Five Little Monkeys Jumping on the Bed (Christelow) . 44, 64
Five Little Monkeys Sitting in a Tree (Christelow) .. 44, 64
Five Little Monkeys with Nothing to Do (Christelow) . 44, 64
Five Silly Fishermen (Edwards) 38, 44
Five Trucks (Floca) 44, 71
Five Ugly Monsters (Arnold) 63, 75
Flannel Kisses (Brennan) 99
Flora McDonnell's ABC (McDonnell) 127
Following the Sun (Stow) 58, 89
Forest Friends' Five Senses (Garelli) 141
Forgetful Ted (Conboy) 107
Four Famished Foxes and Fosdyke (Edwards) 135
Four in All (Payne) 43, 137
Fraction Action (Leedy) 80
Frederick (Lionni) 94
Freight Train (Crews) 10
A Friend for Minerva Louise (Stoeke) 35
Frog and Toad All Year (Lobel) 94
Frog and Toad Are Friends (Lobel) 3, 4, 95
Frog Face: My Little Sister and Me (Schindel) 147
Frogs Jump: A Counting Book (Brooks) 50, 137
From Anne to Zach (Martin) 127
From Here to There (Cuyler) 115, 117
From One to One Hundred (Sloat) 58, 70
Funny Faces: A Very First Picture Book (Tuxworth) .. 150

G

Game Time! (Murphy) 87, 107
A Gardener's Alphabet (Azarian) 120
Gathering: A Northwoods Counting Book (Bowen) ... 50, 92
George Paints His House (Bassède) 9
George's Store at the Shore (Bassède) 49
Get Up and Go! (Murphy) 75, 87

Index by Title **159**

The Giant Carrot (Peck) 113, 146
Give Me Half! (Murphy) 80
Give the Dog a Bone (Kellogg) 55
Glad Monster, Sad Monster: A Book about Feelings
    (Emberley) 11, 149
Go Away, Big Green Monster (Emberley) 11
Goblins in Green (Heller) 8, 124
Goldie Is Mad (Palatini) 151
Good as Goldie (Palatini) 148
Gotcha! (Jorgensen) 27
Grandma Went to Market: A Round-the-World Counting
    Rhyme (Blackstone) 50
Grandma's Purple Flowers (Burrowes) 93
Grandmother Winter (Root) 101
Grandmother's Song (Bauer) 146
The Graphic Alphabet (Pelletier) 128
Gray Rabbit's Odd One Out (Baker) 4
Gray Rabbit's 1, 2, 3 (Baker) 60
Grayfur: The Story of a Rabbit in Summer (Potter) 97
The Great Divide (Dodds) 79
The Great Pet Sale (Inkpen) 62, 74, 82
The Greatest Gymnast of All (Murphy) 28, 30
The Greedy Triangle (Burns) 21, 25
Green Bear (Rogers) 13, 17, 94
Green Wilma (Arnold) 17
The Grouchy Ladybug (Carle) 89, 107, 111
Grow! Babies! (Gentiru) 146, 147
Growing Colors (McMillan) 13
Growing Like Me (Rockwell) 147
The Grumpy Morning (Edwards) 90
Guess What I Am (Axworthy) 1
Guess What I'll Be (Axworthy) 5
Guess Who's Coming, Jesse Bear (Carlstrom) 103
The Gummy Candy Counting Book (Hutchings) 47, 54

H

Hairy, Scary, Ordinary: What Is an Adjective? (Cleary) 138
The Handmade Alphabet (Rankin) 128
Handsigns: A Sign Language Alphabet (Fain) 123
Hannah's Collections (Jocelyn) 4, 39
Happy to You! (Cohen) 154
Harold and the Purple Crayon (Johnson) 18
A Hat for Minerva Louise (Stoeke) 35
The Hating Book (Udry) 152
Hello, Red Fox (Carle) 10
Henry and Amy (Right-Way-Round and Upside Down)
    (King) 3, 30
Henry Keeps Score (Skinner) 113
Henry the Fourth (Murphy) 72
Here Comes Spring and Summer and Fall and Winter (Murphy) 94
Here Comes the Year (Spinelli) 105
Hey, Little Baby! (Buck) 147
A High, Low, Near, Far, Loud, Quiet Story (Crews) 29
Hilda Hen's Scary Night (Wormell) 35, 92, 154
Hippos Go Berserk! (Boynton) 50, 64, 72
The House from Morning to Night (Bour) 89
How about a Hug? (Carlson) 149
How Are You Peeling? Foods with Moods (Freymann) 149
How Big Is a Foot? (Myller) 110, 114
How Big Is a Pig? (Blackstone) 29
How Do You Say It Today, Jesse Bear? (Carlstrom) 104
How Hungry Are You? (Napoli) 80
How Long? (Dale) 86
How Many Ants? (Brimner) 69, 72
How Many Birds? (Curry) 67, 73
How Many Bugs in a Box? (Carter) 51
How Many Feet? How Many Tails? (Burns) 37
How Many Feet in the Bed? (Hamm) 68
How Many Fish? (Cohen) 38, 44
How Many How Many How Many (Walton) 59

How Many Snails? A Counting Book (Giganti) 2, 4, 39
How Much, How Many, How Far, How Heavy, How Long,
    How Tall Is 1000? (Nolan) 48
How Much Is a Million? (Schwartz) 49
How Much Is That Guinea Pig in the Window? (Rocklin) 82
How the Second Grade Got $8,205.50 to Visit the Statue of
    Liberty (Zimelman) 83
How the Sky's Housekeeper Wore Her Scarves (Hooper) 12
A Huge Hog Is a Big Pig (McCall) 134
Hullabaloo ABC (Cleary) 122, 143
Hundred Days of School (Harris) 39, 47, 74
The Hundred-Pound Problem (Dussling) 114
A Hundred School Days (Rockwell) 48. 70
The Hundredth Day of School (Medearis) 47
Hundredth Day Worries (Cuyler) 38, 47, 69
Hurricane Music (Bottner) 143

I

I Can Count 100 Bunnies and So Can You! (Szekeres) 48, 59
I Feel Happy an Sad and Angry and Glad (Murphy) 150
I Knew Two Who Said Moo: A Counting and Rhyming
    Book (Barrett) 60, 133
I Love Colors (Miller) 13
I Love You, Mama, Any Time of Year (Carlstrom) 93
I Saw the Sea and the Sea Saw Me (Cash) 141
I Smell Honey (Pinkney) 142
I Stink! (McMullan) 127, 145
I Thought I Heard... (Baker) 143
I Walk at Night (Duncan) 91
I Wish I Were Big (Bowman) 111
Ian Penney's ABC (Penney) 128
If You Give a Moose a Muffin (Numeroff) 32
If You Give a Mouse a Cookie (Numeroff) 32
If You Give a Pig a Pancake (Numeroff) 32
If You Made a Million (Schwartz) 83
In My Garden: A Counting Book (Schumaker) 58
In My New Yellow Shirt (Spinelli) 17
In November (Rylant) 106
In the Park (Lee) 95
In the Snow: Who's Been Here? (George) 32, 100
Inch by Inch (Lionni) 114
Inchworm and a Half (Pinczes) 81, 115
Inside and Outside (Pluckrose) 28
Inside Outside Upside Down (Berenstain) 27, 28
Into the A, B, Sea (Rose) 128
Into the Castle (Crebbin) 27
Is a Blue Whale the Biggest Thing There Is? (Wells) 113
Is It Larger? Is It Smaller? (Hoban) 112
Is That You, Winter? (Gammell) 100
Is There Room on the Bus? An Around-the-World Counting
    Story (Piers) 57
It's about Time, Max! (Richards) 107
It's Fall! (Glaser) 98
It's Me, Marva! A Story about Color and Optical Illusions
    (Priceman) 8, 142

J

The Jacket I Wear in the Snow (Neitzel) 101
James and the Rain (Kuskin) 55
January Rides the Wind: A Book of Months (Otten) 104
Jasper's Beanstalk (Butterworth) 103
Jelly Beans for Sale (McMillan) 82
Jeremy Kooloo (Mahurin) 127
Jesse Bear, What Will You Wear? (Carlstrom) 89
Jim Meets the Thing (Cohen) 153
Josefina (Winter) 60
Jump, Frog, Jump! (Kalan) 32
Jump, Kangaroo, Jump! (Murphy) 80, 81
Jungle Drum (Wundrow) 144
Just a Little Bit (Tompert) 114

Just a Minute! (Slater) 87
Just Add Fun! (Rocklin) 79
Just Enough (Daniels) 138
Just Enough Carrots (Murphy) 113
Just Like You and Me (Miller) 3
Just Look (Hoban) 117

K

Katy and the Big Snow (Burton) 99
Keep Your Distance! (Herman) 115
Kente Colors (Chocolate) 10
The King Who Rained (Gwynne) 140
The King's Chessboard (Birch) 40, 78, 83
The King's Commissioners (Friedman) 38, 68, 69, 78
Kipper's A to Z (Inkpen) 125
Kipper's Birthday (Inkpen) 87
Kipper's Book of Colors (Inkpen) 12
Kipper's Book of Numbers (Inkpen) 39
Kipper's Book of Opposites (Inkpen) 30
Kipper's Snowy Day (Inkpen) 100
Kites Sail High (Heller) 137
Kiss It Better (Oram) 150, 152
A Kitten's Year (Day) 104, 146

L

L Is for Loving (Wilson-Max) 130, 150
Leon the Chameleon (Watt) 9
Let's Be Enemies (Udry) 152
Let's Count (Hoban) 54
Let's Count It Out, Jesse Bear (Carlstrom) 51, 64, 73
Let's Go, Anna! (French) 52
Let's Fly a Kite (Murphy) 34
Let's Fly from A to Z (Magee) 126
Let's Look at Shapes (Lorenz) 23, 26
Letters (Dena) 122
The Letters Are Lost! (Ernst) 123
Lights Out! (Penner) 77
Like Butter on Pancakes (London) 89
Lily and Trooper's Summer (Spetter) 97
Lily and Trooper's Winter (Spetter) 102
The Lion and the Little Red Bird (Kleven) 8
Listen to the City (Isadora) 144
Listen to the Rain (Martin) 144
The Listening Walk (Showers) 144
Little Bear and the Big Fight (Langreuter) 151
A Little Bit of Winter (Stewart) 102
Little Blue and Little Yellow (Lionni) . . . . . 16, 17 [two entries], 20
Little Farm by the Sea (Chorao) 93
Little Farmer Joe (Whybrow) 153
Little Fern's First Winter (Simmons) 102
Little Gorilla (Bornstein) 111
Little Green (Baker) 17
The Little House (Burton) 5, 86
Little Miss Muffet's Count-Along Surprise (Clark) 51
Little Mouse Has a Busy Day (Lavis) 89, 107
Little Mouse Has an Adventure (Lavis) 27
Little Pig's Bouncy Ball (Baron) 115
A Little Pigeon Toad (Gwynne) 140
Little Rabbit and the Sea (Bishop) 138
Little Rabbit's First Time Book (Baker) 106
The Little Scarecrow Boy (Brown) 71
Little White Dog (Godwin) 11
Little White Duck (Whippo) 14, 32
The Littlest Duckling (Herman) 43, 71
Lizzy's Dizzy Day (Keenan) 74, 76
A Long Trip to Z (Testa) 130
The Long Wait (Cobb) 73, 78
Look at the Moon (Garelick) 92
Look Book (Hoban) 117
Look Once Look Twice (Marshall) 33, 127
Look Whooo's Counting (MacDonald) 56
Looking Down (Jenkins) 117
The Loudest, Fastest, Best Drummer in Kansas (Davol) 143
The Loudness of Sam (Proimos) 150
Louella Mae, She's Run Away! (Alarcon) 133
Louie's Goose (Ehrlich) 96
Love Songs of the Little Bear (Brown) 92
Lucille's Snowsuit (Lasky) 101
Lulu's Lemonade (deRubertis) 116
Lunch! (Fleming) 11
The Lunch Line (Nagel) 82

M

The Magic School Bus Explores the Senses (Cole) 141
Magpie Magic: A Tale of Colorful Mischief (Wilson) 9
Maisy Drives the Bus (Cousins) 61
Maisy's Colors (Cousins) 10
*Mandarins and Marigolds: A Child's Journey Through
   Color* (Wallis) 14
Many Luscious Lollipops (Heller) 138
Marshmallow Kisses (Brennan) 96
Marvelous Math: A Book of Poems (Hopkins) 41
Mary Margaret's Tree (Drawson) 93
*Mary Wore Her Red Dress and Henry Wore His Green
   Sneakers* (Peek) 13
Math Curse (Scieszka) 41
Math Riddles (Ziefert) 41
Max's Money (Slater) 83
Max's Toys (Wells) 59
Me Counting Time: From Seconds to Centuries (Sweeney) . . . 85
Me on the Map (Sweeney) 117
Mean Soup (Everitt) 151
Measuring Penny (Leedy) 109
Merry-Go-Round: A Book about Nouns (Heller) 136
Michael Rosen's ABC (Rosen) 128, 132
Midnight in the Mountains (Lawson) 101
Millions of Cats (Gag) 40, 48
Millions of Snowflakes (Siddals) 58, 102
Minerva Louise (Stoeke) 35
Minerva Louise at School (Stoeke) 35
Minerva Louise at the Fair (Stoeke) 35
Ming Lo Moves the Mountain (Lobel) 34, 115
The Minister's Cat ABC (Dodd) 122
A Mink, a Fink, a Skating Rink: What Is a Noun? (Cleary) . . . 136
*Miss Bindergarten Celebrates the 100th Day of
   Kindergarten* (Slate) 48, 129
Miss Mouse's Day (Ormerod) 89
Miss Spider's ABC (Kirk) 125
The Missing Mitten Mystery (Kellogg) 15, 100
Missing Mittens (Murphy) 70
Mission: Addition (Leedy) 74
The Mitten: A Ukranian Folktale (Brett) 99, 111
The Mixed-up Chameleon (Carle) 7
Moira's Birthday (Munsch) 41
Moja Means One: A Swahili Counting Book (Feelings) 62
Mommy Go Away! (Jonell) 112
Monster Math (Maccarone) 66
Monster Math (Miranda) 56, 69, 76
Monster Math Picnic (Maccarone) 46, 74
Monster Math School Time (Maccarone) 107
Monster Money (Maccarone) 82
Monster Munchies (Numeroff) 57
Monster Musical Chairs (Murphy) 76
Month by Month a Year Goes Round (Shields) 105
Moo in the Morning (Maitland) 90, 144
Moonstick: The Seasons of the Sioux (Bunting) 93
Mordant's Wish (Coursen) 31
More Bugs in Boxes (Carter) 10
More, Fewer, Less (Hoban) 113
More or Less a Mess (Keenan) 4

More Than One (Schlein) 40, 41
Morning, Noon, and Night (George) 89
Mountain Town (Geisert) 93
Mouse Count (Walsh) 63, 67
Mouse Magic (Walsh) 9, 20
Mouse Paint (Walsh) 14, 20
Mouse Party (Durant) 133
Mouse Views: What the Class Pet Saw (McMillan) 35
Mrs. McTats and Her Houseful of Cats (Capucilli) 38, 73, 121
Mucky Moose (Allen) 145
My Baby Brother Has Ten Tiny Toes (Leuck) 56
My Colors; Mis Colores (Emberley) 11
My Crayons Talk (Hubbard) 12
My Day, Your Day (Ballard) 2
My Eyes Are for Seeing (Belk-Moncure) 142
My Fingers Are for Touching (Belk-Moncure) 145
My First Book of Time (Llewellyn) 85
My First Garden (Bogacki) 111, 117
My First Phonics Book (McGuinness) 134
My Five Senses (Aliki) 141
My Five Senses (Miller) 141
My Friend and I (Jahn-Clough) 149
My Friend Bear (Alborough) 110
My Friend Lucky (Milgrim) 30
My Little Sister Ate One Hare (Grossman) 53
My Many Colored Days (Seuss) 14, 150
My Mother's Pearls (Fruisen) 86
My Numbers; Mis Numeros (Emberley) 52
My Opposites; Mis Opuestos (Emberley) 29
My Shapes: Mis Formas (Emberley) 22
My Spring Robin (Rockwell) 96
My World of Color (Brown) 10
The Mystery of the Flying Orange Pumpkin (Kellogg) 18, 98
The Mystery of the Stolen Blue Paint (Kellogg) 16

N

A Net to Catch Time (Banks) 86, 88
Newton (Tyger) 144, 153
Night City (Wellington) 92, 108
Night Day: A Book of Eye-Catching Opposites (Tullet) 31
Night Driving (Coy) 91
Night in the Country (Rylant) 92
The Night Journey (Dowling) 91
Night Lights (Schnur) 58
Night-Time Numbers: A Scary Counting Book (Roth) 57
The Night Worker (Banks) 91
Nine Ducks Nine (Hayes) 45, 65
Nine Naughty Kittens (Jennings) 55
Nine O'Clock Lullaby (Singer) 87
*...Ninety-eight, ninety-nine, one hundred! Ready or Not,
 Here I Come* (Slater) 62, 69, 70
No Fair! (Holtzman) 40
No One Told the Aardvark (Eaton) 2
No Time for Mother's Day (Anderson) 85
North Country Spring (Lindbergh) 95
Not Enough Room! (Rocklin) 23
Nothing Scares Us (Wishinsky) 154
Now I'm Big (Miller) 148
Now It Is Morning (Whitman) 90
Now Soon Later (Grunwald) 86
A Number of Animals (Wormell) 60
Number One Number Fun (Chorao) 38, 73, 76
Numbers (Dena) 38, 51

O

October Smiled Back (Peters) 105
Of Colors and Things (Hoban) 12
Ogres! Ogres! Ogres! A Feasting Frenzy from A to Z
 (Heller) 124, 132
Oh! (Henkes) 100
Oh, No, Anna! (French) 11
Old Bear's Surprise Painting (Hissey) 8, 33
Old Black Fly (Aylesworth) 120
Old Hat, New Hat (Berenstain) 138
Ollie All Over (Roche) 28
On a Wintry Morning (Chaconas) 99
On Beyond a Million: An Amazing Math Journey
 (Schwartz) 49, 84
On Market Street (Lobel) 126
On the Same Day in March (Singer) 4, 106
On the Stairs (Larios) 62, 72
Once upon a Springtime (Marzollo) 94
One Afternoon (Heo) 143
One Cow Moo Moo! (Bennett) 50
One Duck Stuck (Root) 57
One Gaping Wide-Mouthed Hopping Frog (Tryon) 59
One Glad Man (Bowdish) 50, 148
One Grain of Rice: A Mathematical Folktale (Demi) 40, 83
One Gray Mouse (Burton) 10, 51
One Guinea Pig Is Not Enough (Duke) 52, 73
One Hole in the Road (Nikola-Lisa) 56
One Hot Summer Day (Crews) 96
One Hundred Days of School (Harris) 39, 47, 74
One Hundred Hungry Ants (Pinczes) 48, 80
One Hundred Is a Family (Ryan) 57, 70
The One Hundred-Pound Problem (Dussling) 114
One Hundred School Days (Rockwell) 48, 70
The One Hundredth Day of School (Medearis) 47
One Hundredth Day Worries (Cuyler) 38, 47, 69
One Hungry Cat (Rocklin) 80
One Hunter (Hutchins) 54, 65
One Is a Mouse (Hunt) 54
One Is One (Tudor) 59
One Lighthouse, One Moon (Lobel) 1
One Lonely Sea Horse (Freymann) 53
One Monkey Too Many (Koller) 39, 74
One Moose, Twenty Mice (Beaton) 50
One More Bunny: Adding from One to Ten (Walton) 59, 75
One More Time, Mama (Alexander) 92
One of Each (Hoberman) 41, 42
One Potato: A Counting Book of Potato Prints (Pomeroy) 57
One Quiet Morning (Pittman) 142
One Red Sun: A Counting Book (Keats) 55
One Riddle, One Answer (Thompson) 42
One Smiling Sister (Coats) 61
One, Two, Red, and Blue (Le Jars)1
One, Two, Skip a Few: First Number Rhymes (Arenson) 37
One Two Three (Geddes) 53
One, Two, Three for You and Me (Girnis) 53
One, Two, Three, Go! (Lee) 55
One, Two, Three Music (Auzary-Luton) 142
One Two Three Pop! (Isadora) 48, 54
One, Two, Three to the Zoo: A Counting Book (Carle) 51
*One, Two, Three What Do You See? An Animal Counting
 Book* (Bohdal) 50
One Two Three Yippie (Jahn-Clough) 55, 65
One Was Johnny: A Counting Book (Sendak) 58, 66
One Yellow Lion (Van Fleet) 14, 59
Only One Ollie (Roche) 57
Opposites (Dena) 29
Opposites (Hendra) 29
Opposites (Schroeder) 30
Our Old House (Vizurraga) 88
Outside, Inside (Crimi) 2, 29
Over in the Grasslands (Wilson) 59
Over in the Meadow (Cabrera) 51
Over on the Farm: A Counting Picture Book Rhyme (Gunson) . . 53
Over, Under & Through and Other Spacial Concepts (Hoban) . . 27
Owl Moon (Yolen) 92, 102

P

P. Bear's New Year's Party! (Lewis) 18, 56, 107
Paddington's ABC (Bond) 121
Paddington's Colors (Bond) 9, 19
Paddington's Opposites (Bond) 29
A Pair of Socks (Murphy) 3, 33
Pajama Time! (Boynton) 2, 29
Panda Big and Panda Small (Cabrera) 29
Park Beat: Rhymin' Through the Seasons (London) 94
Pass the Celery, Ellery! (Gaga) 123, 133
Patrick's Dinosaurs (Carrick) 6
Pattern (Pluckrose) 33
Pattern Fish (Harris) 33
Patty's Pumpkin Patch (Sloat) 130
The Penny Pot (Murphy) 82
Pepper's Journal: A Kitten's First Year (Murphy) 87, 146
Pick a Color! (Bulloch) 10
Pickles to Pittsburgh (Barrett) 110
The Pie Is Cherry (Rex) 138
A Pie Went By (Dunn) 133
A Pig Is Big (Florian) 111
The Pig Is in the Pantry, the Cat Is on the Shelf (Mozelle) . . 62, 107
Pig Pigger Piggest (Walton) 139
The Piggy in the Puddle (Pomerantz) 135
Pignic (Miranda) 127
Pigs at Odds (Axelrod) 72, 81
Pigs Go to Market (Axelrod) 37, 78, 81, 114
Pigs in the Corner (Axelrod) 33, 34
Pigs in the Pantry (Axelrod) 116
Pigs on a Blanket (Axelrod) 72, 86, 106
Pigs on the Ball (Axelrod) 21
Pigs Will Be Pigs (Axelrod) 72, 76, 81
Pip's Magic (Walsh) 153
Play Date (Santos) 103
Please Be Quiet (Murphy) 144
Polar Bear, Polar Bear, What Do You Hear? (Martin) 144
Polly Molly Woof Woof (Lloyd) 154
Pond Year (Lasky) 104
Possum's Harvest Moon (Hunter) 98
The Practically Perfect Pajamas (Brooks) 135
Prairie Primer A to Z (Stutson) 130
Princess Prunella and the Purple Peanut (Atwood) 135
Puddle's ABC (Hobbie) 124
Puffins Climb, Penguins Rhyme (McMillan) 134, 137
The Pumpkin Fair (Bunting) 18
Purple Coyote (Cornette) 18
The Purple Hat (Pearson) 18
Purple Is Best (Rau) 18

Q

Q Is for Duck: An Alphabet Guessing Game (Elting) 123
Quack and Count (Baker) 45, 72
A Quarter from the Tooth Fairy (Holtzman) 82
The Quiet Way Home (Becker) 143
Quilt Alphabet (Cline-Ransome) 122

R

R Is for Radish (Coxe) 135
Rabbit's Good News (Bornstein) 95
Rabbit and Hare Divide an Apple (Ziefert) 81
Racing Around (Murphy) 115
Rain (Kalan) 12
Rain (Stojic) 142
Rain Dance (Appelt) 49
A Rainbow All Around Me (Pinkney) 13
Rainbow Joe and Me (Strom) 8, 142
Raven and River (Carlstrom) 95
Ready, Set, Hop! (Murphy) 40, 75, 76, 113
Red Are the Apples (Harshman) 11, 98
Red Is a Dragon: A Book of Colors (Thong) 14
Red Rhino (Rogers) 15
A Red Wagon Year (Appelt) 104
Red's Great Chase (Lia) 15, 28
A Remainder of One (Pinczes) 80
Re-Zoom (Banyai) 115, 116
Ridiculous! (Coleman) 99
Roar! A Noisy Counting Book (Edwards) 52
Rock It, Sock It, Number Line (Martin) 62, 66
Roly-Poly Puppies: A Counting Book (Moore) 56
Room for Ripley (Murphy) 116
The Rooster Who Went to His Uncle's Wedding: a Latin
    American Folktale (Ada) 31
Rose and Sebastian (Zarin) 154
Round Is a Mooncake: A Book of Shapes (Thong) 24
Round Is a Pancake (Baranski) 24
Round the Garden (Glaser) 32
Rupa Raises the Sun (Chall) 90
Rusty's Red Vacation (Asbury) 15
Ruthie's Big Old Coat (Lacome) 15, 112

S

Safari Park (Murphy) 75, 79
Sam and the Tigers (Lester) 8
Scamper's Year (Kindley) 94
Scaredy Cat (Rankin) 153
Sea Shapes (MacDonald) 23
Sea Squares (Hulme) 54, 78
Sea Sums (Hulme) 74, 76
The Seasons of Arnold's Apple Tree (Gibbons) 93
Seaweed Soup (Murphy) 5
The Secret Birthday Message (Carle) 21, 27
Seven Blind Mice (Young) 15, 35, 145
The Seven Chairs (Lanteigne) 45, 71
Seven Stars, More! (Mallat) 39, 45
Seymour Bleu (Deeter) 7
The Shape of Things (Dodds) 22
Shape Space (Falwell) 22
Shapes, Shapes, Shapes (Hoban) 23
Shark Swimathon (Murphy) 77
Ship Ahoy! (Sis) 16
Ship Shape (Rogers) 13, 23
The Shortest Kid in the World (Bliss) 111
Shota and the Star Quilt (Bateson-Hill) 25, 33
Shrinking Mouse (Hutchins) 117
The Silly Story of Goldie Locks and the Three Squares
    (Maccarone) 23
Sir Cumference and the Dragon of Pi (Neuschwander) 24
Sir Cumference and the First Round Table: A Math Adventure
    (Neuschwander) 23
Sitting Down to Eat (Harley) 62
Six Empty Pockets (Curtis) 44
Six Foolish Fishermen (San Souci) 41
Six Hogs on a Scooter (Spinelli) 45
Six Sandy Sheep (Enderle) 44, 64, 97, 135
Six Silly Foxes (Moran) 45, 150
Six Sticks (Coxe) 44
Slower Than a Snail (Schreiber) 139
Snow! (Ford) 100
Snow (Wallace) 102
Snow Comes to the Farm (Tripp) 102
Snow Dance (Evans) 99
Snow Day (Bliss) 99
Snow Day! (Joosse) 100
Snowball (Crews) 99
The Snowy Day (Keats) 100
Snowy Flowy Blowy: A Twelve Months Rhyme (Tafuri) 105
So Happy/So Sad (Paschkis) 152, 154
So Many Bunnies: A Bedtime ABC and Counting Book
    (Walton) 63, 130
So Many Cats! (de Regniers) 61, 73

So Many Circles, So Many Squares (Hoban) 24, 25
Some Smug Slug (Edwards) 135
Some Things Are Scary (Heide). 153
Some Things Change (Murphy) 5
Sometimes (Baker). 148
Sometimes I Feel Like a Mouse: A Book about Feelings
  (Modesitt) 150
Sometimes I Feel Like a Storm Cloud (Evans) 149
Somewhere in the World Right Now (Schuett) 85, 89
Soup's Oops! (Hines-Stephens) 137
Spaghetti and Meatballs for All! A Mathematical Story
  (Burns) 78
Splash (Jonas) 39
Splash! A Penguin Counting Book (Chester) 51
Splish, Splash, Spring (Carr). 95
Spot Can Count (Hill) 54
Spot's Big Book of Colors, Shapes and Numbers (Hill) . . 12, 22, 54
Spots: Counting Creatures from Sky to Sea (Lesser) 55
Spotted Yellow Frogs (Van Fleet). 26, 33
Spring: An Alphabet Acrostic (Schnur) 96, 119, 129
Spring Song (Seuling) 96
Spring Thaw (Schnur) 96
Spunky Monkeys on Parade (Murphy) 68, 79
Squarehead (Ziefert) 24, 25
Stay Awake, Bear! (Bishop) 92
Stay in Line (Slater) 47, 75
Stella, Queen of the Snow (Gay) 100
Stellaluna (Cannon) 2
Step by Step (McMillan) 148
Stop—Go, Fast—Slow (McLenighan) 30
The Story of a Blue Bird (Bogacki). 16
The Story of Little Babaji (Bannerman) 7
Subtraction Action (Leedy) 76
Summer: An Alphabet Acrostic (Schnur) 97, 119, 129
Summer Stinks (Kelley). 97, 125
Summer's End (Boelts) 96
Summertime: from Porgy and Bess (Gershwin) 97
Sun Dance Water Dance (London) 97
The Sun Is My Favorite Star (Asch) 88
A Sunday Stroll (Borgese). 86
Sunshine and Storm (Jones) 149
Sunshine, Moonshine (Armstrong) 88
Super Sand Castle Saturday (Murphy) 110
Surprise! (Noll). 57
Switch on the Night (Bradbury) 91, 152

T

Taiko on a Windy Night (Derby) 91
A Tasting Party (Belk-Moncure) 145
Tea for Ten (Anderson) 49
Teeny Tiny Ernest (Barnes) 110
Teeny, Tiny Mouse: A Book about Colors (Leuck) 12
Tell Me a Season (Siddals) 14, 89, 95
Tell Me What It's Like to Be Big (Dunbar) 147
Telling Time with Big Mama Cat (Harper) 107
Ten Apples up on Top! (LeSeig) 46, 55
Ten Black Dots (Crews) 38, 46, 51
Ten Dirty Pigs: An Upside-Down, Turn-Around Bathtime
  Counting Book (Roth) 57
Ten Dogs in the Window: A Countdown Book (Masurel) . . 3, 66
Ten Flashing Fireflies (Sturges) 46, 59, 67, 77
Ten Friends (Goldstone) 46, 74
Ten Go Tango (Dorros) 52
Ten in the Bed (Dale) 64
Ten in the Bed (Geddes) 46, 65, 76
Ten Little Bears: A Counting Rhyme (Hague) 65
Ten Little Bunnies (Spowart) 58
Ten Little Rabbits (Grossman) 53
Ten Minutes Till Bedtime (Rathman) 66
Ten Monkey Jamboree (Ochiltree) 46, 75

Ten, Nine, Eight (Bang) 63
Ten Oni Drummers (Gollub) 53
Ten out of Bed (Dale) 64
Ten Play Hide-and-Seek (Dale). 51
Ten Red Apples (Hutchins) 65
Ten Rosy Roses (Merriam) 15, 66
Ten Seeds (Brown) 64
Ten Silly Dogs: A Countdown Story (Flather) 65
Ten Sly Piranhas: A Counting Story in Reverse (Wise) 67
Ten Terrible Dinosaurs (Stickland) 67
Ten Times Better (Michelson) 46, 79
Ten Tiny Monsters: A Superbly Scary Story of Subtraction
  (Samton) 66, 77
That's My Dog! (Walton) 16, 138, 139
That's What Happens When It's Spring (Good) 95
There's a Nightmare in My Closet (Mayer) 153
There's an Alligator Under My Bed (Mayer) 153
There's Something in My Attic (Mayer) 153
They Thought They Saw Him (Strete) 8
Things That Are Most in the World (Barrett) 139
Things That Make You Feel Good, Things That Make You
  Feel Bad (Parr) 150
Thorndike and Nelson (Jackson) 151
The Three Bears (Barton) 42, 138
The Three Billy Goats Gruff (Finch) 43
Three Friends/Tres Amigos: A Counting Book/Un Cuento
  para Contar (Brusca) 50, 64
Three Kind Mice (Sathre) 43
Three Little Kittens (Alter) 42
Three Little Kittens (Galdone) 43
Three Little Kittens (Siomades) 43
Three Pandas (Wahl) 43
Three Pigs, One Wolf, and Seven Magic Shapes (Maccarone) . . . 23
Three Yellow Dogs (Cohen) 17, 42
Thump, Thump, Rat-a-Tat-Tat (Baer) 115, 116, 142
Thunder Doesn't Scare Me (Bowdish) 152
Tick-Tock (Anderson) 86, 106
Tickly Prickly (Becker) 144
Tiger and the Temper Tantrum (French) 151
The Timbertoes 1 2 3 Counting Book (Hunt) 54
The Timbertoes ABC Alphabet Book (Hunt) 125
The Time It Took Tom (Sharrat) 15, 87
Time to Sleep (Fleming) 100
The Tiny Seed (Carle) 146
To and Fro, Fast and Slow (Bernhard) 28
To Root, to Toot, to Parachute: What Is a Verb? (Cleary) 137
To See the Moon (Bacon) 104, 146, 147
To the Island (Agell) 88
Today I Feel Silly and Other Moods That Make My Day
  (Curtis) 149
Today Is Monday (Carle) 103
Toddler Two-Step (Appelt) 60, 63
Tomatoes from Mars (Yorinks) 16
Tomorrow's Alphabet (Shannon) 5, 129
Too Big! (Masurel) 112
Too Big, Too Small, Just Right (Minters) 30
Too Many Cooks! (Buckless) 78
Too Many Kangaroo Things to Do! (Murphy) 75, 79
Toot and Puddle: You Are My Sunshine (Hobbie) 149
Tops and Bottoms (Stevens) 31
Touch the Poem (Adoff) 144
Tough Boris (Fox) 152
A Triangle for Adaora: An African Book of Shapes (Onyefulu) . . . 23
A Trio of Triceratops (Most) 43, 136
Tucker off His Rocker (McGuirk) 28
Tumble Bumble (Bond) 37
The Turning of the Year (Martin) 104
Turtle Splash! Countdown at the Pond (Falwell) 65
Twelve Snails to One Lizard: A Tale of Mischief and
  Measurement (Hightower) 109, 114

Title	Pages
Twelve Ways to Get to Eleven (Merriam)	39, 47, 74
Twenty Is Too Many (Duke)	76
Twenty-Six Letters and 99 Cents (Hoban)	62, 82, 124
Twice my Size (Mitchell)	113
Two Bad Ants (Van Allsburg)	35
Two Fine Ladies Have a Tiff (Zehler)	151
Two Girls Can! (Narahashi)	42
Two Little Trains (Brown)	2, 6, 27
The Two of Them (Aliki)	85, 145
Two Times Two Equals Boo! A Set of Spooky Multiplication Stories (Leedy)	79
Two Ways to Count to Ten: A Liberian Folktale (Dee)	67

U

Title	Pages
Underwater Counting: Even Numbers (Pallotta)	68, 70
Uno, Dos, Tres: One, Two, Three (Mora)	56
Up the Mountain (Agell)	88

V

Title	Pages
The Very Hungry Caterpillar (Carle)	5, 38, 103
The Very Kind Rich Lady and Her One Hundred Dogs (Lee)	47
The Very Noisy Night (Hendry)	143
The Very Small (Dunbar)	111
Voices in the Park (Browne)	34
Vroomaloom Zoom (Coy)	143

W

Title	Pages
The Wacky Wedding: A Book of Alphabet Antics (Edwards)	131
Wake Up and Goodnight (Zolotow)	90
Wake up, Grizzly! (Bittner)	6
Wake up, Little Children: A Rise-and-Shine Rhyme (Aylesworth)	90, 96
The War between the Vowels and the Consonants (Turner)	120
Warthogs in the Kitchen: A Sloppy Counting Book (Edwards)	52
Warthogs Paint: A Messy Color Book (Edwards)	20
Watch Out! Big Bro's Coming! (Alborough)	34, 110, 116
Watch William Walk (Jonas)	136
The Way I Feel (Cain)	148
We're Going on a Lion Hunt (Axtell)	26
A Weed Is a Seed (Wolff)	35
What Can You Do in the Snow? (Hines)	100
What Color Was the Sky Today? (Ford)	5, 8, 89
What Comes in 2's, 3's, and 4's? (Aker)	42 [2 entries], 43
What Goes Around Comes Around (McGuire)	32
What Is a Triangle? (Dotlich)	25
What Is Round? (Dotlich)	24
What Is Square? (Dotlich)	25
What Makes Me Happy? (Anholt)	148
What Pete Ate from A–Z (Kalman)	125
What Size? (MacKinnon)	30, 112
What the Sun Sees/What the Moon Sees (Tafuri)	90
What's Opposite? (Swinburne)	31
What's Smaller Than a Pygmy Shrew? (Wells)	113
What's up with That Cup? (Keenan)	109
What's What?: A Guessing Game (Serfozo)	31
When a Line Bends, A Shape Begins (Greene)	22
When Autumn Comes (Maass)	98
When I Am a Sister (Ballard)	5
When I Feel Angry (Spelman)	151
When I Was Little: A Four-Year-Old's Memoir of her Youth (Curtis)	147
When I Was Young (Dunbar)	86
When I'm Afraid (Aaron)	152
When I'm Angry (Aaron)	151
When It Is Night, When It Is Day (Tyers)	90
When It Starts to Snow (Gershator)	100
When Spring Comes (Maass)	95
When Summer Comes (Maass)	97
When the Big Dog Barks (Curtis)	153
When the Earth Wakes (Rucki)	94
When the Moon Is Full: A Lunar Year (Pollock)	105
When the Wind Stops (Zolotow)	6
When Will It Be Spring? (Walters)	96, 102
When Will It Snow? (Hiscock)	100
When Will Sarah Come? (Howard)	87
When Winter Comes (Maass)	101
When You're Not Looking...A Storytime Counting Book (Kneen)	55
Where Are You, Little Zack? (Enderle)	38
Where Did Bunny Go? (Tafuri)	102
Where Does It Go? (Miller)	28
Where Is Mortimer? (Bryant-Mole)	27
Where's My Teddy? (Alborough)	110
Where's Spot? (Hill)	27
Where's that Bone? (Penner)	28
Where's the Fly? (Cohen)	27, 117
Where's Your Smile, Crocodile? (Freedman)	149
Which Way, Ben Bunny? (Smith)	34
A Whiff and a Sniff (Belk-Moncure)	145
White Rabbit's Color Book (Baker)	9, 19
Who Hops? (Davis)	137
Who Invited You? (Fleming)	62
Who Is the Beast? (Baker)	2
Who Sank the Boat? (Allen)	114
Who Wakes Rooster? (Meeker)	90
Whoever You Are (Fox)	2
Who's Afraid of the Dark? (Bonsall)	152
Who's Counting? (Tafuri)	59
Why Mosquitoes Buzz in People's Ears: a West African Tale (Aardema)	31
Why Not? (Wormell)	32
Wibbly Pig Is Happy! (Inkpen)	149
Wildflower ABC (Pomeroy)	57
Window (Baker)	5, 86, 146
The Wing on a Flea: A Book about Shapes (Emberley)	22
Winter Lullaby (Seuling)	101
Winter Storytime (Kohn)	71, 101
Winter Visitors (O'Donnell)	66, 101
Word Play ABC (Cahoon)	121, 139
Word Wizard (Falwell)	119
The Worrywarts (Edwards)	136

Y

Title	Pages
The Year at Maple Hill Farm (Provensen)	94
A Year for Kiko (Wolff)	105
A Year in the City (Henderson)	104
Yellow Hippo (Rogers)	17
Yolanda's Yellow School (Asbury)	16
You and Me (Manna)	3, 30
You Are Cordially Invited to P. Bear's New Year's Party! (Lewis)	18, 56, 107
You Are Here (Crews)	6
You Can't Take a Balloon into the Metropolitan Museum (Weitzman)	17
You Can't Take a Balloon into the Museum of Fine Arts (Weitzman)	17
You Can't Take a Balloon into the National Gallery (Weitzman)	18
You Go Away (Corey)	29
You Smell and Taste and Feel and See and Hear (Murphy)	141
You'll Soon Grow into Them, Titch (Hutchins)	112, 146

Z

Title	Pages
Z Is for Zombie (Kutner)	126
The Z Was Zapped: A Play in Twenty-Six Acts (Van Allsburg)	130
Zin! Zin! Zin! A Violin (Moss)	62, 144
Zoë and Her Zebra (Beaton)	121
Zoom (Banyai)	115, 116

About the Author

Melanie Axel-Lute has been a librarian for over 25 years. Formerly head of Children's Services at South Orange Public Library, she now devotes her time to writing, dancing, and teaching. She was born in Massachusetts, grew up in Pennsylvania, and currently lives in New Jersey with her husband Paul, also a librarian. She has two grown children as well as that mainstay of all writers—two cats.

www.ingramcontent.com/pod-product-compliance
Lightning Source LLC
Chambersburg PA
CBHW080411300426
44113CB00015B/2479